At Home in Australia

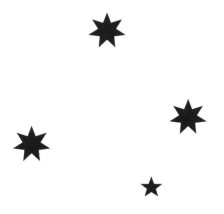

At Home in Australia

Peter Conrad

The Publishers are grateful to the National Gallery of Australia, Canberra,
for its generous support for this publication and in particular to Gael Newton,
Senior Curator, Photography.

First published in the United Kingdom in 2003 by Thames & Hudson Ltd,
181A High Holborn, London WC1V 7QX

www.thamesandhudson.com

British Library Cataloguing-in-Publication Data
A catalogue record for this book is available from the British Library

ISBN 0-500-51141-1

Designed by Derek Birdsall
Typeset by Omnific

Printed and bound in Singapore by C S Graphics

Contents

Acknowledgments

Quite unexpectedly, early one morning at the beginning of 2001, Gael Newton – who is Senior Curator of Photography at the National Gallery of Australia in Canberra – telephoned me to ask if I would write a book about the Gallery's photography collection. I wake up every day hoping to be surprised by life; on that day, it would be truer to say that life stunned me. Gael and I had met twice the previous year, once in Sydney and then a few months later in Paris, though without discussing any kind of collaboration. Why, I wondered now, should she be prepared let me loose in her personal protectorate? With her bicentennial exhibition *Shades of Light* and the book that accompanied it, Gael virtually invented the study of Australian photography. How would she put up with an amateur's invasion of the field? But I didn't ask these questions, for fear she might change her mind.

Although Thames and Hudson agreed at once to publish the book for the Gallery, negotiations proved complicated. The book was saved by Ruth Patterson, who providentially swooped into London and persuaded all concerned to shake hands. She has my deep gratitude.

During my time in Canberra in December 2001 and January 2002, Paul Costigan scanned, drove, cooked, uncorked bottles, spread blankets on the ground to protect our picnics from the bull ants, and sent me home each evening with armloads of photographic books and magazines from his personal collection. Anne O'Hehir, assigned to me as a minder, proved to be a cheerful, endearingly cheeky companion. I returned to London to write, with the pre-eminent historian of Australian photography as my patient research assistant: it was Gael herself who answered queries, and went off in trivial pursuit of facts I thought I needed to know. She demanded no concessions in return. At no point did she attempt to influence my choice of photographs, or my interpretative approach to them. I am still astonished by her generosity, and can only hope that she does not regret that telephone call.

Once more, I must record my admiration for the perfectionism of everyone at Thames and Hudson. I thank Jamie Camplin for his invigorating belief in the book, Helen Farr for keeping a keen eye on the details, Tamsin Perrett for her clear-headed scrutiny of the text, and Derek Birdsall for a design that so deftly and perceptively integrates text and illustrations.

Those images dictated my words, so my final acknowledgment has to be to the photographers, living and dead, who showed me what Australia looks like, helped me to understand what it means, and convinced me, despite my current address, that I still belong there.

1: A Family Album

At home in Australia, we had a treasure chest in our house. At least that was how I always thought of it, on the wintry evenings in Hobart when I was allowed to take it down from its hiding place. It belonged on the mantelpiece, out of view around the corner of a chimney breast, usually concealed by a vase of showy, blowsy, sneezy flowers. It was a plain wooden box with a lid that did not quite fit, handmade by some apprentice carpenter, varnished and polished but blotched by sticky, inquisitive fingers, discoloured as well by smoke that escaped from the fireplace. Childhood invests the most ordinary objects with yearning, hope, and a fierce joy. The contents of the box were precious, alluring testimony to worlds elsewhere in space and time, worlds beyond my experience and before my existence. It was where my parents kept their photos.

After their deaths, I took very little from the house. There was little enough to take: my parents' proudest possession was their garden, which like a pining animal died soon after they did. When it all devolved on me, the sense of ownership and inheritance dismayed and confused me. During the years when I lived in the house with them, I never had a key to the door. Why would I have needed one, since there was always someone at home? Now the place was empty, and the things left behind in it suddenly seemed to have no purpose, to be – as my mother would have said, though she would not have said it about her own belongings – good for nothing. We erect walls, attach a roof, and furnish a small world for ourselves. Inside the house, we tell ourselves that we are at home. It is an investment in the idea of permanence, and we soon enough discover our mistake. I could hardly bear to sort through my patrimony: the chipped plates with the floral pattern almost scrubbed off, the spoons with the apostles by which I'd always been so intrigued, the atlas that my father kept beside the television set so that he could look up the locations of the latest wars. I lacked the courage even to open the wardrobe or the chest of drawers that contained clothes. But I seized on one particular talismanic ornament, which I had always coveted – a salt and pepper shaker painted with images of the Sydney Harbour Bridge – and of course I took the box of snapshots.

It contained my history, or at least as much of a personal past as I would ever have, for neither of my parents, who had childhood wounds that were still raw, liked to reminisce. Sorting through the box now I am reminded of a plaintive comment made by the film director Peter Weir in 1979. He was contrasting the epochal heritage of the Aboriginals with his own slippery, foundering hold on time: 'I have no past. I'm nobody. I ask my parents who these people are in the photograph album and they can't remember. Nobody knows. I have no culture'. When I unpacked the box after I inherited it, I found to my dismay that its contents did not extend back very far. The past that in my childhood seemed so remote and alluringly foreign consisted only of the decade before I was born. Here was my father in his soldier's uniform, lined up with a row of lookalikes. I hadn't realized, during my first perusals of the box, that his face was a preview of mine. Now I was older than he was during the war, he had become my younger, obsolete self. Here he was again, frisking a Japanese captive in New Guinea: the highest excitement, probably, of his life. There was my mother dressed as a nurse, standing under an apple tree. Once, long before, I had sneaked a look at one of their wartime love letters. 'Do you remember that night in the orchard?' my father had written. I stopped reading at once, afraid that I was about to be given a forbidden glimpse of a primal scene: it's a mercy that some moments are not photographed.

Then – since the camera had taken over the function of the family Bible, recording births, marriages and deaths – came the inevitable scenes with babies being held up to the light: my parents with me, with my many cousins, with the babies of their friends. Now, unable to ask for their help, I cannot tell which of the interchangeable babies is me. The one who is crying, I suppose. A few months later, my mother took me into Hobart – strapped into a pushchair, kitted out in clothes she had made herself and topped by a white woollen beret she had knitted – where a street photographer sweet-talked her into posing with me. The anxious expression identifies me to myself. It's a pity that the photographer did not suggest to my mother that she might move my hand: in the picture, I have a tight, retentive grip on my nascent privates. Whenever the image was shown around in the family, people delicately refrained from noticing this. That man in the street captured a truth. One way or another, I have spent the rest of my life engaged in variants of the activity that used to be called 'playing with yourself'. Walter Benjamin recognized that photography, with its keen eye for the physiological truths that are betrayed by chance gestures or fleeting expressions, unerringly incriminated its subjects. 'Is it not the task of the photographer – descendant of the augurs and haruspices – to reveal guilt and to point out the guilty in his pictures?' he asked. That humble, nameless Hobart operative certainly did so.

If I construct a chronology, a pause follows at this point, after the war, the wooings, the births, and my first public investigation of my genitals. The defining events were all over; a life unphotographed, not worth commemorating, was being lived. The next photographs to be taken were my own, dating from the time in early adolescence when I had a box Brownie. The first exhibit is a picture of our house – their house I should say, mine only for a few weeks, now a home for strangers unknown to me. I remember my mother's unease when I went across the street to take it. She said the windows weren't clean, though I suspect she was worried for other reasons. Why had I detached myself in this way, looking back at a house I would not be living in for much longer? What would I see, or what would the cold eye of the camera see on my behalf? My parents aimed to be inconspicuous. The photograph, when I study it now, shows me uncomfortable truths. At this early stage, my father grew vegetables in the front yard, where the garden was eventually to be; there was still a fence of wire mesh, which my parents later – more relaxed now, less defensive, not worried about dogs with diarrhoea or thieves intent on stealing their cauliflowers – removed. Yes, photographs do desecrate the world, or at least this one does. I am confronted by the house without its special, fond aura of associations. It is a carton of weatherboard, with a buckling metal lid and a chimney whose bricks were never quite true. The concrete path through the vegetables is muddy.

So it is no wonder that the next photographs, which I must have taken later, have made desperate, contorted efforts to revise the reality or break free from it. For one taken in the backyard – beside the shed that used to be our outside privy, entangled with passion-fruit vines – I must have stretched out flat on the ground, and earned myself another scolding. The angle was an effort to make a familiar scene mysterious, to tilt the shed sideways and make the rotary clothes line topple. The last in the series records my first trip in an aeroplane in 1962: framed in the window, my initial sighting of what we called the mainland as the Melbourne suburbs flatly unravelled below. Though the photograph is grey, I can still see the opalescent glinting of all those swimming pools, and the baked red and orange tiles of the rooftops. I probably lost the camera, or at least abandoned it, soon after. Anyway, my own unphotographed existence began.

The box – now installed on another mantelpiece, in London, above a fireplace that was long ago blocked up – has not lost its appeal to my imagination. But these days, when I look at the photographs, they no longer seem so personal. I cannot recognize my nappy-clad self, let alone the other people in the archive: the crowd of friends with my father at a football match, the acquaintances who moved to Queensland and sent back pictures of a house on stilts. The private souvenirs have become documents, and what they document is a fraction of Australia's history. They are about a group of people, myself included, huddling together in order to feel at home in this strange new country.

The camera from the first was enrolled in the effort to make Australia knowable, to domesticate its wildness, to balance the equation between us and it by creating affinity, empathy. A camera is a chamber, and a shuttered one like my parents' house after the blinds were drawn down. Could the whole of the bright, dazing continent be cramped into that little room? The camera took possession of views. Anyone using it participated in the grand colonizing feat of the explorer in Patrick White's *Voss*, who makes the country his 'by right of vision'. It contained things, scaled them down. Most of my early photographs are small, not much bigger than postage stamps, further diminished by the white borders around the edge of the paper. To see anything in them now I need a magnifying glass. But reductiveness is among the magical, alchemical powers of the art: it provided me with a microscopic Australia that could be squeezed into the box.

Photography served the purpose of enclosure, which was the first imperative of settlement (so scandalously flouted, as the colonists thought, by the continent's Aboriginal inhabitants, who had no conception of a house and treated the earth itself and the stories it told as their unwalled, roofless home). The idea of home was imported from elsewhere and imposed on the recalcitrant country. Hence all those nineteenth-century photographs of house-proud settlers in their fragile shacks, or of fences valiantly keeping the bush at bay. Inevitably the shared, collectively-created home came to be broken apart. Someone leaves it, saying goodbye too curtly and conclusively; he sees the world differently, or wants to see a different world, and his snapshots with their extravagant angles are symptoms of maladjustment or of a longing so painfully urgent that – in my case – I can still feel it. The camera usually goes along with him on that exile which Australians refer to as expatriation. In my case it didn't: instead I tried to fix images verbally. The camera I lost or grew tired of remained in the past, and now the scenes that slowly formed themselves inside it, like memories glimmering into visibility as we dream, seem to be depictions of homesickness.

To me, the photographs in this book are interchangeable with those in my box. Nicholas Caire's allotment in Gippsland, photographed in the 1880s, could be the only slightly less makeshift property I photographed in Hobart in the early 1960s. The timber of our house was better barbered, and the ragged palisade of the bush had been pushed further back from our door. Admittedly my parents had no such line-up of offspring – a crop as regular and seasonal as the vegetables beside which they were assembled – but I can see my father patrolling those dusty paths, taking stock of cabbages, caulies, and onions that wore stockings on their heads like burglars. The vegetables were his own brave act of cultivation, supplanting the wrecked cars that dribbled oil in front yards in other houses on the block. I cannot look at the soft, fuzzy hydrangeas, azaleas and fuchsias photographed by John Kauffmann in the early twentieth century without remembering my mother's efforts, after the vegetables had discreetly retired to the backyard, to grow those same flowers and to properly pronounce their names.

You first make yourself at home by rigging up a shelter. *Piccaninny Walkabout*, a children's story photographed by Axel Poignant in 1952, shows the process at work in central Australia. The Aboriginal family crouches in a humpy made of bent stringy-bark, and the children lost in the bush overnight sleep beneath entwined stakes backed with paperbark. When I look at these photographs, I remember the rain lashing our roof, the wind plucking at the nailed strips of corrugated iron, and the prickly, bent twigs of an overgrown bush that just before my mother's death forced a way, as if housebreaking, into the crevice of an ill-fitting window. But of course the Aboriginals in Poignant's story do not share my scared, embattled response to the land. Their homes are notional, transparent, lacking doors and locks. They have no reason to worry about keeping the rest of the world out. D. H. Lawrence in *The Boy in the Bush* – his revision of a manuscript by Mollie Skinner, describing the colonizing of Western Australia during the 1880s – delights in the shoddy dwellings rigged up by the settlers: a forked stick holding up a roof of bark walled with brushwood, or a windowless, shutterless tin shack. Such dwellings at least contain no parlours, and banish the bourgeois domesticity that Lawrence despised. Inside a more solid, less permeable and impermanent house he is scathing about the photograph album, which by the end of the nineteenth century was a compulsory possession for any 'respectable householder'. Jack, his hero, dismayed by the images of dead Victorian worthies, vows to 'go up to the Never-Never…where there aren't so many people, and photo-albums'. He wants to cross back over the border into wildness, savagery. The photograph album, which reminds us of a personal past and entitles us to our place in the world, stands in the way of this regression. I suppose that is one reason why I was so moved by our little archive. It kept a roof over our heads, and guaranteed the firmness of the house's foundations.

Allowing for accidents of birth, I am tempted to claim the family tree in Helen Elizabeth Lambert's photograph as my own. Mrs Lambert was the wife of the commodore of the Royal Navy warships stationed in Sydney. She presented the photographs she took between 1868 and 1870 to the designer Viscountess Jocelyn, who assembled

1

Nicholas Caire

Bush Hut, Gippsland c. 1887

Viscountess Frances
Jocelyn, decorator and
compiler, attributed to
Helen Elizabeth Lambert,
photographer
*The New South Wales
Vice-Regal family; (the Earl of
Belmore, the Countess of Belmore,
the Lady Therese, Lady Madeleine,
Lady Mary, Lady Florence Lowry)*
from the album
*Who and What We Saw at the
Antipodes* 1868–70

them in an album entitled *Who and What We Saw at the Antipodes*. The children suspended
from this flimsy eucalyptus bough, like baubles on a Christmas tree or insects in transparent cocoons, were not even hers: this was the family of the Governor of New South
Wales, the Earl of Belmore. The Belmores were victims of transplantation if not of the
transportation to which the convicts were condemned, and their oak-like dynasty does
not seem to be flourishing in our hotter, drier, dustier hemisphere. The drooping gum
leaves are broken and bitten; the coiling creepers sketched onto the page do not manage
to unite these bleached people or incorporate them in the country. The photographs in
this album were hostages to a future in which, safely repatriated, the Belmores and the
Lamberts would be able to look back or down on who and what they saw at the nether
end of the earth. Still, what haunts me here is those stringy, abraded leaves. For all photography's earnest efforts, the family can fray.

   During the two weeks I spent in Canberra looking at photographs, I kept on
imagining I had uncovered portraits of people I knew. It is a common delusion. Gael
Newton often has to gently rebuff Australians who write in to the National Gallery
saying that their grandmother is one of the frumpy, disgruntled matrons waiting to
redeem her coupon in Max Dupain's *Meat Queue*, photographed in 1946. Numerous
middle-aged Australians with beer bellies want to have been, once upon a time, the
dripping, elongated Adonis who clambers out of the pool in Dupain's photograph of

Newport Beach. One correspondent is even sure that his wife's head belongs on the decapitated trunk of a nude Dupain photographed during the 1930s. Martyn Jolly has described the 'consensual hallucination' of some Sydney elders who decided in 1992 that they were the group of boys photographed on Bondi Beach by Sam Hood sixty years before, even though there was no evidence for the identification.

Such misconceptions, I think, should be encouraged. These images and stories belong to us because they are about us; we have seen them in our dreams. Remembering, which involves making mental photographs, is a collusive, contagious activity, because our memories are interchangeable. At Christmas in the desert, White's Voss broods over the recollected image of a tiled stove in his parents' house back in Germany. The sight is insignificant, ordinary, but – in the absence of a domestic hearth – consoling. Voss describes it aloud, and his companions listen gratefully: 'they no longer demanded narrative, but preferred the lantern slides of recollection. Into these still, detached pictures entered the simplest members of the party as into their own states of mind'. In 1992 Poignant's widow Roslyn returned to Arnhem Land, where her husband had photographed a corroboree forty years before. She wanted to show the photographs to the descendants of the dancers and obtain their permission to publish an essay about the encounter. One night she was walking home when a voice hailed her from the darkness: 'Are you the lady with our memories?' She denied it, not wanting to claim that Axel's rolls of film had stolen a tribal past, but the unseen man who addressed her had understood the truth.

I think of the photographs in this book as a family album for the nation. Nineteenth-century photographers attempted a census, an all-encompassing roll-call. First came surveys of the terrain, since in Australia the background is always to the fore; explorers loaded their horses with cameras. Then came the inventory of society, as itinerant studios housed in wagons trundled around country towns offering the homesteaders a chance to see what they looked like. Ideally, everyone and everywhere should have been honoured, made known, visually mapped.

Once at least, fossicking in the Canberra storerooms, I fancied I had stumbled upon myself. How could I not think so, since the image on the title page of Lillian Louisa Pitts's jokey album *My Summer Holiday* is labelled 'ME'? Certainly the squint – belonging to the Goulburn Valley boy Pitts cast as the fictitious Frank – is mine: I was always overwhelmed by the dazing light and the glaring size of the Australian sky from which it

3
Lillian Louisa Pitts
Title page from the album
*My Summer Holiday at
Merrigum,* Victoria c. 1915

cascaded. Frank, at large in the unfallen garden, has the kind of summer holiday I should like to have had. Whereas I spent the long stifling afternoons indoors reading, he murders cats, punctures tyres, and makes himself sick by overeating. Just to ensure that the Fall will occur, he steals some apples: how eager we are to grow up, to acquire a forbidden knowledge! At the end of the album, having caught pneumonia after nearly drowning, he is becalmed in remorseful convalescence: 'I was let sit in the sun with a picture book,' he scribbles underneath one of the snaps, 'and that is how my holiday ended.' For him, images are a meagre compensation. That is where he and I differ. For me, they are substitutes for reality, and often improvements on it.

Mostly, however, it was my parents I was on the lookout for. Mothers and fathers are generic beings, classifiable – as Australians are if you look at them with the required detachment, studying them through a mental camera – by the exemplary qualities they are supposed to possess. And because I was hoping to see their faces again, I did: photographs conserve our memories.

It wasn't exactly my mother's face I saw, more her legs and the elegiac late-afternoon shadow she cast on the bowling green in Paul White's 1978 photograph. So long as the image ends at the waist, I can tell myself that it could be her without risking disillusionment. There could be no better memento. Bowling for her was all about the enjoyment of the lawn, of its disciplined carpet of grass, a Platonic green that was a perfected version of the nature strip she toiled to keep tidy outside the house. Her own lawn continued to grow after her death, like the hair and fingernails of a corpse. 'She always kept it nice,' said my cousins, who wrote to me describing the arrangements they made to have it mown while the house was being sold. The drooping hands of White's subject could be my mother's, gnarled by arthritis. My own hands remember what their papery skin felt like. Perhaps, with its milky haze, this is a photograph of her current abode: spectres in starched uniforms and rubber-soled shoes glide smoothly over the Elysian Fields. White's photograph replaces one that I doubt I will ever be able to look at, though it waits in my box inside a sealed envelope. It is a snap of my mother's coffin beneath its mound of flowers, taken for me by one of the cousins.

4
Paul White
Lawn Shot No. 1 1978

5

Edward Cranstone
Civil Constructional Corps
Worker from the album
Design for War, vol. III
1942–44

My father surprised me inside one of Edward Cranstone's *Design for War* albums. Compiled after the bombing of Darwin in 1942, these volumes document the efforts of a land army to prepare the country for a possible Japanese invasion by building munitions factories and aerodromes in the tropics. Once again, the identification was physical, a churning reaction to the sweat-stiffened, insect-gnawed brim of the hat with its military medallion, and the gravelly roughness of his facial hair, which used to scratch me in the early days when embraces were still permitted. Cranstone's handwritten caption is *A.W.C.*, referring to the Allied Works Council, which recalls my father's proletarian truculence. Once when I asked him before an election how he decided who to vote for, he said 'I'm a worker', and probably banged his fist on a laminated table top. I suppose I already knew that this is not what I would be. No, this can't be him after all. The grin is a disqualification. He seldom smiled, even in photographs.

I chose the photographs in this book because I felt a sense of recognition when I looked at them; they evoked memories and made feelings articulate. Unlike Voss's companions, I allowed them to move; I demanded narrative. Following their lead, I watched as they organized themselves into a story, or perhaps enacted a drama. What I saw in them, looking back when I got to the end, was a tug of war between opposed feelings – a yearning to be absorbed into Australia and a need to stand apart, conducting an introverted, idiosyncratic argument with it; a battle between filial membership and the ingratitude of the prodigal son (or daughter) who happens to be different and wants to be an artist. Over a century and a half, they illustrate the country's emotional or psychological life. They also add up to a history of civilization or culture in Australia, because they show how the terrain has gradually been kneaded and sculpted into a homeland for the mind and spirit, a place that allows us to reconceive it and is adaptable to our desires. Writers and painters began the process, struggling to reach an accommodation that was natural and instinctive for indigenous people. The camera – which made everyone who picked it up an archivist, a missionary, and an artist – enabled photographers to join in this activity. My father and mother, who acquired cameras of their own in later life when they had the funds and leisure to go touring inside Australia, had a rule when taking photographs. Their subjects were usually one another, but they made sure to vary the composition. 'You've got to have a nice background,' I remember my father saying. Photography is about relating that background – the new country's baffling and exhausting spaces, its bizarre fauna and exotic flora – to the human foreground. If the equation is balanced, we feel at home.

6

Unknown photographer
*Members of the Photographic
Society of New South Wales*
c. 1900

But the work of colonization was begun by the axe: if you cannot tame the obstructive background, why not chop it down? Art also deals with reality by aggression or denial. André Breton, writing about Picasso, argued that artistic creativity 'affirmed the hostility which can animate one's desire with regard to the external world'. Members of the New South Wales Photographic Society, out for a weekend ramble in about 1894, are dressed too genteelly to be bushmen cutting their way through the undergrowth, but they could belong to a hunting party, lounging on their tripods as if they were shooting sticks. In Africa, the expeditions of white hunters have given way to photographic safaris: the purpose in both cases is to shoot the wildlife. Behind its chain-link fence, Karen Turner's scruffy zoo offers, once you pay the additional fee, the same opportunity to capture native specimens. Instead of pelts, you can carry home images as souvenirs. Of course the camera's conquering agenda has been euphemized. Inside the wire, koalas are allegedly available for cradling. For all its implausibility – koalas are cantankerous animals, not at all like cuddly toys, liable to urinate on you as you tenderly gaze up at them – the sign on the fence promises reconciliation: a peaceable kingdom, or perhaps a democracy of all created beings, where the woman with the bush hat and the beatific grin hugs the bear to her breast as a surrogate child.

7
Karen Turner
Animal Park 1979

8
Harold Cazneaux
Self-portrait with Camera
c. 1905

The recognition I felt often depended on a guess about something that remained out of sight. Photographs cannot show you what lurks behind the camera. Why this particular image, framed that way? What emotional current connects photographer and subject, the self and the external world? On rare occasions, the photographer abandons invisibility and admits the subjectivity of the camera's vision. Cazneaux, at home in his bedroom, aiming the camera at a mirror on his dressing table – a domestic altar, with a framed photograph already in place as a votive image – can expose the solitariness and solipsism of the practice. Photography is a quest for those 'objective correlatives' that T. S. Eliot thought Hamlet was ineffectually seeking: an attempt to locate aspects of reality that turn, when the photographer looks at them, into symbols. It creates what Baudelaire called 'correspondences': how else can we feel that we belong in the world? By looking at himself in a mirror, with the camera held close to his face like a child balanced on his shoulder to give it a better view, Cazneaux acknowledged this pining for reciprocation. All the windows that photographers look through are mirrors too, even if we cannot see the reflection. Mirrors offer the chance of self-consciousness, though we are wrong to trust the faces they hold up to us. They can only show us ourselves in reverse, back to front.

In the Tasmanian highlands during the 1930s Fred Smithies – whose photographs preserved not only images but would, he hoped, help to preserve a threatened wilderness – lingered at what he called the *Artist's Pool, Cradle Mountain*. The name given to the mountain is a metaphor, a verbal charm enticing brutish geology into a maternal affinity with men: it is a fond dream, almost a dreaming. And to nickname that stretch of water the 'Artist's Pool' is to hint that art has a similar purpose. The pool is artistic because it reflects the trees, recomposing them upside down like objects inverted on the wet, coated paper inside the camera. Things liquefy in the artist's consciousness, merging with emotions, drowning or dispersing into impressions. Smithies made the wishful transference work by leaving himself out of the photograph, though it is pervaded by his feeling for the place. Is the artist then just an incorrigible narcissist?

9
Fred Smithies
Artist's Pool, Cradle Mountain
c. 1935

David Stephenson, an American who lives in Hobart, has found it harder to balance subject and object, artistry and the obtuse power of Australian nature. Stephenson's home is on the foothills of Mount Wellington, the extinct volcano that lours over Hobart, determining the city's weather and the moods of its citizens. The mountain was the first thing I saw every morning during my childhood, and it was generally so stark, rugged and unapproachable, despite its closeness, that I thought of it as a gigantic extension of my father. In Stephenson's 1984 self-portrait, he has placed himself near the summit, against the cracked pillars known as the Organ Pipes. Once more, the name is a pious or possibly a fearful metaphor: is the mountain an organ for the gales to play on, or an organism able to give voice to the savagery and fury of the land? Stephenson's photograph is vast enough to include all of the vista, with an arrested avalanche clearing an aperture in which Hobart is framed. But the photographer himself is hard to find. He knows that the landscape of his adopted country permits none of the sublime,

triumphant gestures of human dominance that American artists allow themselves on the cliffs of the Hudson River or in Yosemite. You can see him, if you look very hard, lurking in a shadowed niche to the right. He is not hiding; the landscape has simply absorbed and effaced him. His decision to call the photograph a self-portrait has an ironic, intimidated deference. Stephenson has picked up the Australian attitude, and recognized the difficulty of subduing this continent with a camera, or with any other human implement.

10
David Stephenson
Self-portrait, Mount Wellington, Tasmania 1984

The camera, if it takes shorter views, finds other ways of coping with reality – refracting it rather than simply presenting a reflection. *Safety Helmets Must BeWorn*, taken at a building site in East Kew in 1973, is one of the random discoveries made by Eric Thake on his ramblings through the Melbourne suburbs. Thake specialized in noticing discarded, dishonoured bits of reality that could be made to look surreal. His streets, like those of Giorgio De Chirico, are enigmatic labyrinths: rather than making you feel at home, the photographs aim to induce a startled, mystified deracination in surroundings that are only too drably familiar. But these posters are more than a curiosity. Thake saw them as a challenge, which he defiantly accepted. 'The "Guru" and I,' he said in a note on the photograph, 'confronted each other with a Yashica camera.' In the middle of this tattered triptych, the adolescent evangelist, bringing divine light to Australia, rebukes the faithless country by aiming a camera at it. The machine, for him, is a symptom of a busy, unfocused, distracted inability to see or to understand. The inscription beneath the image wonders

> If people have seen God,
> why do they create
> so many different pictures of God.

and goes on to assert that

> God is one.

No matter how many persons God may consist of, Maharaj-ji is certainly not among them. While claiming to be the reincarnation of Krishna, he spent the 1970s converting donations from his acolytes into cars, jets and gold-plated toilets, storing the surplus in Swiss bank accounts. Exposed as a fraud, he has recently re-branded the Divine Light Mission, which is currently called Elan Vital: health passes for spirituality nowadays. At his global headquarters outside Brisbane, the portly, middle-aged Maharij-ji sells the baseball caps and T-shirts he has endorsed, and permits worshippers – who file first through a metal detector – to kiss his feet. New countries are touchingly innocent, and therefore vulnerable to such confidence tricksters.

The divine light remains, presumably, unphotographable. Pasted to the fence, the Perfect Master is taking a census of passers-by, or of the crowds he expects to recruit. But Thake, retaliating with his own camera, disproves the unitary proposition on the placard. God is multiple; in Australia a multitude of faiths or genealogical legends cohabit, vying to account for the earth. And photography has its own mission, demonstrating polytheism in action. It enables us to create different pictures – of God or koala bears, or of our friends and families. It shows that there is no single view, no general rule, no authorized version, and thus dispenses with belief in a divine tyrant holding a monopoly on truth. It also has its own second comings, giving us back the past and keeping alive dead faces that would otherwise evaporate in thought. It is at the very least magical, and may even be mystical, as Frank Hurley – who travelled to Antarctica with Shackleton and Mawson and photographed the battlefields of both world wars – realized when he bought his first camera and 'gazed wonderingly at the miracle of chemical reaction on the latent image during the process of development'.

Here, Hurley felt, was 'a key...that would perhaps unlock the portals of the undiscovered World'. For me, words were the key to undiscovered worlds, which by definition lay far from home. The photographs I like are fictions, even if they only intend to serve as documents. They multiply reality, which is why the guru in Thake's image obnoxiously disapproves of them. The photograph that for me is closest to home is the one that is the furthest from documented actuality: enchanting to me because it is so fantastical, so unlike its purported subject. In 1959, completing a commission from Broken Hill Associated Smelters, Wolfgang Sievers photographed the sulphuric acid plant at the electrolytic zinc works on the Derwent River in Hobart. We could see the works from our house. All night they exhaled boiling smoke into the sky, and lit the darkness with a green glare. They also poisoned the river, and sent the workers in suburbs like ours home with festering cancers. I knew none of that, and for me the zinc works on their bare hill were a horizon of lurid, sordid excitement, like the skyline of a tempting city. It was always the destination I longed to be taken to when we went for Sunday drives with relatives who had cars. We drove listlessly yet desperately, imitating the marooned suburban families in Patrick White's *Riders in the Chariot* who 'would drive around, or around. They would drive and look for something to look at....So the owners of the homes drove. They drove around.' Like those trapped characters, we travelled in the hope of arriving at a photo opportunity, a scene – usually a nice show of flowers at the Botanic Gardens – that the eyes could gratefully close on, sealing it in the memory. No one but me ever wanted to look at the zinc works; everyone else looked away, holding their noses. But a few times I managed to persuade whoever owned the car to take a detour past the slag heaps and between the blackened sheds

11
Eric Thake
Safety Helmets Must Be Worn
1973

inside which chemicals seethed, motors chugged, and sparks electrocuted the air. For me, this was the laboratory of Faust or Frankenstein. It is something of a let-down to discover now that the acid circulating in those towers was due to be turned into super-phosphates, fertilizers for Tasmanian lawns.

The filth, the ugliness, the stench, and the violence of the industrialized process elated me. Sievers saw the place very differently, and thus showed that the zinc works, like God in Thake's photograph, were not one. Having fled to Australia from Berlin in 1938, he brought a steely, dynamized religion of his own with him. He subscribed to the aesthetic credo of the Bauhaus, and was a member of what Paul Strand in 1922 called 'a modern Church', which worshipped 'a new Trinity: God the Machine, Materialistic Empiricism the Son, and Science the Holy Ghost'. The man with a camera, entrusting his own creativity to a mechanical eye, was the priest of this technocratic cult. Whereas I adored the grime of the zinc works, Sievers sanitized the factories he photographed: he loaned the workers razors or clean shirts, and once sent them off to scrub their fingernails before a close-up. His zinc works are the headquarters of some cosmic demiurge. Did he persuade someone to polish those gleaming tubes? Looking steeply

12
Wolfgang Sievers
Sulphuric Acid Plant,
E. Z. Industries, Hobart 1959
© Wolfgang Sievers,
1959. Licensed by
VISCOPY, Sydney 2003

upwards through the intestinal pipes and the transparent gantries, Sievers photographed a radiant, unpolluted sky. He knew that he was deploying one of the camera's magical talents, which enables it to alter the world, and he occasionally gave the photograph the subtitle *Snakes*. The metaphor ensures that these are unvenomous serpents: they bring scientific knowledge, for which — reversing the biblical story — there is no doomy penalty.

Eventually Sievers decided to refuse such commissions, which had required him to flatter the companies that hired him, reassure their stockholders, and ignore the evidence of environmental damage and reckless profiteering. The photographic studio opened by Charles Wherrett in Hobart in 1872 evangelized for the new art by inscribing the motto 'Light and Truth' above its portrait rooms. But did Wherrett's customers want to expose their faces to the light of truth? Photography had already learned how to misrepresent reality, which turned out to be its most saleable skill. In 1865 an Adelaide photographer used double exposure to duplicate himself, appearing twice in the same print with different costumes and gestures. I admire Sievers' version of the zinc works because it demonstrates the potent trickery of imagination. Vision is not the same as sight, and, as the heroine in *Voss* insists, it must be allowed its rights, its privileges and prerogatives. A chemical change occurs inside the camera, as it does inside those pipes at the acid plant. An object is transformed into an image, a grubby truth into a gleaming fiction. Murray Bail in *Eucalyptus* celebrates art's superimposition on our apparently drab, indescribable landscape as 'a hectic, apparently essential endeavour', but unfairly refuses to allow photography any part in this redemption of Australia: it 'remains parallel to nature', rather than converting it into human terms or making it serve human needs. When does photography become an art? When it alters reality, or relativizes it. When, defying the edict of Thake's Messiah, it reveals that there are more worlds than one, and shows us how to frame and focus our own private Australia.

Of course, as I realize with a twinge of conscience, if I praise the camera for constructing fictions then I am licensing it to tell lies. This indeed was one of its earliest endeavours in Australia, almost — before the guru's arrival — a divine mission. Photography ordered Australians to smile, and challenged them to be optimistic. In 1914 Kodak sponsored its first Happy Moment contest, which Cazneaux entered. A prize of £100 was offered, with other cash rewards for 'people whose snapshots prove that they have spent the Happiest Moments this Summer'. Advertisements rallied customers to buy vest-pocket cameras for themselves or box Brownies for their children, and diagrams of faces warped into comic and tragic masks identified the kind of people who might win and those who certainly would not:

> Only the man who has most fun;
> Only the really happy one;
> Only the man who laughs all day
> Can hope to take the prize away,
> And, as that's all there is to do,
> Why can't that happy man be you?

The last line contains an implicit reproach. Owners armed with Kodaks were enjoined to

> Snap your fleeting joys,
> And show how happy you can be
> By river, countryside, or sea.

The pictures that won prizes were of children like the spurious Frank Stephenson fondling pets, enjoying piggyback rides, splashing in paddling pools. At home, the Happy Moment adjudicators were partial to snaps of babies' bottoms in bathtubs or domestic clusters at the fireside. Outdoor pursuits like camping, fishing and boating trips also secured commendations from the judges: photography was supposed to be good for you, like a sport. The *Australian Photographic Journal* in 1896 recommended the activity for its healthfulness: practised out of doors, it could be sedately athletic. Hence the formation of walking clubs like the one in New South Wales. *Harringtons' Photographic Journal* in 1918 rallied amateurs for excursions under the title 'With the Camera in Arcadia', inviting 'ladies and gentlemen and boys and girls over 14, the more the merrier, all to bring their cameras'. Merriment was as compulsory as the possession of a camera.

Photography had its own strictly-policed physical and emotional regime; the cameras' eyes were blinkered, directed to ignore anything unconducive to happy thoughts. When John Williams began to attend meetings of camera clubs in Sydney in the early 1960s, he still found 'just these men taking pictures of their children and flowers'. How can there be a culture without discontent? Still, my perusal of that box of smiling faces, all arrested in a black and white childhood that never ends, has made me think again about the superiority of unhappiness. Vanessa Amorosi paid homage to those early contests when, just before singing her anthem about heroes at the opening of the Sydney Olympics in September 2000, she predicted 'It'll be one of those Kodak moments'. The ceremony was a protracted Happy Moment for the whole country and for whoever else happened to be watching overseas. The world for a while was unified by the cameras, as television synchronized experience and created a buoyant communal emotion, and the private album opened out into a national and international archive. Everyone who saw the parade imagined themselves marching, smiling, waving, and taking photographs of the people in the stands, whose flashbulbs popped as they took photographs of their own.

Though Kodak threatened to disqualify the grumpy, unhappy man, there is a tragic theory of photography, which contradicts that comic pursuit of happiness. As soon as the present moment is stilled, it is relegated to the past; it dies. The photographic subject is a corpse – literally so in J. W. Lindt's memorial portrait of Joe Byrne, a bushranger who belonged to Ned Kelly's gang, taken outside the police station at Benalla in 1880. Already dead for two days, Byrne with his clenched, bloodied hands was propped up against a cell door to be photographed. Decomposition had not yet begun, so close-ups were taken and sold as mementos. On the left, the artist Julian Ashton complacently strolls away from a scene he too has transcribed in the sketchbook under his arms. The photograph is a rearranged Australian crucifixion: a thief hangs between two bare trees, with a rabble of onlookers clustered around. The children, for whom this is a happy moment, could be Frank Stephenson's ancestors. The image suggests the ghoulishness of the art, which tampers with time and revivifies the dead (or at least prolongs the life of cadavers). Byrne's awkward posture makes him look as if he is moving: his legs are bent, his hips swivel. Are his hands about to retaliate by reaching for a gun? It is the photographer Lindt has pictured, self-decapitated by the black cloth he crouches beneath, who seems less than human, only questionably alive. His bulky legs supplement the props of his tripod so that he looks like a mechanomorph. His coat, hung on that wintry tree, casually mocks the dead man. A photograph is a husk or a sloughed skin, a surface peeled off a body that was once alive. When someone dies, the worst task is to dispose of their clothes.

Photographs cannot escape from our temporality. Happiness inevitably saddens when looked back on. Kodak advertised its Verichrome Safety Film in the 1955 *Australasian Photo-Review* with an image of a boy cuddling a kitten. The caption read 'Snapshots remember when you forget'. But what if you want to forget? When I first returned to visit my parents after years away, I noticed that they had taken down their wedding photographs from the bedroom wall. 'No one has them up any more,' my mother told me. 'It's a bit old-fashioned.' Unlike me, my parents did not belong to the company of those Kierkegaard calls 'the unhappy rememberers'. Or was it that they flinched from the memory of happiness because it had not lasted? Perhaps it was the funereal black and white that depressed them. My father now refused to watch mono-chrome films on television. 'They're behind the times,' he said. Modern and modestly well-off, he insisted on seeing life in colour. By now my parents each had a small plastic camera, with which they chronicled the seasonal state of their garden and took an inventory of relatives at family gatherings. The photographs came out in bright colour — colour that appears now, when I leaf through their albums, to have detached itself from the flowers and lawns or from the cardigans and jumpers of my cousins; it swims in the air, in blobs and clouds and floating blotches of radiance, like the tints added to old postcards of scenic views to cosmetically prettify them. No wonder colour has always been an ethical issue for photographers, resented by many as a distraction or a euphemistic evasion. The world, despite my father's comment on those old films, is a black and white place. I like that severity and starkness. I am the kind of man who owns nothing but black socks and white underpants.

Cartier-Bresson, whose original title for the book we call *The Decisive Moment* was *Images à la Sauvette*, thought that he was capturing images in a 'sauvette', the grill in the plughole of a sink that salvages your wedding ring if it comes off while you are washing

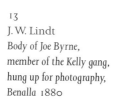

13
J. W. Lindt
*Body of Joe Byrne,
member of the Kelly gang,
hung up for photography,
Benalla 1880*

up. But the replica is never able to replace the person or object or occasion it commemorates. Photographs of home are precious if you no longer live there. None of us does, no matter how close to home we stay, because home, like childhood, is a paradise we only learn to value when we lose it.

Hence the luminous, alluring, insubstantial and uninhabitable holographic house constructed by Paula Dawson. Thanks to laser beams, lenses and mirrors, its rooms and their furniture occupy three dimensions. But they are made of light, tinged green to give them the tonality of decay or melancholia; this immaterial house cannot be entered. Irony puts quotation marks around Dawson's title *There's No Place Like Home*, which refers to the anthem Dorothy chants when repatriating herself to black and white Kansas in *The Wizard of Oz*. Dawson does not mean that home is irreplaceable. What she implies is that there is actually no such place, except in your own fond, self-deceiving reveries. To illustrate the point, she worked on this apotheosis of suburban Australia while away from home: born in Brisbane, she constructed her house of holograms at an optical laboratory in France in 1979–80. Yet she believes in a shared subjectivity – a communal pool of memories like that in which Voss and his companions immerse themselves when he summons up the mental picture of that tiled stove. The occupants of this transparent house have melted into air, leaving their coffee cups and newspapers behind them. It was tactful of them to disappear: we can populate this cubicle with ghosts of our own. Once again, the image induces a sharply painful recognition. We had one of those upright ashtrays, which my mother used to empty and dust each morning. My father died on a dented leather couch like that one, unceremoniously taken while watching the football on his colour television set. The books must belong to some other family, but the walls are those of the house

14
Paula Dawson
There's No Place Like Home
[hologram installation]
1979–80

I grew up in: thin, flimsy, hardly a barricade against the empty, unknowable continent outdoors.

The pained empathy I feel when looking at Dawson's house – or imagining it, since it exists now only in photographs of the switched-off holograms – reminds me that photography is the body's eye. But images can also be the mind's eye, especially if that mind digitally deconstructs the house and displays our notion of home as an abstraction, unrelated to visible reality. The translation can be seen at work in Adam Wolter's *At Home with Detail*, made in 1992. Wolter describes this as 'a slow-scan "live" digitization out the back window of my home'. Suburban Brisbane has been pixilated, digitally reduced to a fog of coloured particles. The diptych makes you see why people must have been so disorientated and angered by the paintings of Seurat: they showed a world suddenly atomized, disintegrated into dots. Because this art is technological, it places its own technical tools on view in that panel of icons, which come from the computer's table of applications. Here, the instructions UNDO and CLR have the same irony as Dawson's quotation of Dorothy's mantra. Having chosen to regard the world in this way, how can you undo the damage? Does clarity exist if our visual field is congested by so many ciphers? Clearance hints at the brisk, unsentimental disposal of domestic assets, a garage sale before you move out. Undercutting the art of painting and its faith in depiction, Wolter calls up a specimen of Deluxe Paint from a swatch and applies it to the scene. My father, who painted houses for a living, painted ours with Dulux. 'It needs two coats,' I remember him telling me, as if the layers of slick paint were an insulation against the cold. The best that Wolter's paint can offer is to smear the exterior. The photograph itself, in its witty way, is the kind of slander known as a smear, because its details call into question our conceit that we can ever be at home.

15
Adam Wolter
At Home with Detail
1992

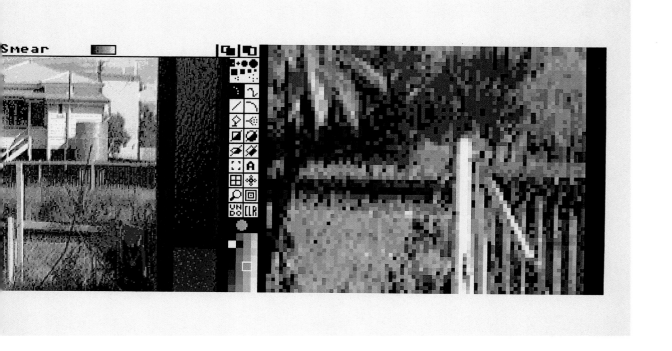

Despite such experiments, people go on building houses, trusting in their solidity, hallowing them by calling them homes, defending them against the threats engendered by Australia itself and stoically suffering their loss. Hence the acts of commemoration performed by Josephine Quigley and her grandson Aaron, photographed by Philip Gostelow in the remains of their house at Warragamba in New South Wales, which was burned by the bushfires that scarred the Blue Mountains at Christmas 2001. As it happens, I could smell those fires even before my plane from London landed in Sydney. At ten thousand feet, the smoke that smudged the sky and blotted out the sun left its taint on the filtered air in the cabin. Every evening on the television news during my first days back in Australia I saw people coping with disaster – and I could not help noticing what it was they chose to grieve over. 'That's thirty years gone,' said a woman whose house was cinders. 'All my kiddies' photos.' Her first regret was the incinerated album. Others told of how, given just a few minutes to evacuate, they rescued the family snaps. Their instinct paid an appropriate tribute to the art. Any photograph, as Man Ray argued in 1934, is the tragic and probably charred residue of an experience, 'like the undisturbed ashes of an object consumed by flames'. All such images have already been through the fire, and have survived.

The framed photograph Mrs Quigley holds up goes with her everywhere: a wise precaution, because if she had left it at home she would have lost it. It is a portrait of her son, killed in a motorcycle accident eighteen months before the fire. When she went to

16
Philip Gostelow
Josephine Quigley with her grandson Aaron at the site of their burnt-out home in Warragamba, NSW 2002

her daughter's house for lunch on Christmas Day, she took it with her. She returned to find her house a pile of ash, except for some scattered sheets of iron from the roof and that tilting chimney. But she did recover the broken crucifix from the wreckage. It had lain on her son's coffin, and formed part of a bedside shrine devoted to him. Her grandson had shared the defunct house with her. If he'd had the chance, he would probably have avoided the suspicion of irony by changing his PIPING HOT sweatshirt, but he too was left with only the clothes he had on. When the debris stopped smoking, he managed to disinter a handful of gemstones from his collection, kept in what Australians call the sun room. The rocks, which he has in his palm, are specimens of abiding, insentient Australia – of what remains when the bushfires, floods and cyclones have done their best to ravage the surface of the earth and dispose of those who live on it. Somewhere underground, the remains of the fire have hardened and cooled into jewelry. Aaron, as if aware that nothing but these foundations can be relied on, wants to be a geologist.

Gostelow's photograph, a piece of home-grown religious art, testifies to the battering Australians so uncomplainingly receive from the fierce elemental gods of their homeland. The gaping hearth cruelly suggests the energy of the bushfire, an output of vital heat not tamed to serve human uses. After a bushfire in the Dandenongs in 1968, the painter Fred Williams wryly noted 'a huge gum tree…smoking like a factory chimney'. The two figures with their sad, scavenged reliquary try to assert a human claim to a landscape that is indifferent to their presence and their imported sanctities. Josephine, for whom the jubilation of Christmas has turned into the sacrificial despair of Easter, might be Mary slumped at the foot of the cross, gripping a token of her son's anguish – except that, as an Australian battler, she is upright, resilient, incapable of collapse. Aaron the would-be scientist has less confidence in the afterlife of images, and deals in stern, stony adamantine facts. The charred colander next to his outstretched hand hints at rituals, small domestic acts of communion, that have been suspended. Any resurrection that occurs will be the result of dry-eyed human courage, rather than relying on a miracle.

On the way back to Sydney after my fortnight in Canberra, I drove past a stretch of bush outside Wollongong that had been scorched by a more recent blaze. The trees, denuded, stood about at stricken, crippled angles. The ground was furred with black ash. But there had been rain the night before, and brash spikes of new grass were already thrusting through the soot. The earth instantly recuperates; fire, as the Aboriginal people have long known, freshens it. The rest of us take longer to rebuild our small worlds, and to regain faith in the notion of home. But Mrs Quigley is surely thinking ahead to that reconstruction, and beside the empty hearth she holds the single possession that challenges her to continue. Once the walls and roof are back in place, what the structure will house is a photograph.

17
Richard Woldendorp
Nullarbor, Great Australian Bight 1988

2: Earthworks

I left Australia by sea. The liner sneaked out of Port Phillip Bay at dawn in the winter of 1968. By the time I had groped up several flights of linoleum stairs to the deck, there was only grey, churning water to see. I remember thinking, proud of my nonchalance, that I had not said goodbye. A decade later, after the invention of the Boeing 747, the return journey showed me what Australia looked like from the air, and made me realize that I had never properly seen it at all.

Richard Woldendorp's *Nullarbor Plain* might have been one of the sights I blinked at through the thick glass window of the plane in December 1979. We had made a stop in Perth, and were on the way across to Melbourne. The plane had emptied, I was trying to sleep, but the brightness that leaked in from that burning, metallic sky shocked me awake again. Staring down, I saw, like Woldendorp, a flattened, featureless, unpopulated expanse of red soil that abruptly broke off and crumbled into the indigo ocean. Ancient geological catastrophes look recent in Australia: looking at the photograph, you can almost hear the rending noise as the rock snaps along that abraded edge, or the splash as it submerges. Those low, searingly white clouds in the distance could have been exhaled by the earth as it heaves, convulses, fragments and recreates itself. Bleary-eyed and foggy-brained, I remember wondering what planet this was. I also remember the choked sensation in my throat when I answered my own question.

On this and later return journeys, it was the aerial view that revealed Australia to me. The serpentine writhing of the rivers that spill themselves into the Gulf of Carpentaria, and the lurid deserts they drain. The strewn boulders and matted forests of south-west Tasmania, and the tectonic rift like a surgical scar across the mountains as a souvenir of volcanic upheavals. The silvery, steaming Hawkesbury River glimpsed at dawn after a flight across the Pacific. Once, on the diagonal route across the continent, the umbilical bud of Uluru directly below, like freshly moulded clay. But Woldendorp's image sums up what I felt on that first trip back. It also confronts you with the problem of comprehending Australia, of imagining the forces that shaped it. I always incuriously assumed that Nullarbor was a native word, and I usually misspelled it Nullabor because that looked more incomprehensibly exotic. From above, it became clear at once that it was a Latinate coinage, meant to be dismissive: Nullarbor, the name it was given in 1866, refers to its lack of trees. For the exhausted explorers, Australia was a place of negative sublimity. But the Aboriginal people saw the plain as the site of a biomorphic saga, not a nihilistic, unvegetated waste. They called it Judara, and attributed its dust storms to the coiling tantrums of a totemic snake, which lashed the earth with its tail. Woldendorp confirms the indigenous account: it takes a myth, not the grudging taxonomy of a learned language, to account for the origins of this place, and for the life that, with or without greenery, seethes from the glinting rock and foaming water.

The Aboriginal people had never seen the country from the air, but that is how — in their paintings, with their ochre tones and arcanely patterned striations — they seemed to conceive of it. The anthropologist Theodor Strehlow pointed out that they 'developed in their pictorial art the habit of looking down upon a landscape from above and not from the side, as we do'. The spirits they dreamed of, not 747s, supplied the altitude. But they were also embedded in the earth, rather than hovering thirty thousand feet above it; they needed to be close enough to bend down and draw in the dirt. As a substitute for that bodily understanding, we have the abstraction of the map. In Woldendorp's image, Australia's serrated outline actually resembles the map of the continent. If the viewfinder could look far enough into the future or the past, you could surely see that gnawed coast stretching all the way to Victoria, where it would betray the wounds left when Tasmania splintered and fell away.

At school we were all issued with plastic maps. (Two were necessary where I went to school: one of 'the mainland', the other of its island appendix. Pleasingly, they were about the same size, which helped me to overcome my sense of inferiority when I thought of that land mass looming above us across Bass Strait.) The maps were aids for geography lessons. We were supposed to trace the indented course of the few, brief rivers that made inroads from the coast, or to pick out the straight lines and right angles — so different from the naturally crumbling and irregular, bulging and tapering outline of the coast — of the borders between the states. But I just liked to look at the map, not to use it. What did that shape signify? Tasmania, at least, could be called heart-shaped (at least until Barry Humphries took to describing the pubic bushes of women as 'the map of Tasmania', or the novelist Richard Flanagan, thinking of the state's suppressed, incriminating history, likened its outline to a mask). But the mainland was harder to decipher. A snooty duchess in Wilde's *Lady Windermere's Fan*, wanting to marry her daughter to the rich heir to a manufacturer of tinned food from Sydney, says that she has conducted research by looking up Australia in her atlas. She remarks on its odd shape, and compares it to a large packing case. I spent a good deal of time, when I should have been studying geography, speculating about what the case's contents might be. The closest I ever got to seeing some organic life in the plastic replica was when my father poured dough into a pan to make johnnycakes: the way the heat made the mixture pucker and run; the trailing extremities at the outer edges. The Australian earth is still cooking, not yet finally formed. The fires beneath it have not gone out.

Using maps in her *Antipodean Suite*, Fiona Hall points to the mental gap between the bureaucratic delineations of statecraft and the amorphous, inconclusive earth with its growing pains, its accidents and amputations. The rivers, probably dry, are wrinkles or worry lines, and the delusive, desiccated lakes on the edge of the desert in South Australia might be pockmarks or dents caused by concussion. Sea horses scattered around the edge of the map on the table frolic in a glazed ocean. By contrast, political Australia has been created with a ruler, or perhaps a pair of scissors, as the states merely approximate to each other rather than slotting into place. My map looked as if it might break along the fault lines of those state borders. I flexed it perilously, but was defeated by that new, indestructible substance, plastic. Instead of respecting the barriers erected by nature – like the convicts who believed that China probably lay just over the Great Dividing Range – white Australia imposed its own impassable frontiers, which carved the land into mutually exclusive sections. A Wild Dog Fence was rigged up between New South Wales and South Australia; Queensland hoped that a fence along its south-western boundary would keep out rabbits. At least Tasmania, given its own map by Hall, has seceded naturally, ripped away from the rest of the

18
Fiona Hall
Untitled from the series
The Antipodean Suite
1981
Courtesy of
Roslyn Oxley9 Gallery

continent instead of being surgically sliced off. The states are pink and purple, artificial colours that are absent from Australian nature. Elsewhere, the raw material of paint – stored in an orange-juice bottle, or sifting across the floor in dusty granular dunes – reconnects the artist with the earth. Even the rusty cans seem to have begun the process of decomposing into nature, from which plastic is immune: Australia has an oxidized landscape.

Wherever you place the map – on Hall's glass table, or on my school desk of shaved timber – it looks adrift, lost, because there is no other country to adjoin it. That, in the more landlocked 1950s, was the shock that came from recognizing where you were. Australia had been relegated to the end, perhaps even turned upside down. Though we clung to the shores, facing away from the interior, the view out to sea was not encouraging: the continent is encircled by estranging oceans like the one that gnaws Woldendorp's Nullarbor. It's not surprising that Hall has changed the waste of water to an aquarium by introducing those sea horses.

Fortifications, South Head shows the bleakness of the view from the mouth of Sydney harbour in the late 1870s: the rampart of North Head, as evenly graded as if it had been planed into shape, and the equally depressed horizon, with only New Zealand beyond. The flagpole, without a banner to flaunt, prods an ownerless sky. Cannons aim at the invincible sea, which still lashes against those cliffs. Trenches have been built so that the citizens of this new world can cower underground, in retreat from its vacancy. The enemy is elemental: the 'trackless infinity' and 'silent immensity' that daunted the globetrotting photographer E. O. Hoppé when he came to Australia in 1930. The guns might also be on their guard against the unknown, fending off threats from the unimaginable place Australians call 'overseas'. But they are diminished by the size of the landscape they must police, and look as ineffectual as water pistols. The dispirited horse has wandered away from its cart, and the soldier turns his back on the inimical vista. At least the lawn vouches for the presence of an imported civilization, bravely trying to put down roots on this exposed bluff.

Untitled – X looks back on this doomed effort. In this image from Debra Phillips's series *Colonization of Time*, a low encampment of colonial buildings on Bridge Street in Sydney, painted by Conrad Martens in 1839, huddles inside a squat wall, but cannot imprint itself permanently on a surface that could be aged metal undergoing a chemical change or perhaps the Australian earth, a mineral bedrock with no topsoil for grass to grow in. Inside the metal frame, the lopsided silver cruciform shape braces the whole panel. Nails driven through it hold the sections of the image together. Those crossed bars propose an analogy between colonization and crucifixion: nature is subdued by being excruciated, and the church extends its agonized, beneficent arms over that model prison at the bottom. But the corrosion that has overtaken the image, spilling down it like gore trickling from a crucified victim's wounds, undoes the combined attempts of church and state to conquer the continent. When the series was first exhibited, the catalogue explained the cross by quoting Nietzsche's claim that 'Since Copernicus man has been rolling from the centre towards X'. The spot marked by X is outer space, the cosmic periphery, a site of alienation: a city at the bottom of the world, or on another planet. Time is the only successful colonist, and it stealthily erases the claims staked by all empires. The cross here is no more effective than the disused, listless flagpole at South Head.

20
Debra Phillips
Untitled – X from the
series *Colonization of Time*
1990

As early photographs acknowledge, the colonizing efforts of the settlers were ignored or rejected by the landscape they attempted to subdue. Charles Kerry's view of the *Grand Arch and Bridge*, taken near the entrance to the Jenolan Caves in the Blue Mountains, conscientiously tries to balance the equation between engineering and brutish geology. The bridge, with its artfully rusticated brickwork, conquers one gulf confidently enough. But where does the little road built across the abyss lead? It curves into another, blacker gulf, which the eye cannot penetrate, leading to a limestone grotto given the heathen name of the Temple of Baal or to a river called the Styx, across which visitors used to be ferried in a punt. And the formality of the bridge's design – its quaintly decorative features, like the differently sized stones that cap its rampart, and the columns jutting out on either side of an arch that cannot call itself grand – is mocked by the avalanche of cracked, pummelled, disintegrating boulders above it. The man-made bridge needs an anchorage, which is why the lines of brick plunge down outside the frame, hoping to find something solid on which to rest. Nature's raw arch of rock is a suspension bridge; its crushing weight hangs inexplicably in the air. Not surprisingly, no tourists can be seen risking themselves on the bridge, or venturing into the cavern.

21
Charles Kerry
Grand Arch and Bridge,
Jenolan
c. 1897

Clarence T. Gosper
Convict's shoe dug at
Blackfriar's Estate, Sydney,
Septr 1890. Pair of convict's
hobbles, weighing 35 lbs.
1893

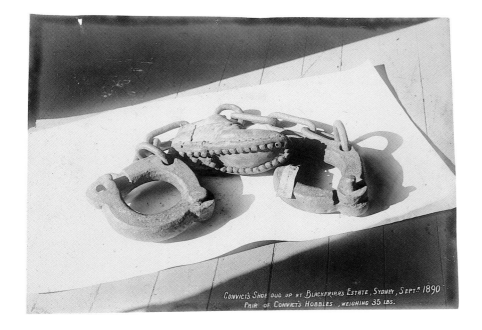

How could those who were not native feel at home in Australia, since the land itself was their penance? They were tethered to it, not rooted in it. The convict's hobbles photographed by Clarence T. Gosper were dug up in Sydney in 1890, twenty years after the transportation of convicts ended. The inertia they induced, the tug of an inescapable gravity, contradicted the Aboriginal sense of incorporation in the earth. The manacles that the shuffling convict had to drag along weighed thirty-five pounds; like a horse's shoes, they redefined him as a beast of burden. This Sisyphus had the rock attached to his ankles, and was not even allowed the sense of achievement that might have come from rolling it up to the top of a hill. But the hobbles also represent the absurdity of a penal system that punished men by devising ever more elaborate ways of demeaning and symbolically laming them, reducing them to uselessness by turning their very bodies into inescapable prisons. Why go to so much trouble? Escape was hardly an option for the convicts; those who did break free usually died in the bush. The system was a theatre of sadistic charades, designed to exterminate the individuality of the men it tormented. It deprived them of any capacity to speak for themselves, or to leave a record of their experiences: they were severely punished if they were caught keeping journals. Artefacts like the hobbles mutely, belatedly testify on their behalf. And even this crude and cruel invention, mockingly exhibited here as a disinterred archaeological treasure, fortified the men who were meant to be disabled. The convicts were braced together, joined at the ankles in a slow-motion phalanx. The chains forged a comradely community in adversity; they helped to manufacture the spirit of mateship that came to define Australian society, and reinforced the salty contempt for authority that underlies it.

To foreign eyes, the Australian earth looked inhospitable, un-nutritious. Explorers perished because they lacked the skills of the natives, who could identify edible roots and grubs and locate reserves of water inside trees or beneath the parched soil. The struggle with a terrain that begrudged newcomers the means of life produced, even in

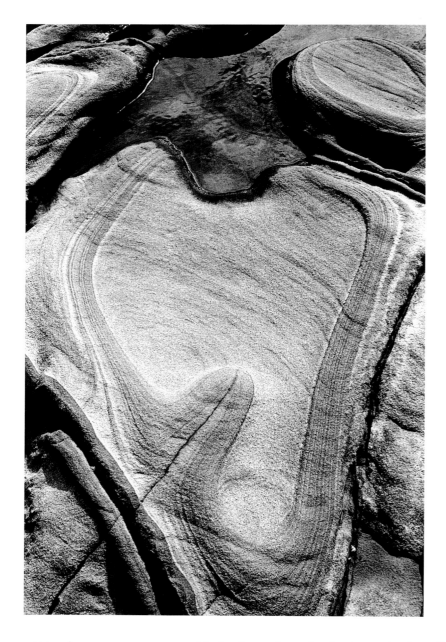

artists, a humorous resentment of the landscape. It was hard to live in, harder still to represent, since it defied imported standards of picturesque beauty. The painter Arthur Streeton likened the bush to 'an army of grey-green ants'. For the frontispiece of his 1968 book *Outback in Focus*, the photographer Jeff Carter chose an image of a belittled mountain range, jutting out of a plain that is its debris. Those hills, Carter comments with typical wryness, 'once towered as high as the Himalayas'; now the cliffs look as if rats have nibbled them. Erosion and abrasion formed the Australian earth, wearing it down – except in mountainous Tasmania, where volcanic upheavals made the surface erupt at sudden angles and confined the settlers to a few river valleys between the peaks. The same forces helped to determine the hardbitten, long-suffering, guardedly laconic Australian character. With a few streamlined adjustments, David Moore's *Eroded Rock* 2 could be the map of Australia seen from a remote height. It no longer floats on Fiona Hall's sea of glass; the surrounding oceans have receded, and are as dry and gritty as one of those ironic Australian lakes that have no water in them. Moore's image could also be a caricature of the archetypal Australian face, with skin toughened and blotched by sun or incised by trenches where muscles have tightened to clamp the mouth shut. That protuberance in the bottom right corner, which suggests the jutting outcrop of Arnhem Land, doubles as an Australian jaw of the kind sported by the actor Chips Rafferty or Patrick White – set like metallic armour, confrontationally extended into a plane far beyond the cavities into which the eyes have retreated, as if the bones were building an extra stubbly defence against the blistering heat, the blinding light, the battalions of blowflies.

The set jaw expresses a stubborn determination. But despite its gesture, the man it belongs to accepts defeat with grim, joking grace. Australia's heroes are not conquerors but gallant losers, like the starving explorers who never found the inland sea they were looking for or the happy-go-lucky recruits who volunteered to be slaughtered at Gallipoli. The earth itself, consuming so many vain hopes, is a compendious cemetery. This is the tragedy of attempted settlement recorded by Hal Missingham's photographs of Western Australia. In *Child's Grave, Broome* the little fence, so brave and wistful and meaningless in this immensity, keeps nothing out, and merely serves to measures the littleness of this particular loss. Despite the shadows of the rude nailed crosses, it is hard to believe that Christian resurrection works in this searing landscape. And what about the beer bottle, tipsily tilted at an angle? Was it being used as a vase? Is it honorific, or just disrespectful littered rubbish? At the cemetery in Broome, Malayan graves were bordered with half-buried beer bottles, and mourners could gather in a tin shed, surrounded by cases that once contained Swan lager. The dead body is an empty, good for nothing but to be thrown away, redeemable at best for a few cents. Missingham's images show nature to be a collective graveyard. White Australians die into it, whereas Aboriginal people are born from it.

24
Hal Missingham
Child's Grave, Broome, WA
1958

A desert is an hourglass, demonstrating our brevity and futility. But in Australia the bleached corpses it has collected perform in ghoulish comedies, undismayed by their own extinction. On the way to Lake Eyre, Jeff Carter once photographed the wreck of a rattletrap car, almost indistinguishable from the red earth, with two skeletal passengers: the ribcages of cattle, with elongated skulls propped unsteadily on them. One of the dead drivers has his long bones laid out so that he can grip the steering wheel. The car has no tyres, and there is no glass in the windshield. A notice hangs where the screen should be, saying 'DANGER HIGH VOLTAGE'. The cadavers grin crazily, enjoying their stationary outing. In his book *My Australia*, Missingham praises the 'wonderful Australian character of inventiveness', of using whatever lies to hand – bones, boots, bottles, scraps of iron, tin drums – to construct elaborate, teetering assemblages. In these rough, sardonic outback improvisations, he finds the origins of Australian art. Contraptions like the one photographed by Carter resemble the bricolage analysed by Claude Lévi-Strauss in his account of the Amazonian tribes. The bricoleur, according to Lévi-Strauss, is constrained by 'the rules of his game', which require him to use 'a set of tools which is always finite and is also heterogeneous'; this is how Robinson Crusoe fabricates a shelter on his island, and any Australian artist who works with the materials available on his larger island observes the same procedures. A beer bottle is pressed into service as a funerary utensil at Broome, and a shoe, containing caked sand not a foot, is redefined as vegetation. Missingham insists on the need 'to discover a form and a symbol', to discern significance in an eroded rock or a nameless grave. The camera has a special aptitude for pointing out the quirky details we might overlook and reading their runes. It saves such humble relics from being effaced by what Missingham calls the 'surface sameness' of Australia.

The beach is a kind of desert, and its flotsam and jetsam – like the waste curated by Carter – tallies what we discard and at the same time reminds us that we too will be discarded. The land works hard to digest Australians, especially around the water's edge. In 1971 Missingham photographed a sandal on Eighty Mile Beach, with shells nestled

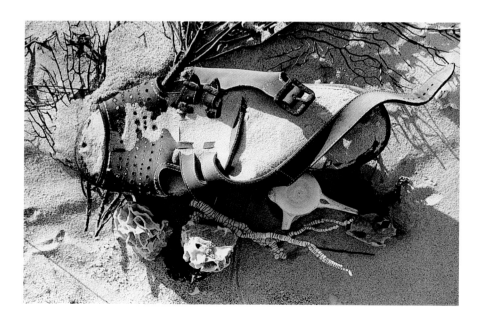

25
Hal Missingham
*Sandal on Eighty Mile Beach,
WA* 1971

Miriam Stannage
The Beach from the series
Weightwatchers
1983

beneath it and rubbery shoots poking through it. Sand thinly coats it, and its undone, free-flying straps might be twisted kelp. The difference between man and nature, life and death, is being erased. This could be a serenely fatalistic reply to Gosper's excavated shoe, acknowledging our disposability and noticing that our footwear outlasts us.

On another beach outside Perth, in 1983, Miriam Stannage photographed her own naked feet planted in sand on which the story of settlement and colonization in Australia has been scribbled. But those traces of conquest – the feet, with their painted toenails, are spread proprietorially wide – will soon be effaced when sand blows over them. Stannage follows other footprints: the paws of a dog, or perhaps some lumbering prehistoric creature, have preceded her. And she settles herself into the bolder, more regular tracks made by the tyres of a car. The rip-top of a can announces the triumph of a civilization that sets out to cover the earth with litter. The bathroom scales are here because the photograph comes from a series on weight-watching; but in this context, its little needle could be an explorer's compass, pointing straight ahead. Or is this a Geiger counter, the needle resting at zero because no buried treasure has been located? Despite the lack of precious minerals, the explorer accumulates curios as she goes, arranging the seaweed, the feather and the shell into her own delicate assemblage of bric-à-brac. These items are displayed on the floral panel with which the scale is inlaid. Even at the beach, Australians dream of gardens, which unlike this circulating sand can be cultivated, controlled, managed aesthetically. Culture implants itself on nature by a series of prohibitions, no doubt disregarded. In the town of Cottesloe, vehicles, surf-boards and spearguns are not allowed on the beach.

The final layer of significance superimposed by Stannage questions what art can do with this random, ephemeral gathering. Does it merely imprint a false order? The design is so rigidly symmetrical, aligned around the needle of the scale which bifurcates zero. Even the dog has almost been coaxed to stay on the same axis, though – alive and therefore disobedient – it veered towards the left. Stannage admits that art attempts to improve nature, perhaps as bossily and ineffectually as the Cottesloe councillors when they put up that sign. But at least the photograph is coloured by hand, as her toenails were, and this personal application of paint contrasts with the stamped, artificial dyes of the floral panel on the scale and the chemical suffusion of the Polaroid. A personal view has insisted on organizing the scene, refracting it and altering its tonal values.

The beach, for most urban Australians, is a desert lying close to home. It is a littoral and therefore a liminal setting, the border between a reality in which we are anchored and the infirm elements. This is where most of the country's dramas – its myths of origin, its last rites – are enacted. At the opening ceremony of the 2000 Olympics, Australia rose out of the ocean and seemed likely to descend into it again when during Vanessa Amorosi's song the arena was playfully inundated by a length of fabric drawn over the heads of the athletes that looked, as it unfurled and ruffled in the breeze, like a rapidly advancing flood. But this last wave was hung up to dry, and when it was completely stretched out the Olympic logo could be seen emblazoned across it. Only Australia, staging a national epic like this, would mime its own destruction.

Max Dupain's beaches function as either Eden or Armageddon. In 1937 he photographed a rainbow arching above the reef offshore from Newport, north of Manly; in 1983 he photographed rock pools at low tide at Toowoon Bay, making the stone look soft, porous, wet as if, like Uluru, it had only recently been given shape. The beach was where Dupain watched society mobilize itself, as the ranks of militarized lifesavers performed in their carnivals. Civilization also arose there: in Australia, culture traditionally attended first to the cultivation of physical fitness. Dupain's father owned a Sydney gymnasium, nicknamed The Tabernacle, and Max subscribed to the eugenic creed, which followed the example of classical Greece by balancing mind and body. He saw his surfers and sunbathers as transplanted gods, revising the myth to make it more at home in Australia. Here Apollo, as well as Venus, is born from the waves, cast up on the shore.

He could not help noticing that the beach is also a place of dereliction and decay, where stone disintegrates into sand and society straggles into the unkempt state of nature. Holidaying at Era Beach, south of Sydney, in 1957, he photographed the tumble-down shacks, sheds and privies at the water's edge. But on this unstable foundation he erected lofty allegories about the superman's advance from earth to sky. He was fascinated by the towers from which lifesavers kept a lookout for sharks – the Art Deco sentinel of white concrete on the esplanade at Manly; the steep timber ladder tapering to a point, like a pyramid of scaffolding, at Blackhead Beach, which he photographed in 1937. The Blackhead Beach tower could be interpreted as a symptom of Australia's paranoia, like the fortifications at South Head. A vigil must be kept to defend the coast; there are enemies both above and below the waterline. But the angle from which Dupain looks up towards that shining sky, and the care with which he posed the watchers on those rungs, turns the tower into an image of aspiration, a Nietzschean stairway that leads, by gigantic strides, from man to superman. This could be the diving board in Leni Riefenstahl's *Olympia*, from which sleek angels somersaulted into the air, seeming to fly

rather than plummeting towards the water: she reversed the film in order to reprieve them from gravity. Earth and water have both been elided in Dupain's photograph. These people stand in the sky – though the boy on the lower rung remains nervously seated, and does not yet trust himself to release his hands; he is also the most over-dressed of the figures, who progressively strip off as they ascend. The empty platform at the top is reserved for a naked god.

Because Dupain saw the beach as an evolutionary launching pad, he took note of a stray religious expedition like that of the three nuns he photographed trudging through the dunes at Newport in 1960. In their black robes, they pause in the glaring white sand against a rampart of frothing white waves. The tallest of them looks up to interrogate the sky, also vacantly white. Did the God she worships create Australia? A scene photographed at Cronulla, south of Sydney, in 1940, is even more ambiguous.

On the Beach, as Dupain called this image, could be an account of creation or destruction, of first or last things; those two explosive moments seem to be close in the youngest, oldest continent, where geology and history do not seem synchronised. This might be a nativity: Prometheus formed the first men from the muddy clay of a river bed, and Dupain's figures, still coated in sand, bask in the sun that – like the fire Prometheus stole from the hearth of the gods – vitalizes and animates them. But this naked couple writhing to separate themselves, like dogs after copulation, are also suffering what look like terminal agonies. Dupain printed the photograph through a crinkled, semi-transparent screen, so their skins are mottled as if by radiation. This is a surreal beach, like those painted by Salvador Dalí. Heat induces decay, a morphological distress that makes the human form melt like wax.

Australian beaches are never simply places of happy hedonism. Nature, as always, is dangerous, which is why the lifesavers conduct their patrols. And although sand soon erases all trace of the people who tread on it, beaches recall the beginning of Australia's modern history and anticipate its end. When Tracey Moffatt photographed the Aboriginal actor David Gulpilil at Bondi, she remembered the landfall of the First Fleet down the coast at Botany Bay and the unpreparedness of the natives to resist invasion. Gulpilil, wearing warpaint and armed with a ghetto blaster, is not at the beach to sunbathe: that is a fad he leaves to the pallid aliens, whom the Aboriginal people thought of as ghosts. He is there to defend terrain. That stand-off in 1788 is re-enacted on the beach; in Peter Weir's *The Last Wave*, Richard Chamberlain – gifted with an Aboriginal power of clairvoyance – foresees an annihilating onslaught of water rolling towards Bondi to submerge white Australia, and the detective in Peter Corris's novel

The Empty Beach, strolling around the pavilion at Bondi 'to kill time', also thinks ahead to apocalypse and retribution: the October bathers look frail, 'as if the sea was playing with them rather than the other way around. Any minute, it seemed, the water could rise up and obliterate them'.

The beach was the place where Australians were meant to gather in 1964 to watch their world end, as radiation sickness wafted down to them after a nuclear war in the northern hemisphere. The date was set by Nevil Shute in his novel *On the Beach*, filmed in 1959 in Melbourne by the director Stanley Kramer. Athol Shmith photographed the set, with Kramer seated at the camera and Gregory Peck – who plays an American submarine commander on a last, elegiac tour of duty – hovering behind. Peck spends much of his time in the film looking through his periscope, as his submarine surveys defunct San Francisco or prepares to surface in Port Phillip Bay. Here he is unseated by Kramer, who commands another viewfinder. Even Shmith defers to the black bulk of the movie camera, with its two aggressive goggle eyes behind which the film unreels. Mounted on a boom, with a seat for the operator, it is revving up for take-off: a replacement for Peck's submarine and also for the fighter jets that, presumably, dropped bombs during the chaotic, catastrophic war. Again the camera, which shoots its subjects, is a weapon. Shmith had glimpsed a world where men were the adjuncts of machines, which perhaps conspired of their own accord to eliminate their feeble, incompetent human users.

The beach in Shute's novel is an abstraction, a symbolic terminus; he took his title from T. S. Eliot's 'The Hollow Men', in which the last representatives of the human race huddle together on a beach, whimpering as they await oblivion. The film, which omits the quotation from Eliot, had to make sense of its title by sending its characters on irrelevant excursions to the seaside. Anthony Perkins complains of sunburn, and his wife recommends calamine lotion; Peck and Ava Gardner romp in the sand. They all sail and picnic under the auspices of something called the Canadian Bay Club. Perhaps this was a frantic effort by the producers to explain to American audiences what and where

29
Athol Shmith
Gregory Peck and Director
Stanley Kramer in
'On the Beach' 1959
© Courtesy of
Kalli Rolfe, Melbourne

30
Frederick Joyner
Vanished Waters
c. 1928

Australia was – just think of Canada, and imagine that it had drifted a bit further south. Despite its muddled geography, the film does catch an authentically Australian mood of quiet despair, a resignation to the cruel whims of nature and the distant edicts of history. Even *Waltzing Matilda*, used on the soundtrack, sounds like a funerary dirge. Our unofficial national anthem is a ballad about the suicide of a thief, who drowns himself to escape from the law after stealing a sheep. A symphony orchestra plays it as the submarine rises to the surface, suggesting that the ocean is now the billabong into which we will all drop. When Peck finally makes love to Gardner, a barbershop quartet off screen sings 'You'll never take me alive' and dolefully describes the swagman's ghost haunting the place where he died.

The world managed to outlive 1964, and its end, for the time being at least, is postponed. Meanwhile, Australia remains the setting for what might be an ultimate confrontation between man and nature. Photographers have recorded the showdown. Nature expresses its contempt for human survival in Frederick Joyner's *Vanished Waters*: a

South Australian river has shrivelled into a pavement of cracked mud. Man retaliates by mutilating or executing nature: in 1953 Axel Poignant photographed a ringbarked forest, its trees flayed and left to stand like gibbets, beneath Mount Warning in New South Wales. In Max Pam's *Effluent*, photographed at Kurramine Beach in northern Queensland in the late 1980s, a pair of thonged feet on a sanitary conduit celebrates this equivocal human victory, like a hunter posing atop a wild animal that has been shot down. Pam diminishes the gesture of triumph by cutting the figure off at the knees. All it can do is trample the earth, though it hovers some way above the scummy, stagnant surface. The pipe could not be more starkly metaphorical. It is a distended urinary tract or a bloated bowel, incontinently leaking. This is the way, on an Australian beach, that the world might end – with neither a bang nor a whimper, but instead to the sound of a trickling rivulet that discharges our waste into the ocean and stealthily kills it. In a poem written in 1938, A. D. Hope likened Australia's 'five cities' (Hobart was not included) to 'five teeming sores', and said that 'Each drains her'. Pam shows the sickly discharge. But his photograph, by way of recuperation, performs its own small alchemical miracle, beautifying the ugliness and once more exercising the 'right of vision' in order to see the world as a better place than it actually is. The stream of effluent shines, thanks to Pam's skill as a printer, and the splash it makes when it reaches the ground produces a dazzling silver mist. And behind the feet, a bleaching wave curls before it breaks, getting ready to purge Australia.

31
Max Pam
Effluent, Kurramine Beach,
Far North Queensland
1986

Photography, which sets out – as Missingham argued – to define forms, confronted an Australian landscape that at first sight looked inchoate, insignificant. Nature was meant to be a supplementary scripture, the open book of God. But when the novelist Marcus Clarke attempted to read Australia in 1876, he saw only garbled scrawls, 'the strange scribblings of nature learning how to write'. Clarke warned that Australians must teach themselves 'the language of the barren and the uncouth', which would enable them to 'read the hieroglyphs of haggard gum-trees, blown into odd shapes'. The director Abel Gance argued in 1927 that film had educated the eyes of modern men and, 'by a remarkable regression', brought back 'the level of expression of the Egyptians'. Marion Marrison's litter of twigs and dry leaves, photographed in 1979, accepts the challenge: is there a pattern and a meaning in these scattered scraps? Though the sticks resemble calligraphic brushwork, they do not write their messages in English. Here is a specimen of what Clarke disparaged as illiteracy, though for Marrison it is a script too ambiguous to be translated into words. Adjustments of scale are necessary, along with a review of cultural expectations. Marrison has photographed the workmanship of what the poet Mary Gilmore called 'the army of the small': those busy, disregarded creatures for whom the dead wood is a living habitat.

Lifting her eyes to the horizon, Gilmore worried that Australia was all frontier. She meant that its terrain consisted of vanishing points, not vistas. Cranstone's aerodrome in *Design for War* illustrates the point: flattened by rollers, swept clear of debris by recruits, the land tapers towards – what? Victory in the air, presumably; in fact, nothingness. The swerving marks made by tyres as they veered to the right suddenly look precious: irregular, and therefore evidence of a human presence, even though they could be the tracks of a plane skidding off the runway.

Hoppé, planning his Australian trip in 1930, worried about the 'pictorial possibilities' of the landscape. Painters shared his concern. In 1948 Sidney Nolan travelled through the outback in quest of imagery. At Tennant Creek, as sun scorched the corrugated iron and the dust swirled, he announced 'This is a bugger of a town – a lot to paint, but a bugger'. The country appears to be deficient in views. The Blue Mountains obligingly form themselves into a crevasse, though without managing the domes, spires, soaring buttresses and cascading bridal veils of Yosemite, which American photographers treated as an open-air cathedral. In 1985 in her series of Cibachromes *The Landscape Re-presented*, Anne Zahalka tested the pictorial possibilities of the region by superimposing the gloomy figure in Caspar David Friedrich's *The Wanderer above the Mists* on a romantic panorama of the Jamieson Valley, with birds wheeling above the blue smoky haze of the bush between a rampart of honey-coloured cliffs. As Zahalka expected, the encounter looks incongruous, unconvincing. The black-suited figure with his tempestuous hair has a self-dramatizing melancholy that does not suit Australia, and the landscape he surveys is disenchanted when Zahalka clears away the mist that fills up the cavity beneath the feet of Friedrich's man and reveals more tediously prolific gum trees. Charles Darwin, on his stopover in 1836, remarked that the Blue Mountains did not deserve their reputation for 'absolute altitude'. Close up, they were merely 'an inconsiderable front to the low land'. Romanticism required dizzier heights, where the solitary consciousness could contemplate its own extinction.

32
Marion Marrison
(formerly Hardman)
Twigs and Leaves 1979
from the series
Bonnet Hill 1975–79
© Marion Marrison
1979. Licensed by
VISCOPY, Sydney
2003

33
Edward Cranstone
*Southern Dromes: Tocumwal Air
Depot* from the album
Design for War, vol. I
1942–44

Though the figure remains in shadow, the valley is flooded with sunlight. Australia is too brightly optimistic to tolerate Friedrich's solipsist, who assumes that nature exists only inside his cloudy head.

Ian North attempted a similar merger of landscapes in 1987, superimposing the Australian bush on one of Monet's paintings of his garden at Giverny, with a Japanese bridge arching over a lily pond. The composition is a triptych, in which the artificial French landscape is accorded centrality. Australia is relegated to the margins and to the bottom of the frame; the Japanese bridge seems to levitate in a beatified haze, like a sacred figure depicted floating towards heaven on an altarpiece. North teasingly encourages an illusion: a mirage shimmering in the dry, ragged bush, as if this were a smaller outpost of the inland ocean that the explorers vainly searched for in central Australia. But the landscapes remain disjunct, one like drab military camouflage, the other liquid and luminous. Darwin, after his visit to Australia, wondered for a while if the country's bizarre flora and fauna pointed to the possibility of two parallel creations. Had rival gods designed the northern and southern hemispheres? Clearly Australia had its origins outside Eden. Biological evidence later convinced Darwin that no creator was responsible for either, but in art his supposition holds good. Romanticism and impressionism, as Zahalka and North reveal, valued topographical and emotional qualities that could not be found in Australia: down here, the ego does not teeter on the edge of precipices, measuring itself against immensity, and neither can it drown in a watery world of indistinct resemblances. Colonial painting, which copied distant, extraneous models, altered Australian nature to make it look more English, and even forced the local physiognomy to fit imported standards. When Robert Dowling painted a sad gathering of Tasmanian natives in 1859, he used European sitters, so the figures look like white colonists wearing body paint. The camera had no excuse for avoiding the truth.

34
Ian North
The Japanese Footbridge and Water Garden, Giverny
from the series
Pseudo-panorama Australia IV
1987

Hoppé's friends thought he would exhaust Australia within six weeks. In fact he stayed ten months. He was baffled at first by the 'vast plains' with their 'scrubby undergrowth', but he learned to appreciate photographic rather than pictorial possibilities. Instead of grand scenic compositions, Australia offered diagrams of empty space: Hoppé photographed the flat, taciturn expanse of desert around Alice Springs, where the steel rails of the Trans Australia Line speed ahead to converge at no discernible destination. Instead of civic monuments, Australia had odd testimonials to the superstitions of its inhabitants: in Melbourne his eye was caught by the occult service advertised in the window of a café, where afternoon tea cost a shilling with a reading of your dried-up tea leaves thrown in.

His journey demonstrated the need for photographers to outgrow pictorial habits, which some of them did by sceptically watching painters at work. In about 1929 F. A. Joyner accompanied the Adelaide painter Hans Heysen on an expedition to the Flinders Range. Heysen, sent by patrons to be trained at the École des Beaux-Arts in Paris, made conscientious efforts to show that the Australian landscape qualified as picturesque. But the photograph artlessly devalues the painter's earnest intent. How can Heysen's small square canvas encompass the range? It surely does not want to; its aim is to select and refine, to make the view manageable. The photograph, being horizontal, can acknowledge the grooved, eroded horizontal foreground, and notice the track looping off at the top right to disappear over a bluff on its way somewhere else. This is a place that is unmapped, uncultivated. No wonder Heysen overlooks his immediate surroundings and concentrates on the distant peak, altering its profile to make it more of a central, ordering principle than it actually is. At least he acknowledges the need for a centre, which Australia in those days supposedly lacked: wasn't its centre a killing vacuum, a 'dead heart' coloured like dry blood?

35
Frederick Joyner
*Hans Heysen Painting in the
Flinders Range*
c. 1929

The pavement artist photographed by Dupain in Collins Street in 1946 is even more self-consciously blinkered than Joyner's Heysen. Dressed in a business suit, he works on the kerb beside parked cars, as if toiling in a notional office. He has annexed the tree as his art gallery, and the sheets of paper tacked to it seek to replace Australian nature with the bucolic fiction of the Treasury Gardens, planted to make Melbourne look like an English cathedral town. His turf is as wistfully deracinated as the drawings he makes, for this is what used to be referred to as 'the Paris end' of Collins Street. (Even the opposite extremity of Collins Street, where the skyscrapers sprout, was admired for resembling somewhere else: Barry Humphries referred to it in 1980 as 'the Cincinnati end'.)

Photography, of course, continued to do its share of pictorial misrepresentation. The Russell Roberts advertising agency employed a team of 'artists, photographers, designers and technicians' to produce 'attention-getting and action-compelling pictures' whose purpose was to sell products by merchandizing a particular image of Australia. Russell Roberts designed a photo-mural 280 feet long for the Bank of Adelaide, sending staff from Sydney to do the requisite tinting: nature's colours were never quite roseate enough, and always needed touching up. The firm's brand of triumphal wallpaper was a collusion between photography and painting, document and fiction. Here the women in their floral print dresses are helping the grass to look greener or mottling the trunk of a gum tree. This, according to the company's division of labour, is a cosmetic chore, appropriate for women. To the side, a man looks after a panel depicting a tougher, more masculine subject, in which that seething chimney vouches for industrial productivity. Before installation, the panels make up a free-standing screen: their purpose is to occlude our view of what happens behind them – to conceal the operations of the economy they celebrate. This mural has its own sly, deceptive agenda. The merinos with their frisking spring lambs make propaganda for an Australian version of pastoral, commissioned by the monopolistic farmers who called themselves pastoralists. These graziers, who supported the Country Party, thought of themselves as the country's natural rulers. By pairing the sheep with the gum trees, the mural pretends that they belong in Australia, where they are unacclimatized parasites. No shepherds are visible, because Australia's pastoral myth did not provide for them: there was only the roving workforce of shearers, or the unemployed swagman who steals the jolly jumbuck in *Waltzing Matilda*. The bank is less interested in those who watch over the sheep than in the absentee landlord who erected the fences, cleared the adjacent paddocks, and established a personal domain. But while the mural tells all these emollient lies, the photograph admits the truth by revealing that the Russell Roberts studio is a workshop of illusion. The designing and embellishing should go on behind the screen, out of sight; here it takes place in full view, which undermines the mural's sales pitch.

37
Russell Roberts Pty Ltd
Women retouching pastoral mural at Russell Roberts Pty Ltd Sydney
1940s

In Peter Dombrovskis's *Painted Cliffs*, photographed on Maria Island in Bass Strait, nature has done the painting, tracing a maternal outline – legs spread, body symmetrically arranged around a seam deriving from that clenched birth cavity – on the yellow, fleshly rock, with vertical contours that suggest the rushing of blood. Dombrovskis, born in Germany to Latvian parents, said in 1995 that he experienced 'a state of grace, a sense of spiritual connection with all around' when wandering through the highlands of Tasmania or the gorges and rainforests of its west coast, and admitted that sometimes 'after being permitted to see and perhaps photograph some particular object of beauty, I often feel it necessary to make some acknowledgement, a sign of gratitude, perhaps a touch or some act of private communion that would appear silly or affected were there someone else to see me'. The goddess of the cliffs seems prepared to receive his embrace. Dombrovskis imported to Australia the belief in nature's divinity proclaimed by photographers of the American west like Ansel Adams and Edward Weston. John Steinbeck, describing a valley on the California coast where he grew up, likened the filtered darkness among the sequoias to the stained-glass windows at Chartres Cathedral, which 'strained and sanctified the sunlight'. Such evangelical metaphors pacified the American wilderness, and explorers tried to impose the same story of spiritual travail and triumph on the wild rivers of Tasmania's west coast. Dombrovskis

photographed a churning maelstrom called The Cauldron, which admits that nature can be hellish; other scenes – at Deliverance Reach or Transcendence Reach, The Sanctum or Freedom's Gate – insist that this is a heavenly region. At Angels' Cliffs, white streaks on the rock face look like hovering spirits. Dombrovskis's best work documents the Tasmanian highlands in winter: snow – as in Ansel Adams's photographs of Yosemite out of season – cleanses the world and makes it coolly radiant.

But Australian nature refuses to be cajoled by churchy nicknames. Children used to be prepared for its cruel intransigence by reading May Gibbs's *Adventures of Snugglepot and Cuddlepie*, in which two gum-nut babies are menaced by an ogre in the form of a Banksia bush. The harried infants take a necrological tour through the bush, encountering crushed baby ants, broken eggs, a snake eating a frog, and a trapped possum. Anthropomorphism is a delusion: 'monster Humans' are here the mortal enemies of Bush Creatures. And perhaps Dombrovskis, for whom conservation was an 'ethic of the land', made a mistake in assuming that the land shared his ethical sensitivity. In 1972 he found the body of the naturalist Oleg Truchanas, who drowned in the Gordon River while launching his canoe. Later he discovered the corpse of another canoeing friend from Hobart, and in 1981 was nearby when a teenage environmentalist was swept away by the Denison River. In 1996 he too died, of a heart attack, in the Western Arthur Ranges. That flagrant spirit on the cliff looks, in retrospect, like a consuming carnivore. Rocks in Australia hungrily demand sacrifices. Plaques on Uluru record the names of climbers who have plunged to their deaths down its slick side. A group of schoolgirls, according to the fable, was gobbled up by Hanging Rock, that stubby tumulus on the outskirts of Melbourne. Joan Lindsay's novel *Picnic at Hanging Rock* describes the pampered girls as intruders in nature, 'no more a part of their environment than figures in a photograph album, arbitrarily posed against a backcloth of cork rocks and cardboard trees', like the natives and settlers J. W. Lindt stiffly arranged in his studio. Photography here signifies disconnection, a false and mediated relationship with nature. At least in Peter Weir's film the figures can move; they fuse with their environment by vanishing into it.

David Stephenson renounced his own American reverence for nature when he photographed Antarctica in the early 1990s. 'Nature does not appear to be benevolently beautiful, or even awesomely sublime,' he said. Frozen solid, it is beyond feeling anything, and its aim is to anaesthetize you. The stark nonchalance of the ice is registered in images that are blindingly blank, an invisible vista extended across ten chromogenic panels mounted on aluminium and entitled *Romantic Projection (The Indifference of Nature)*. Here Stephenson found a chilling inversion of the white heat that makes central Australia uninhabitable – for Antarctica is also technically a desert, thanks to its lack of precipitation, and it sags below sea level because of the impacted weight of its ice. The sight enforced a disorientated abstraction: no pictures or descriptions had prepared Stephenson for 'the total alien strangeness of the view'.

In the air, the camera is alienated from Australia. Woldendorp, looking down, sees architectonic patterns of erosion or geometric scrawlings that could be evidence that some inhospitable planet has inhabitants, though they surely cannot be human. At Cape Crawford in the Northern Territory, he came upon a Manhattan of towering sandstone clumps, a city without occupants. Near the airport in Alice Springs, he saw a series of incisions on the red earth, sliced through the topsoil so that water could seep in.

38
Peter Dombrovskis
Painted Cliffs, Maria Island
c. 1990

The explanation weakens the photograph by disregarding its strangeness: if you do not know the purpose of those entrenched squiggles, they look like tribal scarifications on the skin, raising welts and ridges as a record of initiatic suffering. A dam near Lake Grace in Western Australia must surely be a monument designed by an extraterrestrial civilization, semaphoring to the void: it is a pyramid of brown stripes with an eye at its apex – a wide-open pupil of yellow water, set inside a ring of whiter earth, with streaks of red soil like angry veins. The exploration of Australia, like space travel, is an education in the relativity of worlds, and in the tenuous, ungrounded irrelevance of humanity.

Photography tries hard to balance subject and object, uniting the person out of sight behind the camera with whatever the camera looks at. Australia complicates this quest for recognition and reconciliation. What if the distance across which photography has to do its work of connecting extends into light years, and the camera lengthens into one of those radio telescopes that audit outer space? Do you dare to make yourself at home on this galactic outpost? Edward Douglas – like Stephenson, a transplanted American – ponders the problem in *Moon-rock*, aligning a grainy television image of the lunar surface with a laid-in view of a monolith in the Australian desert. Film of the moon-landing in 1969 was augmented by simulations with animated models. Sceptics and wits alike suggested that the whole elaborate expedition had been staged in a television studio. Perhaps the landing itself was filmed on location in Australia. The few trees and bushes would have had to be grubbed up, and the colours adjusted: rather than being coldly silvery like the moon, Australia is red like Mars. At least this unearthly earth has not been colonized, and the actors playing astronauts have not left an American flag behind them.

Ian Provest in *Omphalos* brings together science and mythology in the hope of understanding Australia and establishing a connection, at once mental and physical, with it. Provest designed a block of sandstone, hollowed out to resemble a squat, stocky telescope, walled it with glass, and inserted a photograph at the base. The stone block has a relief carving of a waratah flower on its rim, which gives it a deceptively domestic appearance: it could be a vase, though it is too large and heavy to fit on a suburban mantelpiece. Squinting into the glazed well, you are immediately disorientated. You seem to be peering down a foreshortened chute that abridges outer space, with a nebular haze obscuring the view. Or are you simply gazing into a green eye that uncommunicatively stares back at you? At the bottom, lit by a fluorescent neon tube, is a digitally-generated magnetic transparency, a diagram that derives from a photograph taken by a satellite that aimed its unmanned camera at the midpoint of the Australian continent. Omphalos was a sacred stone in Apollo's temple at Delphi, thought by the Greeks to mark the earth's centre. Shaped like a navel, it marked the rupture between men and the physical world from which they had detached themselves; it is through the umbilicus that we absorb our mother's nourishing blood when we are in the womb. From the satellite's aerial future, Prevost has looked back to the buried past. With our heads so high in the sky, is it possible to keep our feet planted on or in that native soil? Doesn't the body in-between the head and the feet stretch to breaking point? And if Australia does have a bud of toughened flesh marking the place where we broke our ties to the land, it should probably be called not Omphalos but Uluru.

39
Edward Douglas
Moon-rock
1973

40
Ian Provest
Omphalos [detail]
1992
from the series
Roam 1991–92
[Looking down at
an illuminated
satellite photograph
of the exact centre
of Australia at the
bottom of the well
in the sandstone
sculpture
(stonecarver Jeff
Thompson)]

41
Charles Bayliss
St Mary's Cathedral c. 1875

3: Which Gods?

Once flags had been possessively planted in the soil of the new country, crosses were raised to sanctify the land. The first Roman Catholic cathedral in Sydney burned down in 1865. In the mid 1870s, Charles Bayliss photographed the construction of St Mary's, its replacement. Scaffolded ribs survey the teeming rookeries of Woolloomooloo; across the road is fledgling Hyde Park, with shrubs inside protective fences and no tree cover. To invoke the park's London prototype was a magic spell, which seems not to have worked. Nor is the roofless building ready to accommodate the Mother of Christ. The mystique of European cathedrals derives from their gradual growth through the centuries, as side chapels or spires or stained-glass windows are added: whether or not they are frequented by God, they store our shared history. If that history lies in the future, a cathedral is just like any other profane building. We build a house for God and his family on speculation, hoping that they might consent to move in.

What will eventually be the cathedral is here just an elongated box, much less substantial than Francis Greenaway's barracks to the left, and overtopped by some of the mercantile structures behind it. The view is dominated by the dry rivulet of an empty roadway. The very lie of the land shrugs off the burden of the new building. A steep hilltop obliged the architect to alter the traditional east-west orientation, placing the entrance to the south and the sanctuary to the north. Even so, miscalculations forced the later addition of thirty steps up to the façade, without which the cathedral would have jutted out into empty space. The feng shui experts might have advised St Mary against taking up residence. Though the cathedral extended along that hill above Woolloomooloo, it never persuaded rowdy Sydney to accept its benediction.

Australia remained in need of hallowing. Harry Phillips, a photographer who specialized in views of the Blue Mountains, reported in 1914 on his sighting of a halo, or halation. Photographing clouds in the valley at Narrow Neck early in the morning, he saw ahead of him a figure with a rainbow-coloured nimbus encircling his head: an augury of the arisen Christ? Overawed, he forgot he had his camera with him and missed recording the advent. Others also watched and waited for revelations, erecting lookouts with reserved seating for believers. Across Sydney Harbour at Balmoral, a Greek amphitheatre was built in the foreshore during the 1920s by the theosophical Order of the Star of the East. According to local legend, the Second Coming was to begin with Christ's arrival through the Heads, and the theosophists were assured a ringside seat on those white tiers. When the amphitheatre was bulldozed in 1951, Christ had still not come.

Edgar Bertram MacKennal, looking at Sydney Harbour in 1927, was tantalized by 'some soul I cannot find, some spirit I have never seen'. The camera – which by the end of the nineteenth century had learned technical tricks that enabled it to portray ghosts or fairies or ectoplasmic revenants – should have been able to make that spirit visible. Nicholas Caire thought of the fern gulleys he photographed outside Melbourne as places where Puck and Oberon might plausibly cavort. But visitors continued to worry about who had made Australia and what the country meant. Agatha Christie travelled through Tasmania in 1922, and remarked that 'If there were nymphs in these woods, they would never be caught'. There were no nymphs in the matted bush or the horizontal forests, which is why none had ever been trapped; the settlers had better luck with Aboriginal women, whom they raped, mutilated, or sometimes tethered to trees so that they would be available to supply rapid sexual relief.

The colonists who infested the landscape with imported species such as sheep and rabbits also introduced classical nymphs. Perhaps they understood that Christianity, with its meek and milky piety, had little chance of survival in a country designed to be a living hell. Or they may have calculated that the gods of the Greeks – lustful, violent, amoral, given to plunder and pillage – were better suited to this terrain. The parks with which all the new cities were supplied became zoos where Christie's nymphs could live in captivity, immobilized on pedestals like whiter versions of the Aboriginal women tied up by the settlers. A robed Victorian dignitary pre-emptively embodies civic virtue on a plinth at the entrance to Bayliss's Hyde Park. When the trees grew up, there would be screened alcoves for encounters between rapacious Olympians and their human victims.

John Kauffmann's *Fantasy* found Pan piping in the Treasury Gardens in Melbourne. The statues are actually there, though the photograph's diffuse light, the thick undergrowth and the misty impressionism of Kauffmann's printing make it look

42
John Kauffmann
Fantasy c. 1920

as if we are spying on something illusory. But the fantasy is hardly wan and wistful, like J. M. Barrie's notion of Pan as a little boy whose innocence never declines into sexual maturity. Pan also made himself at home in Kensington Gardens in London, where the statue of Barrie's ephebe is skinny and meatless, with a reed in his mouth through which he might be harmlessly blowing bubbles. His colonial relative is an older, hairier, more menacing creature. His shaggy thighs and cloven hooves mark him as a mutant, half bestial and half divine; as a goat-god he is accompanied by one of his bearded flock. He has a proper set of pipes, and it is easy to imagine their shrill tone, able to incite the carnal riot known as a panic even though he is camped so near to the sober, pompous headquarters of the Victoria state government. He leers as he plays.

Australia bred a grizzled satyr of its own in Norman Lindsay, the cartoonist and essayist who evangelized for pagan bawdry by illustrating ribald writers like Petronius or Rabelais and in 1933 published a diatribe called *Pan in the Parlour*. Lindsay, declaring war on Christian wowserism, introduced Nietzsche to the southland. Australia has always been a battleground for strange gods – Dionysus, Isis (worshipped by theosophists, who thought that all religious doctrines derived from India), the Wandjinas and the sacred snakes or dingoes of the Aboriginal people, Thake's guru with his divine light. Nietzsche's creed favoured tragedy, valuing ecstatic self-destruction rather than the sacrificial pacifism of Christ. Lindsay tailored Nietzsche to Australia by insisting on comic indulgence: paganism meant sexual promiscuity, skinny dipping, and plentiful libations of booze.

Cazneaux photographed Lindsay in his garden at Springwood, his property in the Blue Mountains. He reposes beside a concrete statue of Pan and a nymph who is probably about to escape from the randy god's assault by metamorphosing into a laurel tree. Pan looks like a true demon of the woods, with his erect tail, demonic horns and grasping hand. Lindsay, by contrast, is harmless enough in his rumpled suit. He has not

43
Harold Cazneaux
*Norman Lindsay at his home in
Springwood, NSW* 1920

forgotten to bring his hat along on his ramble, acknowledging that the Australian sun is dangerous for white intruders. With his open book and lolling pencil, he is an academic daydreamer, allowing himself to fantasize about licentious episodes like the one behind him because they take place in a dead culture. And statues are bloodless, as well as being unable to move: this rape will never happen. Pan's arm is frustratingly frozen, and he – like the faun played by Nijinsky in Debussy's ballet – can only grip a corner of the nymph's filmy drapery, rather than fastening on her body.

In 1935 Lindsay invited the twenty-four-year-old Dupain to Springwood. Dupain – who replied in a letter written at Newport, where he lay naked on the hot sand like his own sunbaker, waiting to scandalize any passing 'virginity monger' – treated this as a summons to Olympus, or (as he wrote) to Hyperborea, the paradisial homeland of Apollo's worshippers at Delphi. He explained that he wanted 'to paint the spirit of landscape…the spirit of life within us'; that he had cast aside his camera because it could not transcribe 'the strong blaring light of Australia' or communicate the exhilaration he felt when rising above the earth into the realm of the 'lyrical, fantastical, Hyperborean'. Rather the Hyperboreans than those Christian missionaries who interpreted Australia as a Bunyanesque allegory of expiation, calling mountains Despair and Misery and marsupial wolves devils. In 1935 it was not yet possible to imagine that the spirit of landscape might be black or ochre-red, rather than marmoreally white.

Dupain photographed his *Sunbaker* in 1937, and included the image in an album of holiday snaps that is a manifesto for the paganism he saw as Australia's true religion. The album includes a scene on a shadow-mottled lawn, on which a book lies beside a white lump that could be a shrouded body. The book is D. H. Lawrence's *The Man Who Died*, which tells the story of a Christ who did not die on the cross and – rather than miraculously resurrecting – woke up the next day in his tomb, ready to assume an undivine physical life. Does the wrapped form on the grass allude to this feat? Lawrence's man is revivified by the carnal heat that blazes from an Egyptian woman, a worshipper of Isis who mistakes him for her paramour Osiris. Making love to her, he basks in her 'womanly glow' and 'mysterious fire', feels he has touched the sun, and realizes that he has 'never before stretched [his] limbs in the sunshine'. When he remembers the chaste, clothed society that oppresses them, he reassures himself by declaring 'There is a law of the sun which protects us'. If Christ had ever made that Australian landfall predicted by the theosophists, he might have chosen to be a sunbather rather than a fisherman.

Instead of a bronzed, sand-crusted male, Cazneaux – despite his wry attitude towards Lindsay – sought to photograph wispier, more evanescent nymphs, and encouraged little girls to impersonate them. He called a portrait of the frolicking Dorothy Woolley *Woodland Nymph*, and photographed Phillida Cooper in ballet slippers and a gauzy tunic dancing with a lily in her hand. Photography was reluctant to give up hope that a spirit might materialize in the hot, aromatic, cicada-loud Australian air. When such spirits did appear, they sometimes found themselves trapped in a deconsecrated reality, unable to vanish before later, less devout photographers snared their image. Hence the flustered embarrassment of Roger Scott's nymph, discovered sunbathing (she is woefully pallid) in the Sydney Botanic Gardens. Those gardens were plantations of predominantly English flowers and trees; now a skyscraper encroaches on this genteel, artificial wilderness, and the average stroller is probably from Japan or Singapore. The statue grabs a towel to hide her shame, but she leaves her rear undefended, exposed to Scott's camera. This is a moment as decisive as any of those photographed by Cartier-Bresson: both fortuitous and providential, a convergence of past and present, nature and culture, Anglo-Saxondom and Asia.

At Bondi Junction, in Mark Johnson's photograph, a goddess has managed to escape skywards and balances on a pedestal between two scything wings. The vertical strip of the shopfront that she surmounts, painted in a colour that registers here as black, looks grim, even demonic: this could be the rearing shadow of a vampire bat. She is accompanied by an occult colleague, crouched in profile on the rooftop balustrade. Why is there a sphinx in the suburbs? No one seems to want to own this tight-lipped enigmatic beast: the stripe of paint on Lagudi's section of the property slices her body in half so that her head belongs to the owner of the adjacent laundry. The familiar is estranged, made uncanny or unhomely (in a possible translation of Freud's adjective 'unheimlich'). One of photography's equivocal achievements is to unsettle us, forcing us to reconsider a reality from which mystery seems to have fled. The blind windows in the façade suddenly look sinister, the cracks in the white plaster hint at seismic pressures below the surface, and the painted arrow indicates the way to perdition. The verandah's line of corrugated iron protects the street from the sun and shoppers from the knowledge of what hovers above them. A goddess treads air up there, but a monster is also poised to pounce.

44
Roger Scott
Botanic Gardens, Sydney
1972

45
Mark Johnson
Bondi Junction
1977

46
Grant Mudford
Waverley (Let There Be Light)
1972

Christianity made dour efforts to regulate Australia. At Waverley, north of Bondi, a cemetery was built on a headland: a dormitory suburb for the dead, who had a prior right – since they were already in a state of grace – to enjoy the ocean view. If you lived virtuously, you might be rewarded with a place in this nursery of crosses. Grant Mudford relishes the irony in his photograph of the scene. The memorial pillar hardly needs to quote God's 'Fiat lux', the command that switches on the light and brings order to the universe in Genesis. The light that dazzlingly bounces off the Tasman Sea and ignites the clouds is already here, whether God calls for it or not. This is the kind of light that Dupain called 'blaring', as if it had the brazen sound of trumpets. The carved block, attempting to blot the brightness out, obscures some genuinely mystical apparition on the horizon: Mudford's clouds boil with energy and seem to have been fired into the sky like puffs of smoke from a cannon. But what radiant cataclysm, at the vanishing point behind the pillar, has goaded them into motion? Enlightenment, according to the religion preached by the cemetery, is preferable to the blaze of the sun. Nevertheless, the masonry covers up the mystery. 'LET THERE BE DARKNESS' would transcribe the mood of the place more accurately. The 1985 film of Corris's novel

The Empty Beach makes seditious use of the cemetery at night. Derelicts swigging from bottles congregate among the graves, as if they had clambered out of them; one of the alcoholics is an old woman ghoulishly wrapped in mothy, cobwebbed finery. At least the quiet, enlightened sleepers are enjoying themselves.

The anthropologist Colin Simpson persisted in making a lineal connection between Australia and Eden, and saw the Aboriginal as an authentic Adam or (to use the nickname he proposed in his account of a 1951 trip to Arnhem Land) 'Adamiji'. Simpson's *Adam in Ochre* included Poignant's photographs of tribal ceremonies on Melville Island near Darwin; Poignant himself toyed with the notion that our biblical history was being re-enacted in the Australian present. His photograph of an Aboriginal mother suckling her child was first called *Mary*, and exhibited with that title in 1947 and 1955. By the time of his exhibition at the Art Gallery of New South Wales in 1982, he had thought better of the provocative caption, and chose to call the image *Aboriginal Girl with New-born Baby*. Since then, the word 'girl' has come under suspicion, and the Canberra print is catalogued as *Aboriginal Woman with Child*. But Poignant's original title best conveys his intention. This is a nativity scene without the abstract, bodiless idealism of Christianity, which worships a virgin womb. The child's mouth is plugged to its mother's breast, and its head is a continuation of that swollen mound. Its bunched fist seeks to be reincorporated in her. The braids around her neck, linking her matted hair with the baby's, show them to be still one flesh, almost umbilically connected. She does not look down adoringly but gazes sideways, calmly relishing the pleasuring of being fed upon.

47
Axel Poignant
*Aboriginal Woman
with Child* 1942

The story behind the image makes the biblical analogy even more pertinent, and at the same time suggests that it must be sacreligiously modified to fit Australia. In early 1942 Poignant joined an expedition along the Canning stock route from Wiluna rail-head to Lake Disappointment in Western Australia. The woman lived on one of the cattle stations along the way. The purpose of the journey was to check on wells, in case cattle needed to be driven south after a Japanese invasion: could the photograph be a scene from the flight into Egypt? Summer rains had made the desert fruitful after a seven-year drought, which might have been a biblical curse. Poignant witnessed what he called a 'miraculous transformation': wild flowers bloomed, and budgerigars shrilled at water-holes. But this was Easter at Christmas, or immediately after it. As always, Christian festivities are not synchronized with the Australian seasons, which is why the title *Mary* does not really fit. Australia's more ancient religion was staged at Covent Garden in London in 1962 when Sidney Nolan painted designs for Stravinsky's ballet *The Rite of Spring*. Planning the dances that propitiate the carnivorous earth, the choreographer Kenneth MacMillan consulted Poignant's photographs of Arnhem Land Aboriginal people paying homage to the Rainbow Serpent.

Richard André photographed the church at Fitzroy Crossing in the West Kimberleys as part of a collective documentation of Aboriginal life called *After 200 Years*, published during Australia's bicentenary in 1988. Elsewhere in the settlement, the residents are seen wearing jeans and shorts at a corroboree, playing country and western music at a disco, and painting artefacts for sale to tourists in Broome. In the book, their capitulation to an imported culture is summed up in the text that accompanies André's image of the church: it quotes one of the faithful, who says that he still values his ancestral faith but thinks that Christianity 'is more important because it is all round Australia and overseas', and has a monopoly on 'the only God'. That 'one God', he repeats, 'is the Saviour', which is the single, blinkered version of the truth inculcated by Thake's guru. Speaking for itself, the photograph is less certain. The inscription beneath the roof enforces exclusivity through Christ's claim to represent the only truth. The cruciform bricks below are a series of full stops, summing up the finality of the utterance. But how truly pious are the flock, here pausing to gossip after a service or straggling home? The church summons them, and organizes them when they arrive; they are now dispersing. Has the man in the cowboy hat – who cocks his leg in a typically equilibrial, balletically graceful Aboriginal pose – even been inside? The woman on the left, who is furthest away from the sheltering structure, strides off on her own, not necessarily following the path prescribed by the doctrine. And the stretching dog, woken up by the people spilling out, could not care less about redemption.

48
Richard André
Junjuwa People's Church 1986

49
Frank Hurley
Frilled Lizard
1914

Commentators on colonial nature wrote disapprovingly of Australia's heathen fauna, which would not have qualified for a berth on Noah's ark. In 1819 in *First Fruits of Australian Poetry*, Barron Field viewed the 'sooty swans' and 'duck-moles' as evidence that 'this fifth part of the Earth' was 'an after-birth/ Not conceiv'd in the Beginning' but 'at the first sinning,/ When the ground was therefore curst'. The kangaroo could at best be considered the playful result of what Field called a 'divine mistake'. Marcus Clarke regretted the truculence of 'our beasts' that, like the kangaroo, had not learned to walk on all fours – or, even more insolently, refused to do so. If this was an alternative creation, it suggested that the world was a zone of Manichean strife. Even the trees apparently suffered from disfiguring diseases. The explorer George Grey thought that the baobab trunk, swelling to store water, must be dropsical or gouty. Clarke, listening to the unholy merriment of white cockatoos, accused them of 'shrieking like evil souls'; almost a century later, James McAuley's poem 'Terra Australis' said that the same bird emitted a screech of 'demoniac pain'. Clarke described Australia as a 'fantastic land of monstrosities'. Even if the suspicion of demonism or deformation is rejected, Australian creatures do often look like Darwinian throwbacks. Frank Hurley's frilled lizard, caught erecting the spiky ruff that signals hostility, belongs with the dinosaurs in Arthur Conan Doyle's lost world (which, after reading the book at school, I assumed began just behind Mount Wellington). It was not only white taxonomists who thought that Australian species must be accursed. The Gagudju tribe explains the lizard's frill of loose skin by insisting that it was condemned to this absurd appearance as a punishment for breaking the law.

Tasmania has its own native devils, one of which – stuffed and therefore uncharacteristically docile – posed for Samuel Clifford. Stereoscopy suits the hostility of the devils, which leap at you in a hissing fury: if you look at the double image through the proper spectacles, the subject rears into relief. Clifford's devil, immobilized in profile, is no longer capable of three-dimensional menace. In 1986 Germaine Greer revoked the curse on this ill-tempered creature. Coming across a devil lying dead beside the road on the east coast of Tasmania, she turned its usual snarl into a 'dead smile' and made it a candidate for holy orders, admiring its 'clergyman's collar of shining white hairs'. She then asked its forgiveness for the usurpation of its terrain, and said to herself 'We have no business here'.

50
Samuel Clifford
Tasmanian Bush 'Devil'
c. 1879

The task of culture in Australia has always been acclimatization to a threatening or unintelligible nature. Initially the speediest and surest method seemed to be extermination. The so-called civilizing process involved massacres: the self-righteous housekeeper Mrs Jolley in *Riders in the Chariot*, thrilled by her moral superiority to a foreign neighbour, feels that 'she would have liked to kill some animal'. Governments supported such high-minded rampages. During the Emu War in 1932, army machine-gunners were sent in to mow down these intruders in the wheat belt; the birds won the battle. Jeff Carter has photographed children at a boundary rider's hut on Fort Grey Station proudly showing off the collection of dingo scalps they have strung from a tree, or a rabbit hunter in the outback bulldozing his accumulated kill into a heap for skinning.

Kangaroos at least were superstitiously venerated as savage gods, admired because of their power and speed. Hal Missingham photographed a specimen he called *Big Red*. With one paw clenched pugilistically, planted on two thin, widespread legs, anchored by what D. H. Lawrence called the tail's 'great muscular python-stretch' and exhibiting a pair of bulbous testicles, he is the resplendent embodiment of virility. The kangaroo was a god with at least one attribute of a machine: locomotion, thanks to the tail's accelerating bounce. In *Snugglepot and Cuddlepie*, kangaroos are harnessed for use as taxis, and Qantas used to claim that its planes hopped across oceans like aerodynamic red kangaroos. Species that were not eliminated could be domesticated – or at least photography pretended that such amity was possible. Cazneaux's *Australian Native Bear Book*, photographed at West Pennant Hills in New South Wales in 1930, performed this service for the koala. The bears are colonized by captions, which place them in conversation pieces: 'Strictly Confidential' shows three koalas on the crowded intersection of a bough, apparently confabulating, while 'Connoisseurship' studies a koala as it savours a gum leaf. The pathetic fallacy sentimentally humanized the animals. Later, in a culture less frightened of nature, humans pay the animals the compliment of imitation. The drag queens in *The Adventures of Priscilla, Queen of the Desert* during one of their performances wear costumes modelled on the lizard's showy frill. Observed without fear, Australian nature is as intricate and as gratuitously beautiful as art. Missingham photographed a silvery spade-tailed gecko walking upside down on the ceiling; it reminded him, he said, of a Fabergé brooch.

Poignant's self-effacement, and perhaps his theosophical faith in the kinship between all created beings, made him the finest photographer of Australian animals. His subjects actually seem to trust him, which is why, overcoming their dread of human predators, they permit him to come so close. The *Cuscus* – a possum from the Cape York Peninsula, often mistaken for a monkey by early naturalists – stares back at him, sharing his astonishment at the oddity of another species. She even tamely permitted Poignant to reach into her warm pouch in a gesture of almost amorous sympathy. Viewed aesthetically, like Missingham's gecko, the cuscus is remarkable for that coiled prehensile tail, scaled at its tip, which suggests the fern resembling a bishop's crozier photographed by Karl Blossfeldt in *Urformen der Kunst*. Such creatures must, after all, have a creator, a designer of almost rococo wit and grace.

A sugar-glider possum in one of Poignant's images perches on the back of a black hand for its inquisitive, cautious close-up. The hand can be mistaken for part of the landscape because it is black. 'When photographing animals,' Poignant wrote in his book about the kangaroo, 'one is often privileged to witness moments in their private lives…. This made me realize that humans have no proprietary right to the world.' It is unusual for a man to concede that animals possess a private life. When we put them in zoos, we condemn them to an existence that is involuntarily public. But Poignant's animals look as if they possess an alert and delicate interior life as well. The concord he establishes between the species extends to an approximation between fauna and flora. Hence the finger-like stamens, pistils and stretching leaves of *Kangaroo Paw*, the floral emblem of Western Australia. In the notes to his book on Australian wildlife, Poignant points out that the kangaroo uses its forepaw for grasping; the same desire for manual contact seems to impel the plant. Poignant's fancied handshake between the species is brutally parodied in a photograph by Max Pam, called *After the Barbecue, Darwin*, taken while he was living in an Aboriginal community in the Northern Territory in 1986. A dark human hand holds in its palm the severed paw of a kangaroo, which has been discarded as inedible. The paw is black and leathery, with pointed, piercing claws that can be used as weapons, though they are defenceless against the guns of hunters. Behind the displayed trophy, to complete the despoiling of nature, is a tree with a name scratched into its bark. Patrick White's *Voss*, setting out from Newcastle, is cheered by the scars on the trees. For him, axes are evidence of civilization: 'The world of gods was becoming a world of men'.

51
Axel Poignant
Cuscus 1954

52
Axel Poignant
Kangaroo Paw, Perth c. 1939

Jon Rhodes, in his photograph of a kangaroo hunt in the Gibson Desert, makes man and animal equal partners in a fight that is conducted for subsistence, rather than to celebrate the gleeful mechanical subjugation of nature. Rhodes spent time at Yaruman in the East Kimberleys during the late 1980s, and documented the hunting and gathering there. The Aboriginal people butcher wild beef, and one happy old man carries off a hoof; they snap the neck of a bush turkey, whose white wing-feathers are used in tribal rituals. When their pension cheques arrive, however, they forget traditional food sources and pile up cartons of Bushells tea and Sunshine instant milk. On the kangaroo hunt, there is an attempt to maintain ancestral decorum, even though the hunter travels in a jeep. His profile – featureless and therefore archetypal, a mould of malleable rock like Uluru – is confronted by the lolling head of the kangaroo that he has killed. The window divides them. Man now lives indoors, insulated from a nature that remains locked outside. The hunter and his prey cannot exchange a glance: the man's eyes are obliterated by shadow, and the animal's eyes are closed. But at least this has not been a death triggered by remote control, like the scattergun rabbit-shooting sprees photographed by Jeff Carter. In another photograph taken by Rhodes at Warren Creek, the hunter literally shoulders responsibility for the killing and walks with a dead kangaroo draped over his shoulders. He is bowed beneath its weight; his hands grasp its forepaws and hind legs to balance the load. This might be a game, or an embrace. The image illustrates D. H. Lawrence's claim that killing is (or ought to be) a mode of knowledge, the consummation of an emotional intimacy.

Nature in Australia is apparently determined to kill off the white intruder, or to gobble up his works. Termites in the outback ingest houses, fences, telegraph poles and railway sleepers, which they regurgitate to form a teetering, catacombed architecture of their own: mounds of soil in which they house their pampered queen. Fending off such threats, men retaliate with pre-emptive strikes, and try to kill as much of nature as they can. At Fyansford near Geelong, Laurie Wilson photographed a row of skinned foxes strung up on a barbed wire fence. Foxes are killed for their pelts, so why string up the flayed bodies? Someone must have thought that it made a nice show. It also signals the advance of civilization, the incursion of men into a world that once belonged to gods and to totemic animals. At Sandfire Flat in Western Australia, Missingham photographed the carcass of what appears to be a goat, flattened and eviscerated, beneath a sign advertising a roadhouse and its amenities. Four miles further on, drivers can treat themselves to showers, meals, petrol, tyres, oil, batteries. We revive, and so does our car. The animal has no such option.

Only in Australia could a version of Golgotha place an animal on the cross: during 1959 and 1960 Clifton Pugh painted a *Crucifixion* series, with a pinioned, decomposing wallaby as the excruciated figure. Destiny Deacon, a native of the Torres Strait Islands, has done something similar for the kangaroo in an assemblage that sadly and wryly imitates an altarpiece. Below is a triptych of road kill. Dead human beings look as if they might be sleeping; we fall naturally into the posture of a still life. But the three kangaroos, deprived of motion by the speeding cars that have struck them down, are pathetically crumpled, useless, inefficient. They do not make elegant corpses. A tail that once served as a vaulting pole is now good only to be boiled down for soup. Above, however, as on all the best altars, is the promise of resurrection. The dead animals are reified as furry toys, arranged in a Disneyesque tableau in the window of the tax-free emporium. The central panel arranges a reunion in heaven between the elder, reaching down for a kiss, and its infant. Is this Bambi's post-mortem meeting with his mother, shot by the hunters? The window beckons customers to an irresistible mercantile notion of the afterlife. Heaven is where you will be free, meaning that you will no

54
Destiny Deacon
Tax-free Kangaroos 1993
© Destiny Deacon 1993.
Licensed by VISCOPY,
Sydney 2003

longer have to pay taxes. The kingdom to come is walled off behind glass: a wise precaution, because the reflections show cars, responsible for the carnage in the three photographs below, passing in the street outside. This is also a heaven reserved for those possessing the credit cards advertised in the window, and it is off-limits to locals: only visitors to Australia can shop in these establishments, on production of their passports and air tickets. So heaven, where these tax-free kangaroos are bound, must be overseas.

Deacon's allusion to Catholic art registers the protest of an alternative religion. The kangaroo is a spiritual talisman, almost a relative, for the Aboriginal people. Their stories of the Dreamtime account for its shape, rather than joking about its deformity like Barron Field. One legend says that kangaroos were blown to Australia by a violent wind. Buffeted in the air, they could not attach themselves to the ground; their hind legs grew longer in a desperate effort to serve as ballast, to reach that elusive home below. The first Aboriginal efforts at artistic representation engraved the kangaroo's tracks on rock, or carved its outline in relief. In rock galleries at Port Jackson, groups of charcoal and ochre kangaroos bound across the sandstone: the images convey a vital delight, catching an animation that defines the animal. The so-called X-ray paintings of kangaroos in Arnhem Land see into the beast, rather than looking through it. They demonstrate an admiring knowledge of the kangaroo's long, curved spine and the neat array of its internal organs. The purpose here is not to anatomize but to declare a fond familiarity: some tribes in the east applied the word 'kangaroo' to their friends. This art, like science, investigates the world and analyses its workings. Like religion, it also points to mystifying connections between nature and the supernatural, which may explain why the kangaroos in Hunter Valley petroglyphs are twice the size of men. The art of the stuffed toy or the photographic souvenir purveys a cheaper, more facile magic. The tax-free kangaroos are taxidermic parodies, their proportions altered so that they look reassuringly like human beings in kangaroo costumes: hence the broad shoulders and crooked arm of the tallest one. And don't the photographs of Australia that these travellers take away with them also mortify the experiences they record?

55
Eric Thake
Rathdowne Street Kangaroo
1967

As a surrealist, Eric Thake would not have sympathized with this complaint about a trampled, phonily simulated reality. Surrealism, according to André Breton's 1923 manifesto, sought to 'escape from the human species'; the Australian menagerie photographed by Thake revised reality by escaping from all other species as well. The kangaroo that seems to have been squashed and splattered across Rathdowne Street in Melbourne never was an animal. A trail of paint has spilled across the bitumen; it could equally well be a Magellanic Cloud in the night sky, above rather than beneath us. But this urban accident has produced the same result as those Aboriginal drawings in the rock galleries, with the tapering head and raised forepaws of the beast launching it into the air and its long hind leg almost dematerializing in flight, like an aeroplane propeller. Road kill does enjoy a resurrection after all.

The camera was an ideal instrument for the French surrealists, who took it with them on what they called their 'spiritual huntings' in fusty arcades, flea markets, brothels and nocturnal parks. Thirty years later, Thake set out on a similar safari in Melbourne, looking – as Walter Benjamin said of surrealist Paris – for 'inconceivable analogies and connections between events'. In the process, he captured the ultimate surrealistic prize: he netted a bunyip, bringing home a non-existent monster. In Aboriginal lore, this incubus represents the malevolence of Australian nature. Marcus Clarke described it dragging its 'loathsome length out the ooze' of a lagoon after dark. Everyone could imagine it, though no one knew what it looked like. Clarke called it a 'sea-calf', like the moon-calf Caliban in *The Tempest*. Thake, seeing the world metaphorically, found approximations to it scattered everywhere. His *Captive Bunyip at Back Beach, Sorrento* is a spar of timber, vaguely alligator-like, gruesomely propped up behind wire mesh. The bunyip he discovered at Mystic Park in 1957 has been decapitated, but continues the fight against human intrusion. The curved tree trunk is like a back aggressively hunched, and the lopped branches are paws planted on the ground; the hollow cross-section could be a pair of eyes or a leering mouth. This wooden goanna might have chewed up the other trees in the swamp, and left that twisted carnage.

56
Eric Thake
Bunyip at Mystic Park 1957

There was another significant sighting of a bunyip in Melbourne a year after Thake took this photograph. Barry Humphries played one at Christmas in a children's play called *The Bunyip and the Satellite*, which had sets designed by the painter Arthur Boyd. Since bunyips are mythical, Humphries felt free to conjure up the creature and embody it in whatever way he pleased. The result, as he remembers, was 'a prancing, bird-like clown', described by a reviewer in *The Age* as the 'Australian relative' of Harlequin, Pierrot and Shakespeare's fools. Scarier monsters, more like bunyips, later incubated inside Humphries: Edna the screeching witch, and the slobbering, belching, farting Sir Les, equipped with an independently operated, articulated penis that pounces on its prey (Kylie Minogue, for instance, during a performance at the Royal Festival Hall in London in 1999) like a lizard erecting the stiffest and most gnarled of frills. By impersonating a freak of nature, Humphries in 1958 began the process of mythologizing himself. He also acted out the genealogy of the artist, a being for whom Australia's prim suburban society had made no provision. Figures like Harlequin in Strauss's *Ariadne auf Naxos*, Schoenberg's *Pierrot Lunaire*, or the dejected performers from the commedia dell'arte in Picasso's early paintings all share the debilities of the artist, who is socially marginal, sexually irresponsible, psychologically unstable. The bunyips incarnated by Humphries are less wan and woebegone than their modernist predecessors; they take pride in their monstrosity and the power it gives them. Both the biblical version of Genesis and the Aboriginal alternative, in which ancestors travel across the land and shape it as they go, are repudiated by the artist, who reserves the right to invent himself. Why should a god be formed from society's ideal image of itself? The deity is just as likely to be generated by our bad dreams.

Australia's native religion depends on its iconography, and the icons we revere depend in part on the devotional photographs we take of them. Emile Durkheim, inventing the sociology of religion in 1912, audaciously remarked that 'there are rites without gods, and even rites from which gods are derived'. Photography is one of the rites that invests an object with a supernatural aura.

In 'Some Religious Stuff I Know About Australia', Les Murray astutely identifies a patriotic faith he calls 'Strine Shinto'. Like the Japanese, we attribute divinity to animals or landscapes, even to buildings and works of engineering. The cult objects Murray names are all inescapable, recurring subjects of photography, which attempts to make visible the spirit that is immanent in them. They include the kangaroo and the gum tree, Sydney's Harbour Bridge and its Opera House, and of course Ayers Rock (which, when Murray wrote his essay in 1982, it was not yet mandatory to call Uluru). Our polytheism is more happily promiscuous than the Japanese variety, and among the 'products of man's genius' that Murray celebrates is the pavlova. Once in Perth some friends made a pav for me which emerged from the oven slightly browned; before the cream and the fruit were piled on, it had exactly the lumpy shape, the sunburnt colour and the slippery smoothness of Uluru. We carved up the sacred monolith and ate it. I cannot imagine a happier Australian communion.

Early images of Uluru – for instance a wood engraving published in 1874 a few months after its first sighting by a white man – are nondescript: vertical ridges scored into its side make it look like a low, level escarpment, and picturesque distractions are contrived by planting thickets of trees in the foreground, positioning an unlikely flock of birds above it and organizing a camel train of explorers in the foreground. The photographs exhibited by the anthropologist Baldwin Spencer at his lectures on the outback during the 1890s were grey and fuzzy, incapable of rendering the rock's bulk or its luminosity. Another anthropologist, Charles Mountford, who climbed and photographed it in 1948, honestly admitted his frustration. Photography appraises its subjects metaphorically, but 'there seems to be nothing to which Ayers Rock can be likened'. Mountford resorted to an oxymoron, and described it as 'an enormous pebble'. Rhetoric made amends for the inadequacy of images. Jeff Carter, in his book of Central Australian photographs, sanctifies the rock by calling it Mecca – though the pilgrims who come to see it are not always devout. He therefore tries another way of ennobling the rock by inappropriately calling it 'a colossus', a gigantic feat of Roman imperial engineering, and he goes on to say that the nearby Olgas – named Kata Tjuta by the Aboriginal people – are 'a masterpiece', without explaining who the master might be.

The rites from which the god is derived are placed on view in Fred Schepisi's film *A Cry in the Dark*, about the death in 1980 of Azaria Chamberlain – taken by a dingo, or sacrificed (as some people luridly imagined) to the rock? Schepisi's camera swoops across the ground, irresistibly magnetized by the rock. Tourists line up to photograph it with cameras of their own, in a galactic frenzy of flashes. They spend the day climbing up it, walking round it, or clambering into its caves, always with cameras in hand. Then they gather again to photograph it looking like a fiery coal at sunset. The rock finally fades to black, retiring into invisibility for a few hours. Having come to the shrine as if visiting an oracle, the mobs of seekers expect revelations that the rock, inertly sunbaking, cannot supply.

When Grant Mudford visited the Northern Territory in 1973, this photographic consecration had not yet begun. Ayers Rock was still nothing more than a large, discarded boulder, evidence of nature's untidiness; the campsite beneath it contemptuously touted the superior virtues of white culture. The shack in Mudford's photograph rigs up

57
Grant Mudford
Ayers Rock [Uluru] 1973

the rudiments of a suburban life in the desert: a fibro box topped with corrugated iron, louvre windows like those used for lavatories, and a tin drum for a dog to live in. The knotted tangle of electrical wires nailed to the guttering boasts of extra amenities. There is even a kitchen chair placed next to the clump of spinifex grass, allowing the home-owner to survey his property; it is carefully angled so as to avoid the view of the incomprehensible rock. The camp bed tactlessly gives the lie to this propaganda for an indoor life. The hut must be a sweaty, stifling cell, so why bother depositing it there? Its only value is as a symbolic act of exclusion, enabling you to close the door on the horror vacui of the Australian outdoors. But the colonial pretences are a sham, since the place is uninhabited, and the lengthening shadows suggest the advance of a solar energy that will soon incinerate these tacky leavings.

Whoever lived in Mudford's hut probably thought that his dwelling upstaged the rock. At best, the monolith could be annexed as a scenic backdrop, as it was by Laurence Le Guay in 1959. His model, swathed in orange fabric, spreads her arms in a generous embrace, complimenting the sandstone on having matched its colour to her outfit. In 1938 in a photograph entitled The Progenitors, Le Guay had allegorically equated industry with sexuality. Two nudes are superimposed on a skyline of pipes and towers; the woman stands up and clutches her forehead, as if she were conceptualizing this overpowering capacity for sudden, dynamic growth, while the male – her inseminator, who stokes these engines – sits back and gazes at her in admiration. Le Guay's fashion shot is another attempt to reimagine Genesis, though it does so less earnestly and with a teasing sense of its own absurdity. The model plays at being a pantheistic high priestess, like Isadora Duncan flamboyantly gesticulating among the ruins of Greek temples in Edward Steichen's portrait of her. But she remains as disconnected from the setting as the woman in The Progenitors, who is merely a transparency, a ghost printed onto the industrial machines. The fabric that the model advertises, manufactured by Courtauld, is hardly appropriate for the outback, and the analogy between its folds and the sheen or texture of the rock face behind her seems injurious. Are we meant to think that Ayers Rock is merely decorative, that the land is wallpaper?

Le Guay's photograph is a serious joke, a parable about how civilization conquers the wilderness, kitted out in high heels and the latest fashions. It was meant to have a sequel in The Adventures of Priscilla, Queen of the Desert, in which the spangled drag queens were to have scaled Uluru in costume, their headdresses flaunting. The climb would have definitively but self-deceptively established culture's victory over nature in Australia. Even gender can now be revised or fictionalized, so why should geology hold out? But by the time the film was made, the right to control Uluru's image had been entrusted to a council of indigenous owners, the Anangu, who considered the sequence disrespectful and refused permission. The drag queens totter to the rim of Kings Canyon instead, though there is less sense of triumph in staring down into a hole in the ground. Still, the film's dialogue adheres to the original itinerary, as a hint of what might have been. When Guy Pearce describes his mountaineering ambitions, Terence Stamp sneers 'That's just what this country needs – a cock in a frock on a rock.' He is right: Australia did need a demonstration that art can rise above nature, without necessarily harming or claiming to subjugate it.

58
Laurence Le Guay
*Fashion illustration for
Courtauld's Fabrics,
Ayers Rock* [Uluru],
Northern Territory
1959

59
Wesley Stacey
Uluru in Morning Mists
1972

Photography manages that feat by finding new ways to look at Uluru. The Aboriginal people see it as an anthology of stories or an epic poem, a song of origins. For them its scars and indentations record the travails of the ancestors who shaped it, with marks left by the spears of warriors or the paws of evil spirits. The photographers claim no such power to manipulate it into meaning, but they can pay tribute to its mutability by finding unexpected vantage points from which to catch its stormy moods. In 1972 Wesley Stacey photographed it from every conceivable position. First it pokes up in the remote distance on a flat horizon, enigmatic and undefined. When Stacey draws closer, it retires behind a fog: vapour rubs it out, a reminder that despite its crushing solidity we can only ever have vagrant, partial impressions of it. A side view of the cleft known as The Digging Stick questions whether a mute image can ever translate the words that are written into the rock. According to the legend, the stick belonged to a group of dancing women who camped here during the Dreamtime; it was absorbed into the soft, porous stone. The photograph can show us the petrified outline of the tool, inky shadows in the cleft. It is helpless to tell us the story, which in any case remains the privileged possession of tribal elders. A concussion on the north side of the rock, like the imprint of a skull, is nicknamed The Brain. But if this is a global mind, its thinking remains unknowable: that space is empty, hollow, like E. M. Forster's reverberant Marabar Caves in *A Passage to India*. The best photographs of Uluru agnostically admit their own inadequacy.

For many travellers to Uluru, conquest replaces contemplation. While climbing, you're relieved from having to look at the rock or trying to understand it. The traditional owners consider the trek to the top to be at best futile, at worst blasphemous. Stacey, to his credit, photographed the return journey, during which you stare down into a gulf and repent the hubris that made you want to clamber up. Danger indemnifies his act of trespass. Bravado has always been a professional credential for photographers, as if mortal peril could somehow atone for the technical facility of their art. The war photographer Robert Capa said that if pictures of battles weren't good enough, the photographer couldn't have been close enough to the firing line. Exhibiting similar nerve, Stacey photographed his dangling lower half. His legs are not long enough to connect his dizzy head with the ground, which his adhesive, rubber-soled shoes cannot reach. He has no spare hand with which to grip the chain; he is too busy holding the camera. What the camera sees should have caused him to lose his mental balance. The lines of perspective, converging back on earth, accelerate like a plunging body. Tracks radiate from the base of the rock, then dissolve into a sunny glare before they reach any destination. Given the cross formed by the path down the rock and the roads below, this could be another Australian crucifixion, seen from Christ's pinioned point of view. Have those spikes been driven through his flesh, as well as into the flaking skin of stone? Suspended, he surveys a world so barren that God has surely forsaken it. The horizon, drearily straight when Stacey photographed the rock from across the desert, here acquires a curve. The prospect of tumbling from the rock is not the only thing to be afraid of; we seem likely to fall off the slippery, rounded earth itself.

61
Wesley Stacey
Looking Down the Climb
1972

By contrast with this vertigo, the Aboriginal artists who stencilled their hands onto the rock gallery at Mootwingee were marking their incorporation in the earth. These stencils reverse the values of light and dark like a photographic negative; the subject opens his hand on the cliff, then sprays paint that he had stored in his mouth across it. Stencils leave a physical imprint, whereas a photograph can only serve as a memento of the light that once played on the subject. Photographs, the moment that they are taken, belong to the past. The rock stencils live in a perpetual present, bridging the gap between ancestry and actuality, because they can be repainted every year – freshened, like grass-land after a controlled burning – to repair the damage done by erosion; and the impression of those palms, feeling their way upwards, is a reminder that the rock itself is alive, like an unfurling wave stilled when the shutter clicked. Stacey's camera studies the art of men whose contact with nature was not mediated by cameras, nor any other machine.

The usurpers, as Peter Elliston's photograph makes clear, decorate rock galleries of their own. My mother had a malapropism for such daubings. Driving me through one of Hobart's blitzed and blighted suburbs, she nodded her head over a world that had become unrecognizable to her. 'Will you look at all that there graffarty?' she said. The impulse, I suppose, is artistic: an angry desire to make a mark, to immortalize your name. But at least in Hobart the tags and curses and diagrams of explosive rage had been sprayed onto the hardbitten concrete walls of bowling alleys and used-car lots, which they brightened up. To paint the balustrade of sandstone boulders at Coogee, down the coast from Bondi, is a graver offence. The city asks to be defaced, since its forbidding existence is what the gangs with the aerosol cans are protesting about. What argument can Nicole, Busta and the others possibly have with nature? Their grudge is the same as that of Jeff Carter's hunters on their indiscriminate shooting sprees in the bush. Their act of desecration punishes the rock for its insentience, its ignorance of them; in a less meditative mood than David Stephenson pondering the Antarctic ice, they are admitting the continent's indifference to them and their irrelevance to it. It is because they cannot articulate this quarrel that most of their scrawls are abstract, like calligraphy in a foreign language or the abstruse equations chalked on a blackboard by a physicist. But abstraction, after all, is the style chosen by modern artists to proclaim their secession from a reality that for them had become, as Gertrude Stein once said, 'really unreal'. The hand stencils want to hold the rock, to go on feeling it even after death. The graffiti at Coogee seeks to splinter and detonate the rock, punishing it for having the temerity to exist at all.

Elliston's sunbakers may not have been responsible for that ugliness, but they have made their own contribution to it by recreating a suburban sprawl. The litter of plastic bottles and cups is a way of staking out terrain: the beach must be made as much like your backyard as possible. The ghetto blaster is compulsory, a source of aural pollution to match the filth inscribed on the rocks. The man's head snugly reposes on his woman's pudenda. He is doing the backstroke on dry land, perhaps because he has not yet learned to walk upright. These are cave dwellers, at home in their midden of non-biodegradable refuse. They look mildly affronted, as if the photographer had peeped over their back fence. Coogee means bad smell: a reference by the Aboriginal people who named it to rotting seaweed cast onshore.

63
Peter Elliston
Couple on Platform at Giles Baths, Coogee, NSW 1992

64
Tracey Moffatt
The Movie Star: David Gulpilil on Bondi Beach 1985
Courtesy of Roslyn Oxley9 Gallery

At Bondi, David Gulpilil performs a similar act of occupation for the Aboriginal photographer Tracey Moffatt. His posture, with his fist clenched against his face, is even more lazily recalcitrant than that of Elliston's man. Blocking the beach behind him, he erects a defensive barricade in front of him, using the same weaponry that Elliston's subjects brought with them: an outsized tape deck, and a brandished can of Foster's lager. But he is even more arrogantly proprietorial than the man at Coogee, because he has stretched himself across the polished bonnet of his car, which ensures that he can come to the beach to drink and listen to music without ever needing to quit his cocoon of machinery. The scene is an ironic reappropriation. With his hair braided and a vizor of warpaint dotted across his face, ridiculing the zinc cream white Australians have to smear on their ill-prepared complexions, Gulpilil parks on a beach that the newcomers think of as a sacred site. This is his revenge on the tourists who climb Uluru equipped with six-packs and Walkmans.

Gulpilil was a talismanic figure in the confrontation between black and white gods that began in the late 1960s, when Australia guiltily came to see itself as a particle set adrift from the primal land mass of Gondwanaland. He served as a shaman for his own people, singing and dancing at the behest of spirits who took up residence within his body. But for the white film-makers who employed him, he was more often a token black, required to defer to an alien culture. In Nicolas Roeg's *Walkabout*, made in 1969, he saves two British children who have been abandoned in the desert, showing them how to unearth water sources and cook grubs. But when they edge closer to white settlement, he becomes obsolete: he watches hunters in trucks gun down buffalo, and weeps. He paints his body and does a mating dance for the girl, hoping for a merger of faiths and races. She rejects him, and he hangs himself. The children walk to the bitumen road and thumb a lift back to civilization. In *The Last Wave* Gulpilil advances from the outback to Sydney, where he lives tribally and takes part in the ritual execution of a man who has broken the traditional law. He appears, holding a sacred stone, in the dreams of the white lawyer played by Richard Chamberlain. Once more Gulpilil is superseded: he can play only the evangelist, and the revelation of the last, laving wave is granted to Chamberlain, who supposedly has a share in this primordial wisdom because he lived in South America as a child. By the time of *Crocodile Dundee* – released in 1986, the year after Moffatt's photograph – Gulpilil had been effectively colonized. Here he has a walk-on as a city boy who attends a corroboree to please his father, a tribal elder. Stumbling through the outback, he grumbles 'I hate the bush!'. He refuses to sacrifice urban trophies like his wristwatch, and wears his jeans to the ceremony. When the heroine, a New York journalist, aims her camera at him, he stops her. She thinks it's because of the usual superstition: a photograph will purloin his soul. Instead, technically more adept than she is, he points out that the lens cap is still on. Gulpilil continues to operate along the vexed border between cultures. In Philip Noyce's *Rabbit-Proof Fence* he plays a black tracker trailing three girls of mixed race, removed from their Aboriginal mother in 1931 to be trained as servants for white society. They have escaped from their keepers, and Gulpilil is engaged to round them up. As a go-between, he eventually persuades the police to call off their hunt.

A life straddling cultures demoralized Gulpilil, who succumbed to drink and drugs, and spent time in custody. Moffatt's photograph at least awards him a retaliatory role he was never able to play in a film. He looks ready to hurl abuse, cans and amplified music at anyone who disputes his right to laze on the esplanade. In fact, warfare was circumvented by diplomacy, legalistic deals, and invented ceremonies to which photographers were privileged witnesses. In 1975 the Aboriginal news photographer Mervyn Bishop was sent to Wattie Creek in the Northern Territory to record a transfer of lands to the Gurindji people. In 1967 Vincent Lingiari had led a rebellion against the station owners; now he was to receive the leasehold of the area he and the other workers had occupied. The Prime Minister, Gough Whitlam, made the handover personally, so there was what press agents call a photo opportunity. But how much visual interest does an essentially clerical transaction contain? The moment was made visually significant by being symbolically staged: Whitlam dribbled some soil from his cupped fist into Lingiari's open hand. Unfortunately it all happened out of the sun in the rough shelter of boughs and leaves that can be seen in the background. The setting was dark and, as Bishop noted, 'Vincent was kind of blending into it a bit'.

The photographer, aware of his own power, therefore persuaded the politician and the elder to perform the rite all over again in the light of day, choreographing the occasion himself. Lingiari had glaucoma, which is one reason why the shelter had been constructed. The glare blinded him, so Bishop directed him to look downwards. While lining up the photograph, he foresaw its iconic future. 'I could see it,' he commented later, 'on the front cover of something.' It became the equivalent of those nineteenth-century paintings that sought to fix and eternalize moments that counted as turning-points of history: Washington crossing the Delaware, Napoleon crowning himself, Nelson expiring on his ship. But when it comes to confecting historical fictions, painting enjoys an advantage. A photograph, even if its subjects are arranged into a tableau, is messily candid. Despite the solemnity of the encounter, Whitlam seems to have slept in his suit, and if you do not know about Lingiari's glaucoma, his downcast gaze looks oddly abashed. The old man's hands also tell two conflicting stories. One of them is open (though the tribute trickling into it could be as fickle as water). The other, preferring to trust paper, tightly clutches the deed of entitlement to those two and a half thousand square kilometers. But who can ever own or even lease the earth? The land outlasts all those who buy, sell or barter it.

65
Mervyn Bishop
Prime Minister Gough Whitlam pours soil into hand of traditional landowner Vincent Lingiari, Northern Territory 1975
© Mervyn Bishop 1975.
Licensed by VISCOPY, Sydney 2003

4: Tree People

By Anglo-Saxon standards, the Aboriginal people failed to qualify as civilized beings. They erected no churches for their gods, constructed no houses for themselves, and sowed no lawns. Darwin, for whom culture was inconceivable without agriculture, castigated them because they did not even 'take the trouble of tending a flock of sheep'. Since they had failed to make themselves at home, the earth across which they roved was freely available for occupation by others. If resistance was offered, the evicted people could be nullified.

The camera accompanied and assisted the extermination. Photographers valued the natives as quaint ethnographic exhibits, removed from their habitat to be studied under controlled conditions. Long exposure times required them to hold poses; they were detained, transfixed, mortified. One way or another, the camera issued them their death sentence. In 1858–59 Antoine Fauchery included a portrait of a boy he called a 'half-caste piccaninny' in his album *Sun Pictures of Victoria*. The boy, who cannot be trusted to remain still, has been directed to steady himself against the axed, fire-blackened stump of a tree. It is the kind of evasive tactic used by classical sculptors when carving figures who were not entirely upright. The bent knee and drooping hand, stiffly simulating relaxation, do not come naturally: black flesh is being forced to imitate white marble. The stump makes its own mordant comment on the scene, since the boy and his people were to have their growth violently interrupted.

Also in 1858, Francis Nixon, Tasmania's first Anglican bishop, photographed some of the island's few remaining Aboriginal people, rounded up at Oyster Cove. Like Fauchery considerately supplying the boy with the stump, Nixon tried to observe pictorial niceties, though his concern for the decorum of costume, posture and framing only makes his subjects look more dejected and unaccommodated. Their body language is eloquent. The women have been told to fold their hands in front of them to prevent fidgeting, but the figure in front at the right has decided on a position of her own, defensively raising her knees so that she can hide behind them. Truganini, the last full-blood Aboriginal, lolls on her side, an odalisque without a divan. Why was she exempted from the sullenly hunched deportment imposed on the others? Perhaps to display her white patterned dress, a colonial cast-off nestling in the dirt. Symmetry obviously mattered to Nixon, and his tidy mind might have organized the group into two rows of three. But the matron standing behind, clad in what could be black bombazine, has been excluded. Did Truganini refuse to make room for her? Because she could

not or would not sit down, the camera casually decapitates her. It was a common fate: Aboriginal people who had died often had their heads chopped off and boiled down, after which the skulls were sent to England for phrenological research. Everything the camera overlooks or for which it fails to find a place – the bundled blankets to the right, or the clump of firewood outside the hut – is a reminder that this race was also being relegated to the edge, pushed out of sight and then discarded. We return to the sad imperative of all family albums. You photograph people, babies included, because they are going to die.

During the 1870s J. W. Lindt compiled an album of Aboriginal portraits in which the fixity and falsity of the tableaux evokes the mortician's art: he might be dealing with stuffed specimens. Two Aboriginal women and a child sit by a humpy mocked up in the studio, with drapes covering their lower bodies, and stare at the camera apathetically. The male who presides over an even more dispirited group wears a headband, has a plaque around his neck, and exhibits tribal scars. But his boomerangs lie indolently grounded beneath his feet, and his expression is depressed. A colleague has slumped asleep over his axe, resting his head on the seated man's knee. Another group poses with a dead kangaroo; they too are imperilled livestock. The edicts of the still life have been applied to human beings. The photograph attributed to Daniel Marquis advances to the next stage. The captive corpse – neatly trussed, further compacting the posture assumed by the woman at the front of Nixon's group – is surrounded by useless weapons and an empty, provisionless basket. The living descendant next to the mummy is blurred: being alive, he moved during the exposure. Cadavers are more photographically compliant.

The original inhabitants were permitted to survive if they consented to turn themselves into inept imitators of their supposed betters. Fred Kruger photographed monarchs like Queen Eliza of the Yarra Tribe, who re-enacts her coronation in an indoor bower of uprooted ferns, with a dilly bag slung over her shoulder. The pole she grips is hardly a substitute for Queen Victoria's orb and sceptre; she is swaddled in a blanket, not wrapped in ermine. The natives Kruger considered civilized are being passed off as eminent Victorians. The woman has an ersatz tiara atop her confected curls, and a spurious medal dangles from the man's lapel. As in Fauchery's portrait, the angle of his leg awkwardly tries to indicate elegance and ease; it looks as phoney as his hedge of facial hair. With her mouth glumly set, his wife, to her credit, is unamused. Walter Benjamin was dismayed by the 'upholstered tropics' in which nineteenth-century portrait photographers sat their subjects. Pillars grew out of carpets, as did rootless palm trees. Studios, Benjamin said, resembled a combination of throne room and torture chamber. Applied to bourgeois Europe, the remark is a witty, extraneous metaphor. In the studios where Lindt and Kruger photographed those dethroned and disorientated subjects, it is literally true.

67
Daniel Marquis (attributed)
Mummified Remains of an Aborigine
c. 1866–80

68
Fred Kruger
Family of Civilized Natives from the album *Souvenir Album of Victorian Aboriginals, Kings, Queens, & etc.* c. 1866–87

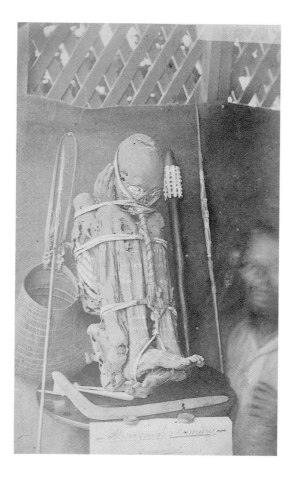

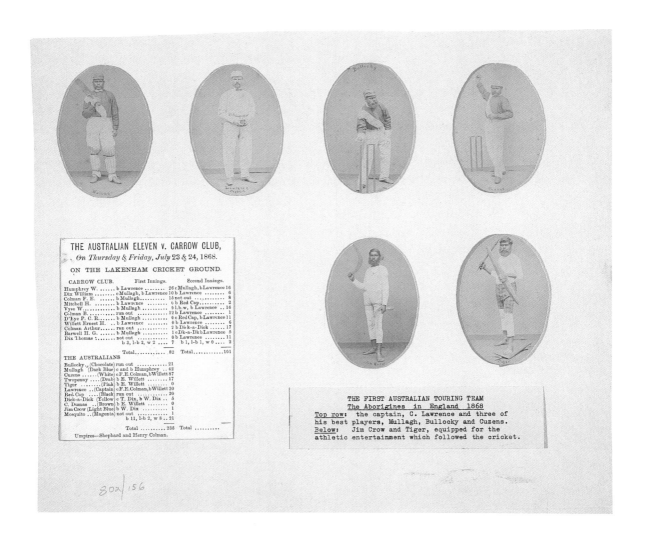

69
Patrick Dawson
Aboriginal Cricketers, First Australian Touring Team 1867

Tame specimens were arranged into bourgeois family groups, or rallied into teams and taught to play games whose abstruse rules inculcated respect for the whimsicality and arbitrariness of the ruling power. The Aboriginal cricketers who toured England during the 1860s advertised the success of the colonial enterprise. Early observers in Sydney noticed that the Aboriginal people were hunters, and complimented their sportsmanship as if they had been chasing foxes rather than kangaroos. But their weaponry could just as well be turned on soldiers and settlers. To allay this fear, the cricketers have been symbolically disarmed. Their spears and throwing sticks are replaced by bats and ball, and mortal hostility is commuted into a good-humoured contest. When the cricketers regressed to savagery after the game – taking off their caps and shoes, stripping down to their underwear and brandishing their boomerangs – the hunt was redefined as an 'athletic entertainment'. Sport, in this case, was not the continuation of warfare by other means. The boomerangs thrown in Lakenham lacked a target, since there were no kangaroos in the vicinity. Denied the status of Homo sapiens, the Aboriginal cricketers were put through their paces as examples of Homo ludens, entertaining their hosts by demonstrating their own impotence.

Mrs Philipson Bellamy, photographed during the 1880s at Parachilna in South Australia by Captain Samuel Sweet, must have often been told that she possessed an excellent seat. Bowler-hatted, bustled and gloved, she perches side-saddle on a camel's hump, gripping the reins as she wills the animal to hold its pose in profile. She resembles Laura in *Voss*, who sits 'sculpturally upon her mastered horse': the equestrian woman symbolizes the control of wildness and of insurgent motion. The camel lifts Mrs Bellamy high above the scruffy, demotic scrub. Here is an icon of colonial demeanour, occupying the landscape while repudiating any contact with it. The camel, also not a native, has haughtily absorbed its rider's sense of superiority. Camels were imported from India and Palestine in the mid nineteenth century as beasts of burden, then left to roam free when the railway, telegraph and cars made them obsolete. This one has apparently declined to go feral, and has worn out the hair on its knees by the labour of genuflecting.

70
Captain Samuel Sweet
Mrs Philipson Bellamy c. 1886

On the ground, deprived of Mrs Bellamy's poise, others found it harder to form a relationship with the land. The overdressed naiad at Katoomba in *Meeting of the Waters* looks back at the photographer in perplexity, apparently asking why she has been positioned there, with her skirt spilling onto the wet rocks. She is supposed to soothe and control the energy that makes the waters froth and bends one of the trees at a broken angle. It is she who decrees the confluence of streams; by her presence, she defines the place as a beauty spot. She looks unconvinced, worried that she might be told to wade across the waterfall.

Sometimes the scenery could be relied on to humanize itself without such nervous intercession. Nearby at Leura, also during the 1890s, Henry King photographed a cataract whose final precipice had been nicknamed Weeping Rock. The pathetic fallacy seems justified in this case: the rock is torrentially tearful. But perhaps the lachrymose fancy does not quite convey the violence of the emotional convulsion. Branches and tangled roots lie scattered at the base of the falls, which carve a trench down the side of the Blue Mountains. What nature suffered here, during

71
Charles Kerry
Meeting of the Waters, Katoomba c. 1890

a recent storm, was evidently a paroxysm, not a gentle crying fit. The mild, temperate metaphors occasionally fail to work their charm; or, with typical Australian irony, they grimace at their own pretence. J. W. Beattie's photograph, subtitled *Ploughed Fields*, is a hardbitten joke. This is an avalanche that has come to rest near the summit of Mount Wellington, a remnant of one of the burned-out volcano's ancient tantrums. We are far above the tree line, at a height where there is scarcely a toe-hold for soil between the rocks, and the shrubs in the foreground do not dare to grow taller because of the punishing winds. To see this as a ploughed field is to shrug about the hopelessness of agriculture in such a setting. Australians refer to scrub congealed in mounds as 'Bay of Biscay country', grimly picturing a bay with waves of dry clay. This field is even less suitable for cultivation. Nevertheless, Beattie has arranged a Wordsworthian encounter between travellers. One man is directing the other – who is still dressed in the city suit he must have worn when conducting business in Hobart, far below – onwards and upwards. Stakes mark the way to the summit, but the stepping-stones are made for giants, and the smaller man will have to stride through this hail of

72
J. W. Beattie
Where Twines the Path – to Pinnacle, Mount Wellington c. 1902

boulders. The fellow confidently giving directions may be teasing the townie by sending him to his doom.

A reviewer appraising the photographs on show at the 1886 Colonial Exhibition in Melbourne lamented Australia's unpicturesqueness. In a Surrey lane 'pictures make themselves', whereas Australia – with its valleys a quarter of a mile deep and trees four or five hundred feet tall – leaves the photographer 'embarrassed by the size of the view'. All it took to intimidate men and enforce their puny insignificance was a single tree, like the one at Neerim around which Caire's bushmen stretch a tape measure. Edmund Burke's theory of the sublime challenged the romantics to transcend their own little-ness by exposing themselves to the power unleashed by oceans or alpine cascades or thunderstorms; the experience was risky but exhilarating, since the individual volun-teered to be a conduit for that power. Shelley asked the west wind to make him its lyre, 'even as the forest is' – to agitate him into wailing song. Such sublimation did not apply to the Australian bush. A tree like Caire's can hardly be measured, let alone imagined, and it is immune to lyrical entreaties. Its base could be the knobbled toes of some sky-scraping monster, capable – if it had not been attached to the ground – of crushing the insects holding the tape.

Tall tales about trees abounded on the frontier. A hollow baobab in Derby, Western Australia, supposedly did duty as a lockup in pioneering days. Caire was fascinated by the battles the settlers fought with these inert, obstructive giants. A Gippsland farmer whose property he photographed has managed to topple two out-sized trees: the stumps, looking exactly like the amputated feet of elephants used as occasional tables, serve as gateposts to his garden. The owner is standing on top of one of them, to boast of a kill. Other bush families, unable to beat the trees, chose to join them. In one of Caire's photographs the settlers have sliced through a trunk but failed to lever its roots out of the soil. Their cabin – built from the sawn planks, with wood left over for a fence and roof shingles – is placed next to the stump: the house remembers the tree from which it is descended. Elsewhere in Gippsland, Caire found some people who, after lopping off its upper extremities, had simply moved into a tree. They hollowed out a room inside it, with a door attached, and stuck a turreted roof on its truncated top. Why bother to clear a space for society when you could simply move into one of these ready-made shelters? In about 1903 Caire photographed eleven people taking afternoon tea in a giant tree. The bole accommodates deck chairs, a folding table, and the formal array of crockery. An axe negligently bites into the trunk, just next to one of the elegantly dressed Edwardian women, a token of the violence that makes such homely hospitality possible. At King Parrot Creek, another of Caire's bushmen sleeps in the burned-out, hollow trunk of a living tree. The inevitable axe is propped beside him. The billycan in which he stews his tea swings on a pole stretched over his fire, with two rabbits strung up, waiting to be skinned for breakfast.

The overturned stump at Botany could be a cross-section of a bourgeois home, with caves as private as bedrooms, a second storey under the eaves that is reached by stairs, and a terrace on the roof. Two of the men have removed their hats, as if they were already indoors. In profile, this ark looks vaguely like a merino sheep. The tree has lost its anchorage, the house has no foundations. What if it suddenly began to move, taking its occupants with it, like parasites on the merino? The studied relaxation of the figures does not quite manage to make the scene look stable. Such games are probably best left

to children, like those photographed by Gerrit Fokkema at Wilcannia, on the Darling River near Broken Hill. The tree is their fort, and they wear its cracked panels as armour; it also serves as their larder, to judge from the paper bag of provisions one of them is holding. The boy in the middle, his head sticking through the hole left by a knot or an amputated branch, pretends to be imprisoned by the tree. His friend on the right, who wriggles free and casts off his camouflage, knows all about coexistence with nature.

Like Robinson Crusoe or the Swiss Family Robinson, the first settlers who lived in the bush insisted on adhering to the standards of a society of which they were no longer members. A pregnant wife stands in the open door of a miner's hut in the Lithgow Valley in New South Wales, photographed about 1879. Her saucepans sit on a bench and her broom is propped against the wall. Some boulders have been manoeuvred into place in the yard to form an oven. In the cleared space, a spindly gum with a few stones arranged around it constitutes a garden. A low rudimentary fence runs off into the scrub: what was it supposed to debar? In his Queensland album, the geologist Richard Daintree photographed two male diggers who have set up house with a doleful hound in a bark hut that leans against a tree stump. Their utensils hang outside, with a chopping block set like a stool beside the barrel that houses their dog. The selector Caire photographed in 1887 at Groajingolong ('a most out of the way locality') lives in a shaky assemblage of logs and bark: the rules of bricolage apply, so no nails were used in its construction. In the absence of companionship, he manages to fulfill both male and female functions. Two saws and a pair of axes are on display, together with picks, hoes, spades and a dismounted saddle, to advertise his mastery of the terrain. But he is also well supplied with pots, pans, a crop of potatoes to cook and a scrubbing board for doing his laundry. In about 1947 David Potts photographed an unkempt, unshaven camp cook in his outback hut. A grubby tea towel hangs from his stove; behind him, dangling from nails driven into the greasy wall, are his eggbeater, cheese grater, a spatula and a battery of grinders and cutters, with a dirty knife negligently stuck into a beam. Lacking a female homemaker, he does his best to maintain domestic niceties.

After Christmas in 2001, the same bushfires that razed the Quigleys' home swept through another property in the Blue Mountains. The man who owned the place returned to find that his house had been spared, not even singed. But the shed in his backyard – where he kept his tools and where he liked to sit, because he felt more comfortable when he did not have to live up to the furniture – had gone. He refused to count his blessings, and grumbled for the benefit of the television news. 'I wish the fire had of taken the house and left the shed,' he said. 'A man needs a shed.' Sarcastic fatalism is Australia's native mood. Civilization is superfluous; it is about superfluity. In the bush, a shed is probably all that it is safe to ask for.

76
Nicholas Caire
Selector's Hut, Gippsland c. 1886

The Brazilian photographer Sebastião Salgado summed up Australia's existential quandary after a brief visit in 1981. 'I've never seen a country as big as this with no people in it,' he said. While taking photographs on the border between Queensland and the Northern Territory, he stared down from a plane and saw only green, writhing rivers in a murky waste. On a remote cattle station, a dentist flew in to pay a house call. Salgado watched him extract a tooth from a station hand who sprawls in an arm chair. A kangaroo skin covers the floor, and there are guns nailed to the wall of the ersatz surgery. Society and its amenities cannot stretch across this empty immensity.

The problem of representing Australia, whether you use words or images, is that the landscape rejects the affinities you seek to cultivate. Its scale effaces any figures set in it: since those figures are your deputies – sent out on an aesthetic version of the colonizing sorties that killed Burke, Wills, Leichhardt and so many other explorers – you have been forewarned. 'Some description of landscape is necessary,' says Murray Bail in *Eucalyptus*. But the desert is a blistering glare, and the bush is a grey-brown blur. How can art exist if the artist cannot give an account of his surroundings? In his story 'The Drover's Wife', Bail investigates Russell Drysdale's painting of the same name, which places a woman with a suitcase in a scorched waste. A man claiming to be her husband identifies her, and wants to know more about the drover she ran off with. But the drover is just a black spot (perhaps Aboriginal?) in the emptiness, and the location is somewhere in an outback that mocks the very concept of locality: 'South Australia? It could easily be Queensland, West Australia, the Northern Territory....You could never find that spot'. Though the husband wants to complain about his personal loss, the 'rotten landscape', as he complains, dominates everything.

When Darwin climbed Mount Wellington, he was relieved to make the acquaintance of some social equals. He admired a 'noble forest' of eucalypts, and some man ferns that, despite their hairy masculinity, opened their fronds into 'elegant parasols'. Those ferns helped to re-enchant the Australian landscape. For Caire, who photographed them in dripping gulleys at Cape Otway or Blacks' Spur in Victoria, they composed themselves into bowers or sylvan dells. But his images were caught between sorcery and science. Is the man in his *Fairy Scene* reposing in a lair of fantasy or about to be consumed by a humid, fetid jungle? In an engraving based on the photograph, published in the *Picturesque Atlas* of 1888, the figure is reversed so that he walks into the undergrowth with a pack on his back. Either way, this confrontation between the almost invisible human individual and the rioting fertility of nature looks unequal. In a note on the photograph, Caire distinguished between male and female ferns, defined by reference to their size. Man ferns outstrip the feeble masculinity of human beings, and shamelessly expose the relativity of species. In 1861 a reviewer in *The British Journal of Photography*, commenting on some photographs taken in the Sydney Botanic Gardens, described the tree fern as a Darwinian missing link, an intermediate stage 'between the ferns and the palms'. Lawrence's hero in *Kangaroo* suffers a terrifying regression when he first wanders into the bush. He feels 'fern-lost', having lunged through evolution in reverse to find himself back in 'the fern age'. 'Will...the fern-twilight altogether envelope him?' he asks. Even after he is disgorged by the bristling swamp, he looks back in alarm at the 'fern-dark indifference' of Australian nature. Such thoughts might have occurred to Caire's diminished figure. The ferns do not shade him with parasols; they extend tendrils or tongues to absorb him. With his arms defensively crossed, he hesitates before committing himself to this seething underworld of spores. The promised fairies remain out of sight. Instead the scene is taken over by hybrids and mutants, which re-enact a brutal and chancy battle for primacy.

In *The Tree of Man*, Patrick White struggles to separate the people from the trees that overtopped and outnumbered them. The novel begins with a man establishing a home for himself between two stringy-barks. His horse, 'shaggy and stolid as the tree…took root', while the man – determined to remain deracinated, unlike the tree – got out his axe and began chopping. Nevertheless, two generations later White admits that nothing has changed: 'in the end there were the trees', which had been there since the beginning. In Douglas Stewart's poetic drama about the Kelly gang, Joe Byrne – the bushranger photographed after his death by Lindt – suggests that the gang's vendetta is

77
Nicholas Caire
*Fairy Scene at the Landslip,
Blacks' Spur, Victoria* from
the album *Colonies* 1878

actually against the bush: 'It's the gum-trees' country. They had it before we came,/They'll have it again when we're gone...'. No wonder that White in *Riders in the Chariot* bemoans the cynicism of the bush. He calls it cynical because it derides human habitation; in the new suburb of Paradise East, where gum trees are being axed to make way for textured-brick boxes, the developers retaliate by asking 'what was land – such nasty, sandy, scrubby stuff – if not an investment?'

In a story by Alan Marshall, the laconic prospector Silent Joe is said to be 'akin to trees'. Nevertheless he consents to say 'Goodbye' at the end of his encounter with the story-teller, and he even waves. 'It was as if a tree had spoken,' Marshall comments. Australian trees may not have the power of speech, but some of them look as if they know how to write. The genus of eucalypts known as scribbly gums have messages scrawled on their bark; the doodling is done by the larvae of a beetle that lives in the tree. What Missingham called the tattiness and 'almost nonentity' of the bush can be overcome by individualizing trees, which are not singled out by our actual perception of landscape. Mr Holland in Bail's *Eucalyptus* offers his daughter's hand to the man who can name every variety of eucalypt growing on his property, which is 'an outdoor museum of trees'. Anyone who successfully completes the test has proved that he understands Australia, and deserves to wed the country. Desire is taxonomic, dealing in types and generalized, generic images. Love particularizes, and celebrates the unrepeatable individuality of the loved one. The architect Glenn Murcutt also insists on looking closely at individual trees – the peeling papery bark of the melaleuca, the honeyed smell of the scribbly gum when it is in flower – rather than briskly disposing of them to make way for houses.

The newcomers thus attempt to relearn the lore of the Aboriginal people, who saw certain trees as the metamorphosed forms of their spirit ancestors. During Charles Mountford's trip through the Mann Ranges in 1948, his guides told him stories to explain the contortions of the bloodwood trees. One with a dead limb sticking out at an angle brandishes the stick used by two women who attempted to trap a mythical water snake. Another with a bulbous trunk commemorates the indigestion of a lizard-man who had gobbled up a whole tribe's share of berries.

Caire, telling genealogical stories of his own, awarded titles to trees: he called one especially distinguished eucalypt 'The Baron', after his friend von Mueller, the government botanist. Other photographers befriended trees, and showed them atoning for the lack of 'society' by imitating the matey virtues of the frontier. John B. Eaton photographed a convivial clump of white gums in Gippsland, calling them *Good Companions*. Stanley Eutrope's *Guardian Gum* protectively extends its branches over an isolated homestead. In *Guardians of the Pool*, Cecil Bostock derived the same reassurance from the behaviour of gums inclining over a meagre puddle: they can be trusted to look after this precious source because they need so little water themselves. Rose Simmonds complimented her trees for being stately as well as tall, and for standing so far apart. At last the bush has learned how to behave when on parade, as if the trees were columns in a cathedral nave. Simmonds arranged another courtly tableau in a bromoil she called *Homage*: a sapling tugs its forelock while a slim, dandified gum that towers above it flaunts its foliage – feudal deportment, better suited to a gentleman's park in England.

There are legendary trees in the outback, ancients of days with tragic stories to tell. At Innamincka, Jeff Carter photographed one into which the knotty, whiskery

78
Rose Simmonds
Tall and Stately 1930s

visage of Burke, who died nearby, has been carved. More anonymous trees have been called upon to exemplify the tough stoicism of the Australian character. There was no need to erect monumental statues commemorating the national epic of travail, duress and disappointment; trees did the sculptors' work, and saved modest Australians from having to pose as supermen. John Kauffmann's stringy *Veteran of the Woods* has been buffeted by winds that bend it backwards, but it has survived. The title implies that it is a veteran of those imperial wars in which Australians, gallantly volunteering as cannon fodder, sought to prove their moral worth. *Victory*, photographed by Kauffmann in about 1918, also commemorates a military triumph, but counts its cost. This tree – leafless, its roots exposed in sandy soil – is a dead recruit abandoned on the battlefield. The twisted, twitching branches in the background are like agonized nerves: for once a tree does not suffer in silence but expresses pain through its lashing limbs.

Cazneaux sought out trees that appeared to have been fortified by their suffering, and cast them in tragic charades. The tree he called *The Lone Sentinel* or *The Sentinel of the Heights* is worn, stricken, denuded of bark lower down and leafless near the top, but with no deputy on the rocky ridge it will not desert its post. The meaning of this physiognomic misery varied; Cazneaux often altered the titles of his tree photographs to bring them up to date with contemporary distresses. In 1937, at Wilpena Pound in the Flinders Range, he photographed a hollow gum, eviscerated like the Spartan boy who uncomplainingly allowed the fox to gnaw his innards. Its arms are upraised in silent protest that it has been left stranded by the eroding earth, but it remains indomitable: it had been there, Cazneaux believed, for five hundred years. The tree seemed to him to embody 'the Spirit of Australia', though because that spirit is immaterial, or perhaps ambiguous, he successively reinterpreted it. In some prints he called it *A Giant of the Arid North* (even though it actually grew in South Australia) or *A Mighty Gum*. Finally he emphasized its fortitude, not its gigantism or muscular might: he changed the title to *The Spirit of Endurance*. The tree now set Cazneaux himself an example, demonstrating how we must accept and cope with our losses. His only son was killed at Tobruk in 1941; according to a legend, which the Cazneaux family disputes, the young man had a tiny print of this photograph in his wallet.

80
Harold Cazneaux
The Spirit of Endurance 1937

Every Australian town has its khaki-coloured war memorial, with a roll-call of the local dead. We tend not to realize that trees are war memorials too. Palms, brought back from the Middle East in 1918 and 1945, mutely mourn the fallen. Missingham photographed a palm tree left to die of thirst near Meekatharra, Western Australia: a blackened torso – all its fronds snapped, the thin filaments of its roots still uselessly clutching the dry ground – in a derelict garden. He called it 'a memorial to the departed'. The remark may recall departed comrades, or perhaps it simply refers to the miner who once lived here and looked after the tree. It could also be hinting at the departure of water, which makes European society, with its lawns and gardens, possible: the war that Australian trees memorialize is a losing battle fought against nature itself.

To personify trees involves a magical act: the vegetable world, safely inanimate, is suddenly animated. Cazneaux photographed a *Striding Gum*, which bends backwards at an extravagant angle, its trunk rippling as if sinews were straining beneath the bark, its branches elbowing competitors out of the way as it prepares to swagger across the ground. This sorcery can be alarming. Why don't those animistic trees, which have the numerical advantage, gang up on us? And even though they hold their poses and pretend to be immobile when their photographs are taken, in what revels – Druidical perhaps, rather than Aboriginal – are they engaging? In Kauffmann's *Fairy Woods* the slim saplings are about to mutate into flesh; in a moment the roots will ease themselves out of the earth and those twisted limbs will start dancing. Mallard's witchy tree is explicitly demonized. The charred triangle at its base opens a crease that runs upwards, so that two cavorting legs separate themselves, lean backwards, and initiate a ribald witches' sabbath, encouraging the angled trees behind to flail and circle frenetically. Dupain experimented with the same spell in his *Flight of the Spectres*, photographed in 1932. Thundery clouds, agitated by streaks of scything electricity, coagulate in the sky above a stand of tormented trees, their white boles blanched in fear. In 1969 Sue Ford photographed a narrative she called *The Witch's Letter*, which retells this recurrent Australian story. Three girls quit the noisy, noxious city with its skyscrapers and fly off to a place without people or cars. In the 'magic bush forest', the maenadic babes dance naked around a scribbly gum, into which the letter has been cabbalistically inscribed. By double- and triple-exposing the images, Ford catches their gyrations 'until', as her caption says, 'they were so tired they were nearly invisible' (which is what happens when bodies in motion are photographed). The bush, like the beach, is a pagan place, home to unorthodox rites. Dupain's bathers worship the sun, and Sue Ford's dancers, having run off to a sacred grove, pay heathen homage to a tree.

These spectral sightings fulfill one of photography's most tantalizing ambitions, which is to trap the image of something that the unaided eye cannot see. At the same time they offer to make visible the elusive and perhaps alarming spirit that lurks behind the country's material reality. In 1925 the American architect Marion Mahony designed a bucolic colony at Castlecrag on the northern foreshore of Sydney Harbour, with the help of her husband Walter Burley Griffin, who devised the urban plan of Canberra. She spoke of the settlement as an earthly paradise reconstructed on Australia's rocky, unpropitious soil. Her first act was to plant trees, rather than, like most Australian settlers, to chop them down. Vegetation was needed to bind the soil together on this bare, eroded bluff. Once the shrubbery had grown up, Mahony imagined phantasmagorical goings-on within it. She was convinced that there were fairies cavorting at the bottom of her

81
Henri Mallard
The Witches' Wood 1957

garden. Hers was a metaphorical faith: the ability to see such wispy sprites was for her synonymous with imagination, and it could also be a symptom of photographic clairvoyance. Theosophists believed in an angelic second sight, the ability to see a healing vibrancy in the air. Photographers, writing with light, sought to transcribe that luminous dance of particles, which in Cazneaux's portraits of nymphs assumes a more or less human, diaphanous form. Photographs capture light; they also seem to exude it. In Dupain's *Flight of the Spectres*, the photons form a blitz of jagged flashes, but in his *Sunbaker*, the light recalls the radiance that first stirred life fertile into being. As so often in Australia, the story being retold is that of Genesis, as one or two isolated human beings strive to make themselves at home in a new, fresh world that looks to them – depending on the weather and their mood – alternately accursed or benign.

Olive Cotton saw no fairies, but for her too photography was a mode of second sight, a visionary intuition that allowed her to glimpse a fugitive spirit of place. In 1992 she photographed a bird launching itself from a burned, broken gum tree that has sent out a new branch at a right angle to the scarred trunk and started to grow again, with tufts of leaves poking into the air. It is 'an ordinary sight', as Wordsworth might have said, but Cotton's 'soaring bird' is also an ancient Platonic image of the soul's release from the body: the tree's carcass expels this volatile rush of energy, on its way elsewhere. In *The Sleeper*, photographed in 1939, Cotton's friend Olga Sharp has nodded off in the grass after a bush picnic, a spray of leaves resting like a brooch on the shoulder of her blouse. She lies on her back, with her hands behind her head; change her sex, roll her over, and she is Dupain's *Sunbaker*, asleep with his face in the sand. The unguarded relaxation of both figures marks an end to the competitive aggression that set men against nature on the frontier. Olga might be dreaming of the bright landscape that hovers above her head, or perhaps – as her epaulette of leaves suggests – the landscape has settled on her and is beginning to grow over and around her, the grass sending shoots through her sprawled, unprotesting body. Light makes the material world transparent. Cotton's *Skeleton of a Leaf*, photographed in 1964, is not skeletal like an X-rayed human body. The leaf, standing upright against the sky, is aerated, its delicate veining laid bare. Instead of bones, it has an irrigation system of filaments through which it is infused with water. It absorbs sun, and after photosynthesis exhales the oxygen that enables us to breathe. The tree of man, whose lumbering size impresses male photographers, looks clumsy and stolid when compared with a single leaf looked at by a woman.

Cotton worked in Dupain's studio, and was married to him from 1939 to 1941. They often received commissions to photograph musicians, such as the Budapest String Quartet, brought out on tour by the Australian Broadcasting Commission; Cotton understood the affinity between their art and her own, as she revealed in 1937 in her *Orchestration in Light*. The trees here make way for the play of light both on grass and in an

82
Olive Cotton
The Patterned Road 1938
© Olive Cotton, courtesy
of Josef Lebovic Gallery

empty but unthreatening chasm, with a distant (and almost audible) waterfall. A tentacular branch overhanging the gulf fingers the air, like a harpist plucking strings to release a vibration. Conductors move air around; photographers, as Cotton's title implies, make music by manipulating something equally insubstantial. Commenting on the image, Cotton explained her synaesthetic translation of the landscape's 'great range of tones, from light through to darkness…into orchestral sounds, from the high treble of piccolos to the deep sonorous notes of double bass instruments'. In *The Patterned Road*, she stops to investigate a configuration of shadows, a calligraphy as obscurely meaningful as musical notation on the page of a score, even though it has been written on a dusty track through the bush. The tree that casts the shadows has spread its denuded arms to conduct the light. Cotton's angle of vision ignores the trajectory of transport and settlement. The lines scratched in the dirt by passing wheels run on ahead to some future beyond the frame, and the river flows in the same direction. But she does not follow the course of history; the marks on the road merely serve as ruled staves, on which the music – those curls and squiggles and slanting diagonals – is inscribed. Rather than looking ahead to the road's destination and fretting about your arrival there, it is more important to sit still and look around you – to put down roots, like a tree.

Caire often nicknamed trees elegiacally, conferring a mythical hauteur on them. A tree he called Big Ben might well have stood up to the clock in Westminster, had it not been destroyed by a bushfire. Uncle Sam, an almost American overachiever, decayed before it had a chance to challenge the sequoias. In 1908 Caire complained when the looming veteran known as Billy Barlow was cut down so that the government could send a slab to the Paris Exposition. He accused loggers of usurpation and regicide: he called his photograph of a tree prostrate among the ferns *A Fallen Monarch*.

Australians, who think of human life as a grim comedy, permit trees to be tragic and encourage them to dramatize their anguish. The log in Dupain's series *The Death of the Tree*, which helplessly batters the air with that carbonized, abruptly foreshortened branch, resembles the calcified victims of the volcano at Pompeii. But photography, with its connoisseurship of surfaces, cannot help finding beauty in misery and ugliness: the burned bark looks rich, almost edible, like crackling on roast pork. There are signs here, as tragedy requires, of recovery and consolation. Though fire has seared the tree's outer layers, the raw flesh it has exposed is a seedbed for those eager thistles. Such cathartic dramas, apparently banished from the comfortably unspiritual home life of Australians, are acted out everywhere in the bush. James McAuley notices that 'the angophora preaches on the hillsides/ With the gestures of Moses', and Patrick White in *The Cockatoos* refers to 'those professional martyrs the native trees', whipped by a wind off the ocean. Hans Hasenpflug, who migrated to Australia from Germany in 1927, photographed an abused tree during the 1940s. Though blackened by fire, it extends two arms in a gesture that might be interpreted as a benediction. Hasenpflug called the image *Amen*.

In 1956 Charles Mountford published *Australian Tree Portraits*, a collection of his own photographs. 'Trees,' he declared, 'are the people of the landscape': whoever said that Australia was underpopulated? His recognition that trees are characters, prototypes for what Alexander Herzen called 'the crooked timber of humanity', prompted him to single out specimens as quirky and grotesquely warped as Patrick White's unsociable egotists. The banksia's seed-pods look like a scary old man, the ghost gum with branches like outstretched arms is genuinely spooky, and the prickly ironwood is 'unfriendly'. But despite these acts of personification, the notes to Mountford's book dismiss trees if they can make no self-sacrificing contribution to human society: the coolibah, beside which the jolly swagman camps in *Waltzing Matilda*, has 'little value to man', the bark of the corkwood is 'too short and friable to have any economic value', and the red mallee is good only for fencing or 'domestic heating'.

The impulse to hug trees is countered, as always in Australia, by an impatience to cut them down to size. A small photographic anthology of *Australian Treescapes*, published in 1950, eagerly appraises trees as timber. Blue gums, photographed by Cazneaux at Babbington Tops, are recommended for wood paving blocks, and cedars are predestined to turn into cabinets. The casuarina, also photographed by Cazneaux, is said to have been called the she-oak because the grain of its wood resembles English oak, but (as the caption says) is inferior, which is why the female pronoun seemed appropriate. Beneath another Cazneaux photograph, of a pastoral estate at Kurrajong, eucalypts are rebuked for being 'rabid individualists', which must be cleared to make way for the cooperative protocols of society. Nature is defensible if it strives to resemble architecture: though the Moreton Bay Figs near the Observatory in Sydney have 'flying-buttress trunks', they cannot compete with 'the precision of the engineering achievement of the Sydney Harbour Bridge', which they frame. The volume includes Max Dupain's photograph of his own house by the harbour at Castlecrag. In this case the caption compliments the feathery trees for softening the building's modern angularity. The sapling gums are deferential, their branches too high to interfere with the severe lines of the house.

The final photograph in the book, by Olga Sharp, shows a sculpturally gnarled and arthritic gum on a barbered lawn beside a suburban swimming pool. 'The trees abide,' says the final sentence of the caption, with biblical gravity, like White giving the bush the last, silent word in *The Tree of Man*. It's not quite the same thing as declaring that the people survive and will go on forever, as Steinbeck does at the end of *The Grapes of Wrath*. In Sharp's photograph only one tree has been allowed to abide, and it is there on sufferance, with imported shrubs lined up in pots to set it a cautionary example. More recently, Graham Howe photographed an unhappy trio of *Disciplined Trees* in a repressive, regimented suburban garden. The pines have been clipped, trussed and made to stand up straight. One of them, trained to forget its natural growth patterns, is razored into the shape of a bell jar. All you can see of the house is a fly-excluding mesh on the verandah: nature must be kept at bay.

The anthropologist James Frazer in *The Golden Bough* praised tribal people for their fellow feeling for trees. If a tree is animate, it must feel pain, so to cut it down is a delicate procedure. European peasants planned such operations as ritual sacrifices, which were necessary to renew the land. Chopping down a decayed King of the Wood, they staged what Frazer calls 'mimic executions', with human beings clad in bark volunteering to voice the tree's pain and atone for the cruelty of men. Artists, who possess what Lévi-Strauss called savage minds, continue to stage such expiatory rites in contemporary Australia. In 1982 Stelarc (born Stelios Arcadiou) performed a 'prepared tree suspension event' on the side of a mountain above Canberra. Naked, pinioned by hooks, with pegs and clamps attached to his flesh to stretch it, he hung upside down from the boughs of a tree. Like Stacey's suspension from Uluru, the scene resembles a crucifixion, with an agnostic rabble of curious gawpers gathered at the foot of the cross. But Black Mountain is not quite Golgotha. Stelarc was not impaled on the tree; it supported him and – thanks to the cords that turned the empty air into a trampoline – allowed him to realize his dream of escaping from gravity. Like all photographic subjects, he is in a state of suspended animation, and could be an evangelical angel hovering in mid-flight to announce good news.

83
Stelarc,
performance artist, and
Norman Ainsworth,
photographer: image
from the performance
*Prepared Tree Suspension Event
for Obsolete Body, No. 6,
Canberra 1982*

The male ego achieves lift-off: Stelarc has freed himself from the tree's anchorage to the ground. In 1979 Jill Orr explored the female equivalent to this mad mysticism by growing into the ground. In her impersonation of a bleeding tree, she inverts herself to bury her head in the earth like a tree's roots. Elsewhere in the series she casts herself as a classical nymph, consumed by greedy nature: her leg disappears into a crevasse, and dirt girdles her groin. Here she shows what the tree of woman looks like. Orr's legs and arms, if she could free them from the soil, would be waving branches, her pubic bush foliage. Her mouth may be open to scream, as well as to drink. Animation alienates us from the earth; to be planted, however, involves the sacrifice of freedom and identity. The woman has been deprived of the facial features that make her a person, and her eyes now do their looking underground. The pantheistic dream of union with the landscape is here a screeching trauma.

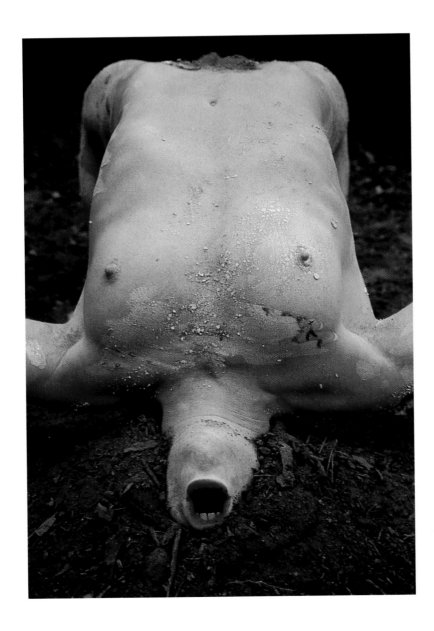

84
Jill Orr,
performance artist, and
Elizabeth Campbell,
photographer: image
from the performance
Bleeding Trees 1979

Frazer noted that Aboriginal people relied on magical invocation to awaken 'the dormant energies of nature at the approach of what may be called the Australian spring'. But since they lived in a desert, they were at best concerned with the revivification of shrubs, not trees. Further south, settlers seldom had time for the commiseration with tree-spirits described by Frazer. Tasmania's forests of mountain ash, as tall as the Californian redwoods, were chewed up into paper pulp during the 1950s. After just over two centuries of white occupation, two-thirds of Australia's native woodland has been toppled. In Wisconsin or Ontario, loggers and lumberjacks dreamed up a mythical giant, Paul Bunyan, who massacred the woods with the assistance of a blue ox called Babe. There is no such figure in Australian folklore. Though the adolescent Ned Kelly in Peter Carey's *True History of the Kelly Gang* prides himself on felling five ironbarks a day and thinks he hears 'a whole empire collapsing' as they lunge to earth, his mystique has nothing to do with his axemanship. The photographs by Caire – or Charles Kerry's *Felling a Forest Veteran*, which has six Lilliputian axemen balanced on planks stuck into a trunk that still defiantly towers above them – reveal how unequal the combat between man and nature was on this final frontier.

Machinery eventually conquered the forest. Wesley Stacey reveals what is left of Myrtle Mountain in New South Wales after bulldozers, skidders, excavators and graders have trampled the trees and grubbed them up for conversion into woodchip. The horizontal amplitude of the image would have suited a panorama. Instead the view is arbitrarily cropped at the top as if to replicate the decapitation of the trees, and the space it surveys is flat and unrecessive. Beyond the few trees that remain there is no dreamy distance, only the mutilated mess of a battlefield. This could be Ypres or Passchendaele as photographed by Frank Hurley in 1917, with planks scattered across the quaking mud and mass graves marked by splintered trees. The purpose of machines, whether they are Howitzers or bulldozers, is to make war on a natural world they have rendered obsolete. You can see why the suitors in Murray Bail's novel are required to romance Mr Holland's eucalypts. The alternative to this sylvan courtship is what the architect Robin Boyd calls arborophobia: the Australian hatred of trees that get in the way of society's advance.

85
Wesley Stacey
*Woodchip Logging Aftermath
(near Myrtle Mountain)* 1980

The Aboriginal climber photographed by Kerry as he vaults up a tree with only a vine to help him is a better bushman than those who have taken over his habitat. Still, his acrobatic exhibition is pointless: there are no fruits to pick or animals to catch on the upper branches, which have already been amputated. Though the usurpers have dressed him in their own clothes, they have systematically stripped the land and chopped it flat. The trees that once stood on it, reduced to palings, now probably creep along the horizon in that squat fence. The trees beyond the fence are maimed and limbless after a fire, and therefore less of a threat to the settlers. As for the tree being climbed, it hardly belongs to nature any more. Planed down, it could be a mast, a flagpole, or perhaps a factory chimney. The dogs, not native, either sniff the air in the hope of identifying something to kill or investigate the tree to find whether it is worth peeing on. They too are trained to conquer, or to annexe territory by leaving their signature on it in urine. Imagine that the Aboriginal man went on climbing and, after a few decades of historical progress, got to the top of the tree. Pan upwards after him, as if tilting the camera, and you might see what the defunct branches have evolved into: the crossed bars of the telegraph network, being wired up by Cranstone's workers. Of course they need ladders (made out of other butchered trees), which the native can do without, though one of them has at least shed his clothes to suit the climate. The vine has been replaced by wires that are tougher, less organic. Trees once harboured spirits. They still have voices, but magic has given way to technology.

87
Edward Cranstone
Men at Work from the
album *Design for War*, vol. I
1942–44

Documenting preparations for war, Cranstone photographed timber-fellers in the bush and skilled choppers slicing and sculpting the trunks into telegraph poles or railway sleepers. In 1848 the *Sydney Mail* published an engraving of a bush photographer on his rounds. Parking his wagon in the scrub, he sets up his camera on its tripod and crouches beneath the cloth. Four male settlers pose stiffly in front of the log pile that is evidence of their small incursion into nature; they have used the wood to build a rudimentary house, which has a roof but as yet no walls. The man who dominates the group leans against his proudest possession, an axe. He and the headless photographer, confronting each other at opposite ends of the engraving across an empty expanse, balance a paradoxical equation. The destroyer and the preserver need each other, since the house that the axe makes possible will not be a home unless there are photographs to hang on the walls.

The niceties are maintained in the tumbledown house photographed by Laurie Wilson. The roof is peeling and rusty, the verandah sags, but the family inside wears clean underclothes. A fence with its regular grid of wire strictly marks the difference between society and unkempt wilderness. Again the axe, conclusively driven into the stump, announces that whoever has claimed this land means business. We had just such a chopping block in our backyard. My father used it to slice logs for the fire, and every Sunday morning, swinging the blade with one hand while he held down the flapping bird with the other, he killed a chicken for us to eat. Fokkema's butcher presides over a similar block at Wilcannia, with cuts of meat strung up on hooks behind him. Its wood is scarred and bloodied: the stump, once a tree, is now a site of execution and brisk surgery. On the floor, sawdust – the tree in a state of ultimate refinement – soaks up the blood.

Axe-wielding is an Australian rite of passage. I underwent my own apprentice-
ship when, as a teenager, I appeared in a film of Nan Chauncy's *They Found a Cave*. The
results were laughably inept; what I could not manage was the casual ease with which
you let the handle slip down through your hands as the blade fell. I was often dragged,
under protest, to wood-chopping displays like the one photographed by Margaret
Michaelis-Sachs. She calls the performance a carnival, which is an ironically apt name
for it: carnival is a licensed orgy, a time of riot during which believers say farewell to the
flesh and its pleasures before Lenten abstinence begins. The pointlessly destructive
energy of the men with axes suits the festive mood. The event hardly qualifies as a sport:
it requires battering force, not skill. Perhaps it re-enacts Australia's settlement,
which could only happen when the trees were brought down. A cross-section of the
population has turned up, dressed in its Sunday best, to watch the logs being scythed
through. Michaelis-Sachs catches the almost churchy solemnity of the occasion, and
the conformist rules it imposed. But by choosing to look over the shoulder of the
couple in the foreground, she registers her own detachment. This man has broken with
the crowd's uniformity by not wearing a hat: maybe he wants to show off the sleek
rivulet of lacquer on his hair. His companion, to her credit, is more interested in him
than in the chopping. The photographer too prefers the intimate foreground to the
sweaty, murderous display in the arena.

The rite goes on being played out, even in an Australia that has outgrown its
origins in the bush. Anne Zahalka photographed a wood-chopping contest in 1999 as
part of her *Leisureland* series, which documents group activities in a culture where relax-

ation is organized, even regimented. Now that physical labour is virtually obsolete, the brawling contest with nature has become a theatrical spectacle. Michaelis-Sachs's men in singlets are replaced by professional athletes who probably have agents and make money from endorsements. Floodlights allow the chopping to continue after dark, a computerized board tallies the score, and the fence is festooned with advertisements for corporate sponsors such as Coca-Cola. But Australia retains its atavistic craving for the sight and sound of trees being felled. In a stadium like Zahalka's, the chopping blocks are miked, acoustically enhancing the axe's bite as it eats into the wood.

Society's purpose is to consume the debris the axes leave behind: we gobble up a natural world that we see merely as a source of fuel. In Geoff Parr's landscape, a hill has been shorn of vegetation, leaving only a telegraph pole to deride the irregular trees that once grew there. The maw of the fireplace gapes, ready to feast on all that butchered timber; it is as if the fireplace had burned up the house to which it originally belonged, and engorged the wooded hillside as well. An industrial economy depends on such reckless gormandizing of resources. In Jules Verne's *Around the World in Eighty Days*, Phileas Fogg pulls apart the steamer that is carrying him across the Atlantic in order to feed the furnace and increase the vessel's speed.

91
Geoff Parr
Fireplace Landscape 1976

Victory for the loggers or choppers consists of reducing a tree to shavings. Artists, engaged in their own competition with nature, employ less violent methods. A tree does not have to be obliterated; it can be changed by the way you look at it, treated as an aesthetic invention, not a natural growth. Missingham applied this vision to a prostrate log he photographed at Mildura in Victoria. Adding insult to injury, it had been used for testing power saws, and the trunk was scored with a dozen deep gashes. But his caption transformed the abused wood into flesh or marble. He nicknamed the torso *Nolan's Venus*: this is the form the hardbitten, horizontal goddess might have taken had Sidney Nolan carved her effigy. 'Standing upright,' Missingham reported, 'she made a fine piece of sculpture.' At Bouddi Park in New South Wales, Missingham photographed a spotted gum, its bark mottled like elderly skin, that is wearing a corset. The hybrid has a shocking plausibility. The stays have been tied around a branch which thanks to a convenient shadow looks bluntly phallic rather than matronly. The laces are loose. Soon enough, rising sap will engorge the trunk and burst them asunder. In 1966, on the coastal road between Cossack and Onslow in Western Australia, Missingham photographed a bare mallee with beer cans attached to each of its brittle twigs. The local wits who played that joke on the mallee probably would have taken angry offence if anyone had called them artists, but their impulse was the same as that of the Optronic Kinetics Collective, whose members painstakingly turned a twisted gum into a cubist installation. Yet despite the efforts of the conceptualists, the tree that they have chosen for their experiment repudiates cubism. Geometry is a human

92
Hal Missingham
Stayed Tree, Bouddi Park, NSW
1967

invention, and those boxes, like an Australian suburb of interchangeable weatherboard homes, expose the schematic, repetitive neatness of our minds, by contrast with the exhilarating freedom of nature. The serpentine contortion of the trunk compresses energy within itself, like the coils of a spring; every box is the same, but each of the tree's leaves – curved or sharpened like a scimitar, not clustering together but claiming its own share of space – is different. The faceless optronic kineticist in the T-shirt is happy to disappear into a collective. The bush remains a gathering of restless, unruly individuals.

The title of Moore's *Impossible Tree* conveys both exasperation and wonder. How can such a rubbery, elastic thing possibly pass as a tree? It is an angophora, native to the coast around Sydney; this was the tree that gesticulated at McAuley like a fanatical preacher, though Moore's example seems to be wildly dancing rather than sermonizing. It bears an uncanny resemblance to Jill Orr upside down in the earth, all the more so because when its bark peels off the angophora is pink like denuded flesh. But the tree does not feel the gasping terror expressed by Orr's open mouth, and it flaunts its limbs like a maenad who has grown innumerable arms. We wound the ground with our feet, or cover it with concrete or bitumen; perhaps we do so because we are alarmed by the growth that erupts through it. Photography is an instinctively surrealist art: it draws attention to objects that exist in the real world but confound realism. The eurhythmic angophora, like Australia, is impossible but true.

95
Maureen Mackenzie
*Charity Mango Line-fishing in
the Mowbray River Estuary*
1986

To be inanimate has its advantages. A tree is a fixture; human beings, with heads like clouds, wander across landscapes from which they are disconnected. We have use for a scenic backdrop only if we see our own shadow passing over it. As the photographer Graeme Hare puts it, explaining his own images of moody, storm-beleaguered trees, 'Landscape is where one projects oneself onto what is there'. Subjectivity supposedly quickens and animates the obtuse, immovable object.

But what if the subject does not recognize a difference between itself and the objects with which it shares the world? Maureen MacKenzie's photographs of Charity Mango fishing form a triptych. It describes an action – the woman gathers up her line, throws it out into the river, then pulls it in – though in each of the frames motion matters less than calm, and the quiet and unflurried performance of a ritual. When she lets go of the line, her arms do not drop. They register a greeting, a pantheistic salute to nature. Photography prefers stationary targets: the Aboriginal people in those nineteenth-century portraits look so achingly uncomfortable because they have been made to imitate the rigidity of corpses. Stillness, however, suits Charity Mango, whose stance matches the tree beneath which she stands, her arms reaching out like its branches and her feet aligned with its stubby roots.

The garden goddess in Stacey's photograph has no choice in the matter. Her feet have presumably been concreted into place in the rockery, and she is held upright by a pole between her legs. Her purpose is prohibition: to keep people off that thirsty, pampered lawn. She had no way of defending her own habitat against invasion, and she is equally unable to protect her own body against intrusive scrutiny. Wearing only the bottom half of a bikini, she accessorizes her nudity with a necklace. Her hands do not attempt to cover her breasts. The sign, which in any case is behind her, can be safely disregarded, like a virgin's initial, mock-modest refusal: she might even be inviting us to assault her (though she would be grateful if we spared the lawn). Behind her, the house, with its blinded eyes, repels the sun. Daylight is unnecessary, since the wiring under the roof connects the inhabitants to the electricity grid. The ornamental maiden should be grateful. Her owners are civilized people.

96
Wesley Stacey
Black Garden Ornament 1970

5: Spiritual Homes

Darwin, making a brief landfall in 1836, considered Hobart 'very inferior to…Sydney; the latter might be called a city, this is only a town'. He admired the potato fields as evidence of cultivation, if not of culture, but was disconcerted by the 'fewness of the large houses, either built or building'. So was I in the 1950s. The suburb in which I grew up was unpacked from boxes on a hill that had been penitentially shaved with a razor. Though the roads were eventually tarred and the backyards disappeared under concrete, we were squeezed between shaggy, frowning mountains. You could see where the settlement surrendered to the bush, as the suburbs ran out in the foothills of Mount Wellington. Yet in 1965, when I visited the national capital for the first time, my home town suddenly seemed almost metropolitan. That evening in Canberra, I set out to walk from the university campus to that tantalizing location called Civic. Misled by country lanes, I never got there. In Hobart, I thought indignantly, we could boast of tramlines, milk bars, musty thrift shops, and houses containing staircases.

At least those notional arcades had been given the right name. Civilization is a civic affair; it requires the existence – or the invention – of cities. New countries, which start human history all over again, have a chance to question this evolution. Eden cannot be urban. Innocence belongs in a garden, and the ungardened bush, like the American frontier, was proud of its distance from the moral contamination and mannered falsity of cities. Australia offered its artists a choice between two opposed moral worlds: Sydney or the bush. They were expected to pledge allegiance to the latter. When May Gibbs imagined a generic city for Snugglepot and Cuddlepie to get lost in, she called it simply Big Bad.

During his tour in 1930, Hoppé conscientiously documented the bush, and lined up the so-called 'wild men' to compose a 'dusky background' for his images. But he expected more of Australia than dusty plains, mosquito-ridden swamps and lunar deserts. 'The spiritual home of the white races', he declared, 'is naturally in the cities built up by their vigour and vision.' In 1858 John Smith had photographed the construction of Sydney University, which was meant to be just such a sanctum. Sandstone griffins and gargoyles lie around awaiting installation, but the cerebral cloisters are bare, like premature ruins. Gothic architecture is cruelly demystified by the pitiless sun. Even after almost a century of institutional consolidation, Hoppé was unpersuaded. Urbane Melbourne struck him as virtually Bostonian, but the lamp posts in Canberra looked as if they still had price-tags attached. In Sydney he called Taronga 'the happiest zoo in the world' because 'its boundaries come right to the ocean-edge and make a natural home for water-loving denizens of the animal world', while across the harbour lay the Botanic Gardens, 'Mecca of typists in the lunch-hour'. The typists could be considered fauna, nibbling their sandwiches among the flora. Where, however, was the white, shining, spiritual citadel? In 1930, no one imagined that an opera house might one day perch on the foreshore.

Traditionally, the centre of a city is occupied by a mound on which a symbol of power and communal ideology is erected, or by a square that symbolizes the congested space of urban society: an Acropolis or a Palatine Hill, a Piazza San Marco or Place de la Concorde. The cities of the newer world experiment with a different ordination of space. Rather than relying on architecture and engineering to separate them from nature, they make room for nature within the walls. New York has Central Park, and every Australian city has its Botanic Gardens where nostalgic citizens can revisit a fanciful version of the countryside. Lindt, who photographed the Botanic Gardens in several cities, noticed the oddity of these encounters. In Adelaide, a Greek temple rears out of the shrubbery, into which it will soon disappear. Trellises for creepers have been nailed to its side, and sheets are slung over the windows of its outbuildings to deter the heat, like blinds on a verandah. In Brisbane, the gardens with their banana plants and prickly cacti expose the folly of transplanting English species to another hemisphere. In Melbourne, an overdressed bourgeois clan pauses at a grass hut. The lawn, trimmed and regular, belongs to civilization, but the explorers brace themselves before venturing into the rank, savage luxuriance of the jungle. You can easily trespass across the border. Once in the Sydney Botanic Gardens – within sight of the skyscrapers of the financial district, minutes from the Art Gallery – I watched a flight of white cockatoos methodically strip a tree of its mandarins, picking the fruit, pecking off a strip of peel and then disdainfully hurling the pulp to the ground, which reeked of orange juice. And on another occasion I looked up, puzzled by a noise in the air, and saw a tree-load of flying foxes dangling upside down, their leathery black wings rustling as if they shared a contagious bad dream.

97
J. W. Lindt
Adelaide, Botanic Gardens, Temple c. 1887

Canberra, planned as a gathering of garden suburbs divided by an artificial lake, made hopeful provision for urban life. Some time in the future, the plastery arcades of Civic were to be the backdrop for a thronging human comedy; they are still waiting. Photographed at night by Fokkema in 1977, the A. C. T. Tourist Bureau is comatose, displaying brochures to non-existent tourists, while the building labelled 'Canberra House' is a bare, unoccupied box. Street lights blur into stars: we might be – we are – in vacant interstellar space. Walter Benjamin said that the photographs Eugène Atget took in the Paris streets resemble documentations of crime scenes. He meant that the city is a site of random and illicit encounters, an incubator of vice and violence. Atget's city – with its tramps, its prostitutes, its secretive, seditious passages and the dead carthorses that occasionally putrefy in its gutters – hardly presents itself as a spiritual home. It is a labyrinth of recondite pleasures feverishly imagined by all those who live there. Fokkema's Canberra, bleached by moonlight or pallid neon, is too clean, too uncomplicated, too orderly. At dusk on New Year's Eve in 2001, I noticed that the police had set up barricades in Civic. This seemed an unnecessary precaution, since there was no one about. My taxi driver put me right, and said they expected a crowd of at least two hundred before midnight. In the event, the party fizzled out because the municipal authorities forgot to order fireworks.

Not long ago, sheep grazed outside Parliament. Now a cluster of tents and vans – with barbecues and formica kitchen chairs scattered about for the occupants, who are campaigning for Aboriginal land rights – recreates a bush clearing on the same stretch

98
Wesley Stacey
Canberra from the West 1980

of grass. Up a slope, the new Parliament House recoils on a hilltop, waiting for the trees to camouflage it. The building does not seek to command the view or to impose its authority through its bulk, like the Capitol in Washington or the Reichstag in Berlin. Instead a flag on a see-through pole waves above a lawn. In 1980 Wesley Stacey photographed Canberra from the west. The city has dwindled to a cluster of white specks between the hills and the flat, baking paddocks. The telecommunications mast on Black Mountain aims its gabbled, insignificant signals at a white-hot sky that absorbs and silences them. The thin clouds, coasting just above the haze of heat, mimic the hills that shelter Canberra, and suggest that they too might be no more solid than vapour. The trees have always been here, and so has the sky. Who needs politicians, and the city they have rigged up in which to conspire and confabulate?

The bush and the outback are inimitable. Australian cities, however, began as facsimiles, metaphorical semblances of places elsewhere that they did not really resemble. Hal Porter likened Hobart to 'such upstairs/downstairs Old World cities as Naples and Genoa', or to San Francisco on a smaller scale, 'quite without the tang, glamour, ebullience, and uproar' – but what good is a city if it lacks spice and vice? The poet Kenneth Slessor defined Sydney as 'a kind of dispersed and vaguer Venice'. Dispersal helps the far-fetched analogy, and so does vagueness, which is a wavy motion, a watery dissolution. The camera, taking stock of Australian cities in their early years, looked at them with the same double vision, registering both the paltry reality and the hopeful idea that sustained it.

In 1872 Henry Beaufoy Merlin photographed a photographic studio in the gold rush town of Hill End, acknowledging both the pathos of the civic enterprise and his own art's complicity in it. The studio belongs to a company that calls itself, on a bold, inky placard, 'A & A'. Two continents, America and Australasia, are joined in the title, but despite this ocean-vaulting grandeur there is no space to accommodate more than those thick initials on the sign, and the words 'Photographic Company' have to squeeze themselves into a corner, twist at an angle and run sideways down the margin. Three employees slouch in an open door, uneasily acting the roles of dandies; the shopfront behind them looks as flat and flimsy as a painted backdrop, which of course it is. Views of Sydney Harbour are strung up on display above a dirt pavement and a gutter choked with rubbish. A photographer exposes the delusion of photography.

The first Australian daguerreotype, made in 1848 by J. W. Newland, shows Murray Street in Hobart sloping down to the wharf. The buildings are substantial enough, and indeed they are all still standing. But photography, however earnestly it might venerate monuments, has a wayward eye, beckoned by ephemera. It is an art that chases fugitive time; it therefore favours whatever is temporary. Across from the colonial offices there are blotched, stripped posters on a brick wall, relics of used-up amusements. The ghosts of horses and riders, having wandered past during the exposure, linger on the street, mingling with the dust. The first glimpse of an Australian city acknowledges that all cities are places of rapid transit, where the record of our existence is soon effaced, like the smudged passers-by or faded posters.

99
Alfred Winter
Sandy Bay from St George's Hill,
Tasmania c. 1870

When I look at Alfred Winter's photograph of the harbour from Battery Point, I become one of those revenants who loiter in limbo on Murray Street. I can spend hours walking through this view. It starts with the skidding descent of the hill beside the unsteady paling fence. I can feel that gradient, now smoothed by tarmac, beneath my feet. Then, crossing a bridge over a rivulet, comes the cold, pebbly beach and what I remember as a yacht club on the esplanade, a place out of bounds to families like mine: the rich had prior rights to the foreshore. Up the hill is the site of what became my university campus. Eventually, on a spit of land jutting into the harbour, a hotel was built, with a casino where my relatives risked their pensions in games of two-up. I stayed on an upper floor during my last trip to Hobart, where I no longer have a home. My recollections give names to streets that had not even been laid out when Winter took the photograph, and allow me into the houses: I am sure I once had sex in the cottage on the esplanade. Yet these perambulations through space and time leave me feeling bereft, like a ghost haunting myself. I only ever saw it like that at dawn, as I wandered home from all-night parties. Though I want to read this scene as a preview of Hobart's future, it is also a review of my past and its succession of perishable moments like faded photographs.

It is the vacant allotments – fenced or bordered by hedges, whether or not there is anything inside the boundary – that upset me when I look at Winter's scene. Early photographs of cities always have aching holes in them, spaces not yet filled in or filled up by human associations. A plot of land that might be densely occupied by your memories was empty once; it will probably soon be empty again. You could be revisiting a room you once lived in, freshly painted by the new occupant. Cities are places of storage, supposed to conserve the past. That is what makes them spiritual homes for Hoppé's white races. (The black races, he implied, need no such shelter: they are domiciled in nature.) Photography, which began keeping records such a short time ago, questions this pretence. The terrain of Sandy Bay is forgetful. Left to their own devices, the trees will reclaim the territory stolen by the cottage-dwellers.

In 1874 Bernard Otto Holtermann built a masonry tower on the northern shore of Sydney Harbour, and with the help of Charles Bayliss installed a series of large-format cameras to form this panopticon. Exposing the largest wet plate negatives ever used and delicately manoeuvring them downstairs to a darkroom in the basement, he assembled a panorama of the city. Twenty-three separate plates joined together to cover the four miles from Neutral Bay to Waverton. In 1876 Holtermann accompanied his panorama to Philadelphia, where it was displayed at the Centennial Exhibition.

Two years later, Eadweard Muybridge made a photographic panorama of San Francisco, looking down from the tower of a plutocrat's mansion on Nob Hill. The privileged vantage-point on this affluent pinnacle had a circular sweep that encompassed the evidence of progress: a grid of streets defying the hilly topography, tracks for cable cars, rows of shingled houses obsequiously clustered on the lowlands, ships docked on the Embarcadero. Describing the shield of Homer's Achilles, Georg Lukács called it an emblem of epic because its carvings, which narrated the process of the armour's manufacture and dramatized the art of war, contained 'the totality of objects'. Muybridge's multiple plates made up such an inventory. Except for odd outcrops of rock where the diggers are at work, nature has disappeared. It is merely a source of mineral wealth or, failing that, a base for human habitation.

Holtermann's panorama testifies to the different conditions of settlement in Australia. Here there is no materialistic triumphalism. Despite his tower, the angle is not dizzy, exalted because exclusive like Muybridge's. The land is low, the horizon straggles away indistinctly. The villages in the photograph are more like encampments that cannot resist the intervening bush. Three churches – Anglican, Presbyterian and Catholic – make common cause in Lavender Bay, deriving comfort from proximity despite their

100
B. O. Holtermann and
Charles Bayliss
*Panorama of Sydney Harbour
and Suburbs from the North
Shore 1875*
[detail: 2 of 23 panels]

doctrinal schisms, but none of their gospels extends very far. The water nibbles holes in the shore and forces the settlements to the fringes (whereas in Muybridge's San Francisco it is the bay that remains at the margins). Circular Quay is a bite-sized indentation, indistinguishable from all the others. If you isolate one of the panels, the city disappears: between the manse of St Peter's and the cliffs behind Kurraba Point, a contorted dance of white tree trunks threatens the fence that tries to keep out wildness, and the bush chokes another plucky, isolated string of dwellings. Beyond Cremone Point and Bradley's Head, uncolonized land resumes, floating on the water as if newly created. At the western edge of the panorama, along the Parramatta River, Sydney promptly gives in to the bush. Its citizens accept the justice of this surrender. In *Back to Bool Bool*, published by Miles Franklin under her pseudonym 'Brent of Bin Bin', a character disembarking from a liner at Circular Quay complains about the deforestation of Hyde Park caused by excavations for the railway tunnel to Bondi Junction. Where are 'the great Port Jackson and Moreton Bay Figs with their marvellous roots, that made Sydney different'? The city's identity derives from vegetation: the novel's hero considers the settlement's initial name of Botany Bay a 'certificate of original glory'.

After the San Francisco fire of 1906, George R. Lawrence photographed the charred waste from a balloon, and the *Los Angeles Times* published his panorama under a headline insisting 'SHE WILL RISE FROM HER ASHES'. Such prophetic certainty is not available to Australians, who were inclined in the nineteenth century to see their country as a curse, rather than God's open-handed gift to them. Australian panoramas meditate on emptiness, rather than the rich, teeming accumulation photographed by Muybridge. On a mount of vision in Montefiore Park, the sickly green copper figure of the Surveyor-General Colonel Light can still be seen imagining Adelaide, with a scroll drooping from his hand. His left leg is anchored by the trunk of a beheaded tree: culture will require the clearance of nature. With his rapt, springing pose, he discounts the damage as he prepares to leap into the future. A panorama from the 1860s compares Light's dream with the unpromising actuality. The garden city consists of a lawn and a fence. A solitary stroller represents its distant populace. The spires of its churches can hardly reach above the horizon. Untrodden paths trail away towards a vanishing point that might be on the Nullarbor Plain.

Australians take a witty pride in seeing through the deceits of a world that purports to be real. Writers experimentally demolish the cities that are supposed to be our mental fortresses. In *Holden's Performance*, Murray Bail dismisses Light's fiat. He calls

101
Unknown photographer
*Panoramic View of Adelaide,
South Australia* 1860s

Adelaide 'a small city and flat', and remembers it dwindling to a luminous blur when, during his own childhood, the tramlines were torn up. The metal grid of rails organized space, and the punctual schedule of the trams made sense of time. When the lines were removed, Adelaide itself, in Bail's account, became a mirage. Peter Carey in *Illywhacker* shows how easily Sydney too can be unbuilt. All it takes is a single act of hooliganism. Scrape at the granite veneer of the Bank of New Zealand in Martin Place and you'll uncover brick; even the ersatz granite is only terracotta tiles. Augustus, to whom Virgil paid tribute in *The Aeneid*, was said to have found Rome brick and left it marble. Carey finds Sydney granite, but leaves it wattle and daub.

The mining town of Solferino qualifies as 'characteristic Australian scenery' because it looks so temporary and unstable. Cabins on stilts warily hover above the ground. Not having founded themselves in this ravaged, exploited soil, uneasily balanced on a slope, they are ready, like wagons, to trundle off elsewhere. The main street is a gap between these habitable crates, and tree trunks roughly bridge a creek. The title of the series must be ironic: scenery should be picturesque, artistically arranged, whereas

102
J. W. Lindt
Solferino NSW, Mining Town from the series *Characteristic Australian Scenery c.* 1872

Solferino is earth in its primordial state – churned-up, random, unmapped. Cities that managed to get themselves built were liable to be reclaimed by nature, like Brisbane during the 1893 flood. The street's inundation mocks the conceit of the merchants whose names are emblazoned on the sides of their shops: the circulation of commodities must defer to the sullen, sluggish current of water. The half-submerged horse and cart and the waterlogged citizens stand still to oblige the photographer, but also because they have nowhere to go. They are witnesses to a disruptive miracle. Floods, once interpreted as a symptom of divine anger, can now be understood as nature's assertion of its superior will, ignoring human amendments to the land. Nevertheless a mystery remains, at which Poulsen stares in awe. The flooded street has settled into a photograph, as the smooth surface of the water mirrors the bodies and buildings that stand above it. Those becalmed, bemused people have been turned into narcissists by the bad weather; they see themselves reversed in a looking-glass world. The trading city they knew has deliquesced into a depthless reflection of itself. Now when the eye inspects the world above the waterline it questions the solidity of those commercial containers and the merchandise supposedly piled up in them. This is photography's existential admonition. It shows us what we look like, and in doing so estranges us from ourselves. It duplicates the world, and thus renders it unrecognizable.

Early photographs sometimes rely on trickery to create the illusion of home. Another Sydney panorama, taken from Blues Point not far from Holtermann's tower by John Degotardi during the 1870s, carefully positions pyramidal clumps of three or four picnickers in each of its panels. The deception works well enough until you notice that the groups are always the same: the dragooned members of Degotardi's family were probably sent from one spot to the next as the exposures were made, swapping clothes and altering their gestures at each stop. There is so much space, with so few people to occupy it.

What repletes the emptiness is death. These presumptive cities long to have a history; they are hungry for corpses, which will invest the ground with memory. George in *The Boy in the Bush* says that dead bones are needed to mature and manure the sand of Western Australia, to hold it together. When a baby is buried, it is 'another sop to the avid country'. The graveyard in the photograph attributed to Daniel Marquis looks forward to a future when there will be a past worth mourning. A column on the hilltop tries to assert the idea of centrality: society derives courage from the ancestors it has interred. But much vacant space remains, and the trees planted beside the appointed tombs of those who are perhaps not yet born have no shade to bestow. Gerrit Fokkema's documentation of Wilcannia begins and ends with graves. The first photograph in his book is of a mound alone in the mallee near a barbed-wire fence, surmounted by a headstone with the florid inscription 'SACRED' – sacred to what? – while the last is of a recent pile of mud, marked by a bouquet but no headstone, inside the town limits. The dead put down roots, or try to: my parents were cremated, because the cemetery near their house only had wall niches left to offer them. My mother took me to see hers, so that I would know how to find it when I came to visit. 'This is where I'll be,' she said, smiling as she put her hand into the gap in the wall. On the way out, she pointed to the resting places of relatives, friends, neighbours. In the colonial photograph, the dormitory is less snug and companionable. The column is stranded in an area that has not been landscaped, and the paths between the graves give up before arriving at the slope.

103
P. C. Poulsen
Brisbane in Flood
1893

104
Daniel Marquis
(attributed)
Graveyard c. 1866–80

Australian space was unintelligible to nineteenth-century photographers unless it could be partitioned and peopled. Kerry, photographing the esplanade at Manly during the 1890s, planted figures as deliberately as the gardener who situated the Norfolk pines, still stunted, inside their little protective fences. On the sand and in the ocean among unbreaking waves, other citizens hold their poses like pieces on a chessboard. Only the shrubs growing from the cliff at an unauthorized angle interfere with this rigid delineation, which gives every square its tenant: a tree or (better yet) a telegraph pole, and a human being who loiters proprietorially nearby.

The fiction is more airily decorative and poignantly wishful at Enmore, an estate in what is now the Sydney suburb of Newtown. The young ladies on the lawn, playing at archery or croquet beneath a rampart of mature Norfolk pines, remain disconnected from each other, and too many games are in progress simultaneously for the tableau to cohere. Shouldn't they be taking turns with the mallets, rather than engaging in a free-for-all? And if the archer drew her bow – which, thanks to the photograph's charmed stasis, she never will – wouldn't she endanger her friends? It is all too solemn and premeditated, lacking the frisky energy and sporting randomness that such enjoyments should have. Anchored by their hats, their hooped skirts and their mallets, the women are conscientiously performing in the mannered charade we call social life, even though they have garbled its rules. (I am reminded of Jeff Carter's sardonic photograph of golf in the outback, where caddies carry extra equipment: a rake to use on the 'green', which is bare dirt, and a rifle – propped on a steer's whitened skull – to scare off the crows that swoop down to gather up the balls.) But the collective invention has not entirely subdued or civilized the Enmore women. The archer, aiming her arrow outside the frame, is intent on an Amazonian career of her own, and another isolated, breakaway figure has crossed the circular, engirdling path and approaches the shadowed bushes. She has escaped from definition: she is a white triangle, as unfocused and uncatchable as a butterfly.

105
Charles Kerry
Esplanade, Manly c. 1890

Unknown photographer
'Enmore', near Sydney, NSW
1860s

Even buildings can have that same volatility, a lightness of being that leaves them bobbing above the ground like helium balloons. In Samuel Wood's souvenir album *Views of Sydney*, the Queen Victoria Markets and the General Post Office in Martin Place are isolated from their urban surroundings by clouds of white gas; like opiate dreams, they levitate on this curling fog. Kubla Khan might have decreed them, or hazily conjured them up. Though Nettleton's Post Office is tethered to an actual street in Melbourne and has a few ectoplasmic pedestrians outside it, it looks equally phantasmal. The angular street corner narrows it into a prow; luckily the foreshortened sides are not quite symmetrical, otherwise – with the line from the flagpole on the roof to the gas lamp on the kerb dividing it cleanly down the middle – it would constitute another cheating photographic mirror image, like the reflected Brisbane street. The ceremonious tier of steps up from the pavement, the lofty range of upper windows and the tower with its hollow staring eyes conduct the eye through an arduous drama of ascent. Three orders of columns – Doric, Ionic, Corinthian – are piled up in successive storeys, as at the Colosseum; the building is determined to be colossal. Meanwhile the pillared arcades, the balconies between the windows and the gratuitously doubled battlements sprawl sideways to fill up whatever space is available. Can the building already be growing in another direction, from beneath that copper-sheeted mansard roof with the fenced lookout on top? Extra columns at street level, bearing no load, function as sentries, standing to attention. This is more than a headquarters for the postal service. A single structure, exponentiating vertically and horizontally, sets out to incorporate an entire society. Imagine the echoing cavities inside it, and – to judge by the smattering of people on the street – how few customers it had. But society is about being enclosed; this Piranesian pile is a monument to the idea of incarceration.

Charles Nettleton
General Post Office, Melbourne
c. 1867

Photographing the fire brigade at Ballarat, Nettleton joked about the fussy ineffectuality of society's defences against nature. The new, jerry-built settlements were highly flammable (and they have remained so: two houses on our block in suburban Hobart burned down during my childhood, and my parents considerately awoke me in time to see the ambulances take bodies away). Ballarat therefore had two troops of firemen, keeping watch at opposite ends of the town. The men at the squat, castellated station rehearse their routines for the camera, clambering up ladders and trailing a hose from the turret. Their scurrying response to an undeclared emergency looks farcical, agitated but unavailing, like a training session for the Keystone Kops. The building on which they are practising has its own mixed motives. Castles are meant to be fortified against threats from the outside, sullenly defensive like the Elizabeth Street GPO. The fire station, however, has as many windows as a bourgeois villa, and there is a promenade at the top of its tower. Across town the architectural imposture is even more beautifully, touchingly absurd. The watchtower, a container for a series of ladders, is held up by buttresses that are vaguely churchy, though the observation deck could be a gazebo or a bandstand. And why the picket fence, which impedes access? The engine house is a folly: a rococo villa – with ornately raised eyebrows above the windows, frilly-topped columns at the corners, and a peaked turret behind its own lacy fence – that functions as a garage. The firemen here do not make believe that their building is on fire, like their colleagues at the neighbouring station. Instead Nettleton has lined them up on the street, as if this human cordon could act as a firebreak. Perhaps because it is formed from volunteers, the phalanx has not been drilled into military precision. The men lean and loll, some with hands in pockets, others with helmets off. They have also left their horses behind, which turns the stationary wagon wheels, larger than any of the men, into obtuse obstructions.

108
Charles Nettleton
Volunteer Fire Brigade,
Ballarat 1860s

109
Charles Nettleton
Volunteer Fire Brigade,
Ballarat East 1860s

110
Charles Nettleton
(attributed)
*Congregational Church and
Burke and Wills Monument,
Collins Street, Melbourne*
c. 1867

Back in Melbourne, another image attributed to Nettleton finds desolation and a killing disorientation at the centre of the city. A monument to the dead explorers Burke and Wills stands at a crossing in Collins Street; a photograph of it from another album in the National Gallery of Australia shows the intersection to be as flat, hot and sandy as the desert in which Burke and Wills perished, and half a dozen stranded passers-by, equally lost, are positioned at intervals around the pedestal like rescuers who have arrived too late. The Nettleton view sees the statue from a different angle, and takes in the Venetian Gothic church that has reared up behind it on another corner. With steps and doors on both sides, the church invites all comers, though there are none; it overemphatically prods the sky with its spires and crucifixes. Meanwhile the explorers, their backs turned to this sanctuary, go on dying of exhaustion and starvation in the middle of the untrodden street.

Photography enjoys making the city disappear. In summer the streets are a simmering desert, in winter a shallow lake. Photographers in Melbourne enjoyed the city's icy rains because they rendered it picturesque, creating slick, glassy surfaces. In Stanley Eutrope's image, Collins Street shines in the drizzle; the pavement is a sky fallen to earth, and the trees grow in a chimerical swamp. In John B. Eaton's *Wet Day in Melbourne*, photographed on Princes Bridge in 1921, the murk is opalescent, and the buildings above the river are softened by mist, like a face photographed through flattering gauze or with vaseline smeared on the lens. Cranstone photographed Princes Bridge at night in the

111
Stanley Eutrope *Collins Street, Melbourne* 1917

mid 1930s with its pillars lit up, its arches festooned with bulbs. In the dark water the reflections lengthen to construct a submarine causeway of white, streaked flames. Here the city drowns; elsewhere it thins to a silhouette or a papery cut-out. Cranstone photographed Collins Street from the T&G Insurance building, the summer sun imprinting the skyline's shadow on the road. Telephone wires, and lines painted to separate the lanes of traffic, rule the space diagonally into a strict grid, which makes the frieze of rooftops all the more improbable: chimneys that could be attenuated mosques, steeples belonging to a church of unknown denomination, and a camouflaging screen of foliage to baffle us. This might be a Potemkin village, or one of those canvas towns hastily rigged up as misleading targets for aerial bombers during World War II. And just off Collins Street, in a cosy basement, more outlandish wonders lie in wait. A uniformed bellboy and a stuffed tiger issue complementary invitations. The bellboy, whose rakish pillbox hat rhymes with the row of dangling coronets, appeals to Empire loyalists who want to see newsreels of the coronation, while the tiger entices customers more interested in the 'jungle antics' that fill up the programme. Somehow the miniature theatre finds room for both, although they look uncomfortably jumbled: the limber Tarzan in the advertisement swings from a vine that seems to be growing between the crowns. In Paris, Atget and Brassaï photographed a surreal city where street doors lead to lairs of iniquity and shop windows display the trophies of recondite vices. Melbourne is more sedate, but a coffee lounge – exotic enough in those tea-drinking days – dispenses an opiate. The pot drips letters from its spout, and at the same time decants illusions.

112
Edward Cranstone
Collins Street, Melbourne
1937

113
Edward Cranstone
Albany Coffee Lounge,
Melbourne
1937

Deeper than that Collins Street cellar, gulfs open to disclose the emptiness on which we tread. In 1977 Wolfgang Sievers photographed excavations for an underground railway station beneath the State Parliament in Melbourne. In a vaulted tunnel that could be the pupil of a dilated cosmic eye, two engineers stand on the edge of the abyss. A shaky ladder drops into the cavity where an escalator for commuters would eventually plunge. Fitting foils over his arc lights, Sievers coloured the tunnel a sickly green, while the rest of the gaping space is blood red. Cities are metaphysical places, great chains of being that extend from affluence to penury, salvation to perdition. Heaven could be a terraced penthouse at the top of a skyscraper, and hell a short, smooth ride away on the escalator that slants down to the centre of the earth. Our spiritual home must have room for an inferno.

Cities are enticed out of the ground by a longing for conviviality and maybe – since we are a species that delights in difficulty, even if this entails the possibility of destruction – for complexity. In *The Tree of Man*, Amy Parker rides past 'a bit of a shack, of wood and tin', with two children paddling in the remains of a flood. A casual but startlingly creative thought occurs to her: 'This is perhaps the beginning of a town'. A town can grow of its own accord as shacks agglomerate, but a city needs to be invented. The act of foundation is religious. It sets a boundary to separate society from nature, and boldly claims a surrogate eternity for mankind. It also requires patrons, supernatural protectors who can intercede with the gods (which is perhaps why interested parties suggested that Australia's national capital be called Shakespeare). We have forgotten who Lud was, though London is supposed to be his town, and no one really believes that Ulysses founded Lisbon on his way home from the wars. But in 1864 the sailor Robert Towns tautologically doubled his own name and immortalized himself at Townsville. The state capitals made do with obscure British dignitaries like Sydney, Melbourne, Brisbane and Hobart; Adelaide was a politician's consort.

In Australia these mythical ceremonies happen in modern times, and can be recorded by the camera. Despite the pious placating of higher powers, the initiative is violent: the city can only exist if the bush is cleared. Amy Parker, sick of 'endlessness', gathers sprays of leaves 'to acquire some reason for her being there'. Meanwhile her husband Stan chops down trees that are abjectly 'waiting for the axe'. At Wilcannia, Fokkema photographed this necessary sacrifice. A stump tersely announces nature's submission. Its truncation makes possible the small victories of civilization displayed in

115
Gerrit Fokkema
The Post Office
from the album
*Wilcannia: Portrait of an
Australian Town* 1982
© Gerrit Fokkema

the street: the wire-mesh fence and the rubbish tin, the portico of the Post Office, and the shady lid above the petrol station next to it. But is Wilcannia anything more than a voluntary prison? The mystified child in Fokkema's photograph remains unsocialized, unsure why you should not walk on this patch of grass or discard litter in the street. Those who are older, inured to the routine of maintaining society and keeping up appearances, no longer ask such questions. Around the corner, Fokkema photographed Mrs Beryl Tweedale – whose surname invokes a neat, villagey little England, bewildered to find itself on this frontier – sweeping the street beside the Post Office. The road is unpaved, so her broom merely stirs up a whirlwind of red dust. Bent over it, her elderly figure casts a long, onerous shadow, which underlines the Sisyphean nature of her housekeeping. It is wasted effort, but there is something heroic in such a doomed campaign. She regards the outback – the area stretching beyond the symbolic black stump that for Australians marks society's border – as an extension of her living room, and is determined to keep it looking nice. Perhaps she also shines the fence of corrugated iron that protects her backyard. Elsewhere in Wilcannia, Fokkema photographed another metal fence, in the moonlight, its silvery grooves rippling like vertical waves. Behind it is a house made of the same material: the equivalent of Ned Kelly's body armour, which was smithied from stolen ploughshares and had a cushioning of quilt inside the headpiece – a barrier, like any house or town or city, against the inimical outdoors.

Les Murray claims that fences were 'a desperate spiritual necessity' in Australia. Others saw them as an unnecessary evil. In Douglas Stewart's drama, Ned Kelly defies the police because they want

> to make the bush
> A different place, fenced and safe and tame
> For good and all. No wild men riding their horses!

116
A. V. Smith (attributed)
*Lake Learmouth, near Ballarat,
Victoria* 1860s

The gang's capture provokes a gloomy prophecy: 'the bush is fenced'. Peter Carey's Ned Kelly cuts his way through the barbed-wire fences of a magistrate's property, and relishes the heady reek of eucalyptus on unselected land. The fences, as Murray admits, 'kept failing to hold'. Australia has its own equivalent to the Great Wall of China: the plural Walls of China in the dry bed of Lake Mungo in western New South Wales. The walls are actually crumbling dunes, incapable of keeping anyone out, even if there were anyone here who wanted to get in. From the three thousand miles of wire meant to debar wild dogs to the sagging palisade of palings between the houses on the block where I grew up, fences were also a psychological necessity. They frustrated feral marauders or nosy neighbours. Even more soothingly, they set limits. Space was no longer a continuum; it had been divided up, graded, owned. The Aboriginal people wandered across an entire continent. Their urban and suburban usurpers preferred to own patches measuring a quarter of an acre.

Australian fences, as at Lake Learmouth, preceded any settlement they might be fencing off. The posts in the photograph reach out to join hands in a long relay race, dividing interchangeable patches of emptiness from each other. This fence corresponds to some remote cartographic and territorial decision. Like the frame around a photograph, it defines the place as a view that is the property of the viewer. Yet it sags and wanders, and emptiness leaks through it. A metaphor used by the novelist Colleen McCullough suggests that fences may have been a medical necessity, though they prove ineffective: she describes outback fences that 'stutter away like stitches in a suppurating wound'. At Government House in Brisbane, the fence imports the ideas of hierarchy and exclusiveness, though the symbolic demarcations get muddled. Shouldn't the trees be outside the fence, and the pampered lawn inside? All that shaggy vegetation conceals the vice-regal mansion. Only the Norfolk pine at the right belongs in this haughty setting: its triangular, tapering shape makes it a diagram of colonial society, the branches narrowing as they ascend to a privileged apex. Otherwise, the ladder of social esteem that clambers up to towards Government House is toppled by the local terrain. The low angle of the photograph turns it into a study of the dirt road, carpeted at intervals with what could be horse manure. Rather than scaling the fence or strolling through the open gate, the photographer remains outside – a dusty, grounded realist.

117
Daniel Marquis
(attributed)
*Driveway to Government House,
Brisbane c.* 1866–78

The fence is a symbol of Australia, and photography enjoys showing how mutable symbols are. Art disregards utility, and prefers to play impractical games with the blunt, single-minded objects we rely on to give shape to our world. When Stacey looks at an unmade fence, he mentally rearranges the clump of metal posts and the barbed wire that is meant to be strung between them: they make up a kind of Golgotha, at which Stacey gazes up – prostrate as if in prayer – from the grass. The posts deputize for crosses, although they lack the beam that would complete the symbol; they also symbolize the crucified body, since stigmatic holes have been drilled through them. The wire coils into a crown of thorns. Leaning at angles, not yet driven into the ground, the posts still manage to stand more or less upright, supporting each other when they stagger and somehow balancing that circle of wire in the air. The ready-made sculpture has to be read anthropomorphically. The posts, leaning together like tent poles, display the interdependence of life in the outback: this is a diagram of mateship. The snagged, dishevelled halo of wire, uneasily resting in mid-air, suggests the tortuous spirituality of Australia. This could be headgear for the visionaries in Patrick White's novels, who are hurt or maddened into mysticism by the stark, cruel land. Whose crucifixion has Stacey photographed? Nature's, presumably, since the fence wounds the earth it slices up. But those who build the fence may tear their own flesh on the wire, injuring themselves to establish a boundary that will not hold for long. All the tragic, futile toil of settlement is summed up here.

Thake makes the same point more sardonically in his photograph of a dead bird pinioned on a fence at Dumosa in Victoria. Fences can baffle dogs, cattle or human beings, but they are no threat to birds. This one has been strung up, its wings knotted around the wire, as a warning to all creatures with no respect for property rights. Also in Victoria, Laurie Wilson photographed a line-up of ten skinned foxes, tied by their back legs to a wire fence at regular intervals. The animals were killed for their pelts, so why were the discarded bodies exhibited? Culture brags about its extermination of nature; the fence is an art gallery. With their valuable skins stripped off, the foxes look as scrawny as rabbits, despite the snaking bone that is all that remains of their bushy tails. Hanging upside down, they seem to be posthumously nibbling the roadside grass, reduced to peaceful herbivores. Thake's bird does accept defeat so easily: it hovers, treading air without needing to agitate its wings. It might be positioning itself for a kill, with its aggressive beak and hooked claws. Or perhaps, like the dove in religious art, it has paused there in benediction, forgiving its tormentors. For all its sunny secular hedonism, Australia is a religious country: a site where matter and spirit do battle, the scene of a battle between man and a nature he did not create and therefore is determined to subdue or destroy.

119
Eric Thake
Roadside Crucifix, Dumosa
1957

This metaphysical combat rages even in the Melbourne suburbs. In the street photographed by John Kauffmann, the trees have been pushed back behind a fence, while the pavement belongs to the battalion of telegraph poles. No one walks or drives through the space, and the poles are fixed; circulation happens in the air, thanks to the singing cables that spool out between the poles. Over the brow of the hill, already on the declining slope, the church is a memento of the creed made obsolete by the worship of electricity, and its spire reaches only half the height of the nearest pole. A choice is proposed: either you can venerate a deity who might possibly be resident above the clouds, or you can take the initiative and wire the sky, stealing the voltage that crackles through it and turning the air into a circuit board for your whispered messages.

By the time Mark Strizic photographed South Melbourne, the technological future foreseen by Kauffmann had arrived. By differently aligning the same

120
John Kauffmann
*Street, Telegraph Poles
and Church c.* 1920

components, Strizic manoeuvres them into conflict. Kauffmann's tree stands aside (though its branches, organic and therefore over-abundant, messily approach the wires). Strizic's pollarded tree has been maimed; the curtailed branches are wracked limbs and outstretched hands, raking the air in helpless protest. Above it, in a reproof to its Laocoon-like writhings, the pole conducts its business in taut, tight lines. The tree is a corpse, which may or may not revive when spring comes; the pole sustains a different, deadly life, thrilling down the wires from those galvanic switches. Another image from the same series contributes to the martyrology of the Australian tree. A pole seen from below is rough, knotted, unshaven, as if still alive in the bush. But higher up, where its branches should be growing, street signs are clamped or screwed into it, and at the top it is braced by criss-crossing wires. It first suffers torture, then electrocution.

121
Mark Strizic
Tree and Telegraph Pole
from the series
South Melbourne
c. 1970

In 1933 Max Dupain began photographing the wheat silos at Pyrmont in Sydney: a local homage to those grain elevators in Buffalo that served as a prototype for modern American architecture, severely functional yet monumental. On one occasion he photographed them through the windscreen of his car, positioning the rubber wiper at an angle; the shafts holding wheat rest on the car's control panel, and the steering wheel stretches the length of the silos. Mobilizing commodities or people, the city of the future is a machine to live in, not a shelter for the spirit. A rear-view mirror looks back unregretfully at the past, framing a slice of brick wall. Dupain's hands are not on the wheel: the urban machine appears to run automatically, needing no operator. For the same reason, Walker Evans said that the camera was the perfect instrument of expression for Americans, those efficient modernists, since it made art without requiring the intercession of an artist. Pyrmont also functioned as the city's backside, where it disposed of its waste: among Dupain's other subjects was an incinerator with Mayan-style ornaments designed by Walter Burley Griffin, whose wife in 1949 interpreted the smoking chimney as a symbol of 'what remains when matter is destroyed.... When the atom was smashed there remained only warmth, light, sound and magnetism.' Here the city burned itself up, evaporating into thermal energy.

Pyrmont was the laboratory in which Dupain watched as the modern world escaped from nature. The industrial landscape he photographed there is also an industrialized landscape, where telegraph poles grow instead of trees and the serrated roof of a factory stands in for the horizon. Photography expresses judgments and articulates emotions through the interplay between black and white, and here the extremes of the tonal range measure the distance between the prostrate past and the bright, electrified future. The scruffy grass in the foreground is black, smudged by shadow. The nearest pole stands up in silhouette, but its wires thin out and disappear into the burningly white sky. Abstraction has revised the topography of the place. The factory roof, with its saw-toothed serrations, could be a geometrical rendering of waves. Above it – so delicately traced on the surface of the print that the eye, unless trained to look into the future, can miss or misread it – a rainbow arches across this expanse of metallic, symmetrical water, evangelizing on behalf of a modernity that promised to accelerate history and revolutionize the world: it is the Sydney Harbour Bridge.

In 1934 *Australian Home Beautiful* issued a brisk decree about the kind of dwelling it thought appropriate for the twentieth century. Brick and plaster, it declared, were cumbrous, clinging to an antiquated idea of permanence. Modern houses were put together from lightweight, manoeuvrable materials like weatherboard, Masonite and asbestos, with strips of corrugated iron for the roof. Standardized and modular, they could 'be disassembled, sold and re-erected elsewhere virtually without waste'. The process is proudly illustrated by Cranstone. A house – or a barracks, a depot or a factory, depending on the future use of the prefabricated frame – consists of a transparent frame lowered into place by a crane, later rendered opaque and watertight. It is, like the hut Stan Parker builds among the bleeding stumps in *The Tree of Man*, 'more the symbol of a house', the minimal diagram of a dwelling. Australian houses have an almost existential lightness of being, a reluctance to impose themselves on the land. In Queensland

122
Max Dupain *Industrial Landscape* 1935
© Max Dupain 1935. Licensed by
VISCOPY, Sydney 2003

Edward Cranstone
Prefabrication
from the album
Design for War, vol. III
1942–44

outback towns, they are sometimes arranged in thin strips, with single rooms set end to end so that the breeze, when there is one, can blow through, and with stilts to raise them a few feet above the earth as protection against floods: the house is a combination of train and boat, not grounded or settled at all.

At least Stan's shack is his own handiwork, rudely personalized by a verandah that looks stuck on and a tin chimney shaped like a matchbox. The new suburbs where my generation grew up were designed by Housing Department bureaucrats and uncrated on tracts of bulldozed bush, with sewers promised sometime in the future. Inside these symbols, as Patrick White says about some fibro cottages, 'human beings went through the motions of living'. Can you make a home from a kit of rudimentary parts? I can't look at Cranstone's photograph without remembering the frailty of our house, which for all its outer claddings – including the skin of artificial brick my father added later – still felt permeable. Like a photographic negative or an X-ray, it announced the shaky vulnerability of our world. You could dent the internal partitions with your fist or foot, and the wind sometimes prised loose a strip of metal from the roof. The concrete steps at the front sank at an angle, and the wooden columns that pretended to hold up the porch twisted arthritically as they aged. It hardly mattered, because everyone but proselytizing Mormons and Jehovah's Witnesses came round the side to the back door. The motions of living that many of us went through in these houses were limited, and rigidly prescribed. You entered the house through the kitchen. After eating, you relaxed for a while in the next room, called the lounge. Then you opened the only other door and went to bed.

The plucky pioneering continues, as in the suburb south of Canberra photographed by Fokkema in 1977. The woman in the driveway is moving in; the trailer she has unloaded is parked on the lawn, and boxes wait on the porch to be unpacked. The houses have what the estate agent would have called picture windows, though the curtains are tightly closed. No one would want to look out at that patch of dry, unmown grass. Fokkema has set the view inside another picture window, using the frame on which the developer probably advertised the name of the little, lucrative colonial outpost he dreamed up: Sunnyside, Mount Pleasant, Edenvale, who knows what? The empty oblong determines the contents of Fokkema's photograph. It does so arbitrarily: along with the house, it includes a strip of the neighbour's lawn, a jumble of adjoining roofs, the festoon of electrical wires, and those low clouds that reflect the scorching heat. Anyone living here will look out through a similar frame, as I did. I had a choice of horizons, both forbidding: the smoky zinc works, less polished than in the photograph by Sievers, and the rampart of Mount Wellington. In another direction, near enough, though not visible from our house, there was a third horizon, wider and narrower but frustratingly fictional. The screen of a drive-in cinema, occupying empty space in the middle of a racetrack, splashed lurid dreams onto the night sky. This – whenever I could sneak out to watch, often sitting in a pine tree on the other side of the highway and trying to read the lips of the magnified faces – was my preferred picture window. Fokkema's frame reminds me of my desperation to fill the space outside our house with a different view.

124
Gerrit Fokkema
Somedaze No. 5
1977
© Gerrit Fokkema

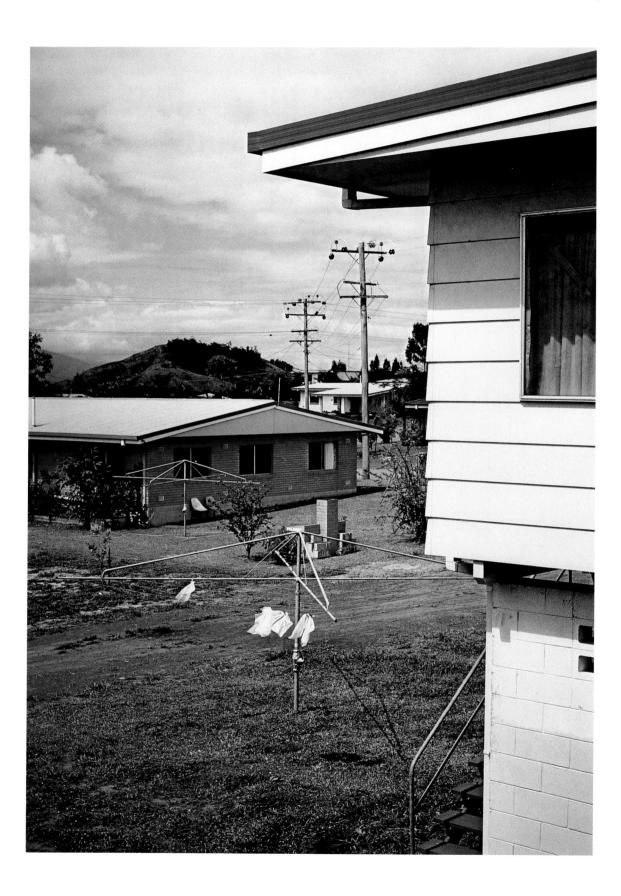

I wish I could have seen it through the bright eyes of Tim Handfield, who turns the suburbs into Pop playlands. In Cairns, the planners have decided that the fence (across which I remember insults being traded and stones or bottles thrown) is no longer spiritually necessary. On the shared lawn, rotary clothes lines take brisk advantage of the good drying weather to whip some plastic shopping bags back into shape. A barbecue acts as a communal camp fire, a shared hearth. This is an agora, a forum; like the coffee shop, the pub and the swimming pool in *Neighbours*, it is the affable, jostling ground of citizenship. The idea of the suburb was too good to be true, assuming that all frictions could be sudsily erased on washing day. Life is only like that in soap opera, which is why the cul-de-sac of Ramsay Street in Erinsborough had to be invented. Cheery conviviality is obligatory here. Those Hills Hoist clothes lines announce the terms of the social contract: no secrets are allowed, since you are expected to hang out your clean linen for the scrutiny of those living next door. When I first went back to visit my parents, having acquired a fussy British concern for privacy in the intervening years, it alarmed me to see my underpants flapping on the lawn as the dryer creaked round in a circle. They had been washed, so they told no tales, but I retrieved them while they were still damp, as if covering up their nakedness as well as my own. I need not have worried, of course. The clothes lines took no notice of individual peculiarities, which they existed to eliminate. Wasn't everyone the same? This environment suits photographic formalism, which discounts content and concentrates on the arrangement of shapes or (as in Fokkema's Canberra) the witty selectivity of framing. It is a synthetic world of Laminex, plastic, plywood and veneer, or nylon, vinyl and polyester: simulations of superseded nature. At Doncaster in Queensland, Handfield photographed a lawn that unrolls and fits into place like exterior carpet. Non-indigenous trees, fresh from the nursery, are as skeletal and transparent as the roof-beams photographed by Cranstone. A fence apologizes for its intrusion by becoming a decorative feature, with its palings set at an angle. The white wall could be a cyclorama.

127
Fiona Hall
Adelaide, South Australia 1984
Courtesy of Roslyn Oxley9 Gallery

In the backyards photographed by Fiona Hall, the fond feigning of the suburban myth is picked apart. The garden supposedly mediates between society and the wilderness, but the grotto in Adelaide is not sure whether its allegiance belongs to the kitchen or to some remote, jagged mountain range. The cooker disguises itself in a rusticated chimney. The beams supply it with a roof, though one that remains open and disables the umbrella that should fit into the table top. The wrought-iron bench was once the base of a sewing machine, now expelled to the garden; a potted plant sitting on a chair wants to migrate into the house. All this would be intelligible enough if it weren't for the spar of chipped, runically scarred rock that nuzzles the trellis. It has reared from beneath the earth under pressure, like the knobs of granite jutting into the air in Central Park; but that volcanic upheaval did not happen here, since it appears to stand on a paved floor. If it has been hauled from far away and deposited here on purpose, you have to wonder why anyone thought the effort worthwhile. Perhaps it is a styrofoam boulder, artfully painted, left over from a production of *Die Walküre*. The searing Adelaide sunlight shines down on a mystery. Over the border in Victoria, vacuum cleaners that have done their duty indoors stand ready to tackle the dusty open spaces of Australia. Still, they will have to do it alone, without the aid of electricity and with no Beryl Tweedale to push them along; their bags deflate, depressed by the task ahead.

128
Fiona Hall
Wantirna South, Victoria 1986
Courtesy of Roslyn Oxley9 Gallery

For my parents – born into agricultural poverty, separated by the war before they could marry – the suburb was a happy ending. Here they grew their roses and potatoes, while their domestic appliances contentedly hummed. When they saw the rest of the world on the television news, they congratulated themselves on their luck. Meanwhile, waiting in a fury of impatience for childhood to be over, I dreamed of leaving. How I would have been tantalized by Jon Rhodes's shark-finned convertible, stranded in a paddock near a Hobart suburb like ours. I never learned to drive, probably because I wanted to go further than that aerodynamic car would take me; I revved up inside my head. D. H. Lawrence, travelling in the opposite direction, described himself passing through 'an open door into the blue beyond. You just walk out of the world and into Australia'. I walked out of Australia and into the world, ungratefully slamming the door behind me.

On early sorties to the mainland, I only ever spent an hour in the blue beyond, before catching sight of the Melbourne suburbs. Bumping down towards the airport at Essendon, I did not allow myself to admit that the rows of houses with roofs of corrugated iron or terracotta tiles, set back behind their tonsured nature strips, were a continuation of Hobart. What mattered was the difference in scale: as in Stacey's photograph, taken from above that same airport, they went on forever, rather than prematurely tapering out into the foothills of a mountain. Suburbia, exponentiating like this, was my first glimpse of infinitude, long before I set eyes on the Nullarbor Plain (and even longer before I saw Richard Woldendorp's photograph of it). The aerial views by Woldendorp and Stacey tell overlapping truths about Australia: emptiness provokes, in reaction, a neighbourly huddle. After taking in what I could see beneath the plane, my eyes always slid away to speculate about what I might see, somewhere in the inscrutable distance, if I ever got the chance. Stacey's smoggy silver haze, curving over the edge of the world, is where I thought the future began. It did not occur to me back then that there would ever be a past, to which I would piningly come home by looking at photographs.

130
Wesley Stacey
Suburbia Forever 1970

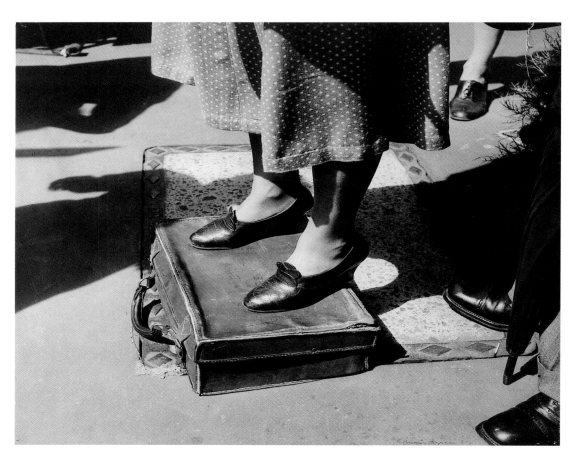

6: National Characters

When Australians feel at home with each other, they start to poke fun, which is called chipping or chyaking. Inside the fence, the group maintains its collective identity by raillery. My father, who seems to me now to have been the most national of characters, used to refer to people as blokes, bastards, mongrels, shavers, jockeys and, most interestingly, jokers. A joker did not have to tell jokes; his function was simply to demonstrate that existence itself was a joke.

Les Murray, listening to all this rollicking derision, has said that a 'spiritual laughter' is one of Australia's 'great gifts to mankind'. I am not sure that it is always spiritual. It is also a primitive initiatic rite, preparing you for life in this arduous place. I hear political subversion in it too, since the jester is the enemy of authority. Hence the pair of punches delivered, as if by robotic boxers with thin extended arms, to Bob Hawke in Lorrie Graham's photograph, taken at the Sydney Opera House during the election campaign. The mood of this laughter is sometimes more nihilistic than Murray might wish (unless you concede that nihilism is a spiritual option). I once stayed at a new hotel in Alice Springs at which the first room I was sent to had an unmade bed, the second no electricity, and the third – as I found after unpacking and undressing – a shower that did not work. The clerk at the front desk beamed as he handed me a fourth key. 'Mate,' he said, 'this whole place is fucked!' He then let loose a volley of that whooping national mirth. The hotel, after all, had a view of a dry river, in whose waterless bed the citizens hold an annual regatta, riding piggyback because there is no chance of sailing. Laughter admonishes us to mock tragedy, which encourages individuals to bemoan their uniquely painful fates. A joke deprives us of our unearned advantages, reduces us to parity with everyone else.

D. H. Lawrence, noticing that most Australian houses were what the English call bungalows, rightly sensed a hostility to 'stair-climbing shams and upstairs importance'. This is why Dupain's title jeers at the woman standing on a case to watch a procession celebrating the fiftieth anniversary of federation in 1951. He writes her off as a 'short dame': why can't she accept our common confinement to the ground, with all its arbitrary inequalities? And anyway, who cares about parading dignitaries? Lorrie Graham batters Hawke's head, whose permed quiff – along with the podium – lends him some extra height, and Dupain prods the woman's feet, wanting to knock her platform out from under her. Laughter polices Australian democracy, and makes sure that people do not get above themselves.

131
Lorrie Graham
*Bob Hawke, Labor Party
Campaign Launch* 1982

132
Max Dupain
*Short Dame at Jubilee
Procession* 1951
© Max Dupain 1951.
Licensed by VISCOPY,
Sydney 2003

The only heroes such a society can tolerate are rogues, subverters of order and propriety like the disgruntled horse-thief Ned Kelly. Some commentators on Kelly have ennobled him by association with classical or romantic prototypes: Peter Carey's Ned is a mother-fixated Oedipus, and Sidney Nolan, overseeing a film about his paintings of the gang's piratical exploits, insisted on a soundtrack using Siegfried's funeral march from *Götterdämmerung*. Photography prefers desecration. Juan Davila, born in Chile, has cut and pasted illustrations from gay pornographic magazines into a series of eight panels about the Kellys, who – looking more Latin than Irish – are glued together by their dabbling tongues. One of their sweaty orgies is stuck onto the cover of a booklet expounding *The Beauty of Australia by Australian Artists*, though the beauties on show are sappier than the usual weathered eucalypts. Another glimpse of the gang's priapic home life has been added to a fortnightly publication on *Australian Cricket*, which – innocent of fetishistic implications – advertises gloves, bats and pads in a bottom corner. The parody is all the more impudent because it eroticizes the national preoccupation with team games.

At Glenrowan, where his gang holed up, Ned's last stand is re-staged outside a shallow mock-up of a railway station. Wesley Stacey's photograph pretends to catch the showdown, with a marksman taking aim and amateur commandos clambering up to the corrugated iron roof, while a toy train peeps inquisitively out of a rusticated tunnel. It is a tableau as predetermined as Lindt's image of Joe Byrne, propped against the wall to be shot all over again by the photographers. The photograph excludes time, and therefore reduces the pretence of furious action to static attitudinizing, but it does manage to contain history, because the scene straddles two centuries. Kelly is fixed in the past, rooted like a helpless tree, his spread legs resembling one of the habitable trunks that Caire photographed in Gippsland. His metal helmet deprives him of a face, and his hands uselessly point his gun in the wrong direction. Carved from wood or moulded from papier mâché, he is inanimate, again like Lindt's Byrne: he is posing for posterity. The kneeling gunman, however, belongs to the present, and is dressed in the fatigues favoured by weekend hunters or recruits to backwoods militias. Slung over his shoulder is a bag that could contain either ammunition or rolls of film and spare lenses.

133
Wesley Stacey
Mythical Sight, Glenrowan 1988

Like a dummy in a booth at a fair, Kelly has been set up so that we can knock him down over and over again with bullets or clicking shutters or coconuts. Though Stacey has teasingly positioned the signpost so that it blocks the price list on the door beside the ticket office, the myth is now for sale. Society invents the hero so that we can pay for the pleasure of destroying him.

Carey's Kelly battled in vain against the fences that parcelled up the frontier. The picket fence at the station in Glenrowan excludes no one; it is low enough to step over, since it has no wish to deter customers. Still, its presence evokes the suburbs with their fussy, notional division of terrain, and turns him into an ornament on someone's front lawn, like Stacey's plaster Aboriginal in the rockery. Eric Thake takes away what is left of the outlaw's mystique by removing him from the bush and locating him beside an urban road, where a shrouded petrol pump plays at being a two-armed bandit disguised by a mask. This bushranger's guns remain in their holsters: he knows it is all a harmless charade. 'These will make me a hero?' asks Carey's Ned Kelly, scoffing at the handful of glass marbles he seizes during his first hold-up.

134
Eric Thake
The Bushranger 1957

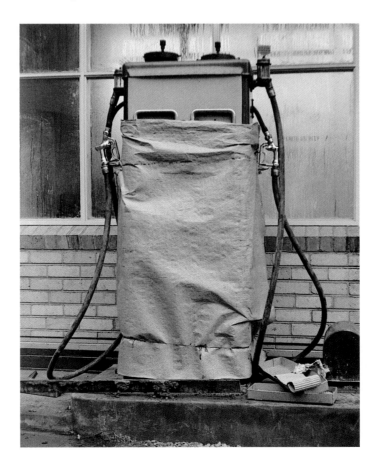

The hero has a vertical career, leading us upwards. Like the firemen in Bruce Springsteen's song about the World Trade Center, he rushes up the stairs and, when those run out, strides on into the sky. Australian battlers enjoy no such ascension. They are horizontal men, flattened by the elements that will eventually destroy them. America, which mechanically conquered the wilderness, produces epics of belligerent triumph about gigantic axemen and iron horses; the Australian equivalent is an elegy that stoically accepts man's defeat by nature. The stories the nation tells itself brood over noble failures, like the journeys of the explorers who never returned or the massacre of ingenuous Anzacs at Gallipoli.

Frank Hurley's meteorologists – photographed in 1912 during Douglas Mawson's Antarctic expedition – are two such horizontal men, knocked to their knees by winds of eighty miles an hour as they return from checking their recording instruments. These are not mountain climbers; clinging to their spiked crampons, they grope and grapple back to the foul-smelling hut that Hurley, in his book *Argonauts of the South*, ironically describes as '"Home"'. The photograph has undergone some pictorial touching up, which only worsens their plight: they are inside a vortex of lashing wind that has been painted onto the print. Hurley was determined to turn the blizzard into 'a subject for a moving picture', and built a protective igloo for his ciné camera. But he too, along with his equipment, was scooped up by the wind, blown over the ice and hurled onto the rocks. This white, howling waste, like the red desert of the Australian interior, belittled men rather than sublimely invigorating and aggrandizing them. As Madigan and his assistant Hodgeman ventured out to do their 'stiff job', Hurley wryly likened them to 'goblins of the storm'. Mawson valued Hurley because he possessed the national talent for spiritual – or perhaps bleakly desperate – laughter. 'Hurley,' Mawson said, 'would joke in the face of death' and could make 'a comedy of the most desperate situation'.

135
Frank Hurley
Out in the blizzard at Cape Denison, adjacent to winter quarters 1912

There is an epilogue to Hurley's image of the blizzard in the photographs taken by John Gollings in 1973 for a Marlboro advertising campaign. The aim was to align the Australian outback and the American West. The United States has always liked the idea of having a hero-worshipping little brother across the Pacific. In 1959, when Fred Zinnemann was preparing to film Jon Cleary's novel *The Sundowners*, the studio tried to dissuade him from using Australian locations, and proposed Arizona instead, with kangaroos loaned from the Phoenix zoo; Zinnemann held out for Cooma and Port Augusta. A few years later, the *National Geographic* photographer Robert B. Goodman looked at the country through American eyes for a picture book called *The Australians*, and was pleased to find cowboys tricked out in chaps at a Queensland rodeo and a deracinated Indian teepee standing in a paddock. But transplanting the Marlboro Man proved trickier. In Gollings's tableaux, his spurred, conquering virility peters out; he pats a dog while smoking, or ruminates over some billy tea rather than aggressively rounding up cattle. The emphasis is on matey solidarity, not the arrogant, mounted solitude of the American ego: three smokers share a light. For the most commercially inapposite of these images, Gollings went further afield, and photographed his Marlboro Man wandering through a crevasse on the Franz Josef Glacier in New Zealand. This is hardly Marlboro Country, as there is no chance that it can ever be colonized. Gollings's model is Voss with a nicotine habit, which will contribute to his defeat: his cigarette prevents him from putting his right hand in his pocket to keep it warm.

After the Mawson expedition, Hurley signed on in 1914 to document Ernest Shackleton's intended trek to the South Pole. Again the epic turned into a gallant fiasco. Pack ice gripped the ship and broke it up; Hurley spent two years stranded, waiting for a rescue party from South America. On his return, he set sail at once for Europe, where during the autumn of 1917 he was to photograph Australian troops in the trenches at Ypres, and arrived in London during an air raid. *Argonauts of the South* sums up the transition between assignments with an existential shrug, like Ned Kelly's comment 'Such is life' before the hangman sprang the trap. 'Emerged from a war with Nature,' Hurley remarks in the last sentence of his book, 'we were destined to take our place in a war of nations. Life is one long call to conflict, anyway.' That 'anyway', accentuated by the pause before it, has a humorous, laconic hopelessness that could only be Australian. The conflict is endless, and though you valiantly fight on, you do not expect a victory. Jeff Carter photographed a black jackaroo at a rodeo, grimly holding on as his horse lunges beneath him. He is wearing a T-shirt that reflects on the absurdism of the event: 'You Pay Good Money To Risk Your Life To Win A Belt Buckle'.

Hurley compared the 'gruesome shambles' of Flanders to the butchery of the whaling stations he had seen at South Georgia during his Antarctic expeditions. It was a ghoulishly photographic scene: photography stills life, and on the cratered, blood-drenched battlefields he often could not tell whether the exhausted soldiers were living or dead. If God existed, he asked, how could such carnage go on beneath 'the omnipotent eye'? It seemed that God had long since ceased to notice human folly; the witnessing eye, powerless to alter events, belonged to the photographer.

Sometimes, unable to tolerate the squalor and anguish on the ground, Hurley superimposed that vigilant eye aerially, combining negatives so that shafts of sunlight fought their way through embroiled clouds to shine down redeemingly on the splintered trees and shredded corpses of Passchendaele. Other photographers – anonymous, unofficial and therefore more confidential – showed the comfortless truth. The troops in the photograph printed on a cigarette card are not relaxing; blinded by gas, they have been discarded here, while behind them, mechanically unstoppable, trucks and horse-drawn carts stumble towards whatever destination the commanding generals have marked on the map. Some of them sprawl on the grass, as if – though they are lost in a disorientated darkness – they were back home sunning themselves at the beach. Others, still sitting up, have hunched shoulders and bent heads. Their posture signals despair, the inanimate misery of those who have been reduced (as Hurley said in his diary) to 'shadows of men'. Dejection and fatigue are not heroic qualities, which is why they are usually excluded from the iconography of battle.

137
Unknown photographer
Gassed Australian soldiers at Villers Bretonneux 27.5.18
1918

If it were not for his gun, the infantryman on another cigarette card could be a swagman humping his bluey in the dusty outback; still, the gun serves a peaceful purpose, because he props himself up on it as he takes what used to be called a spell. He is small, which makes him look unequal to his load, but obviously practised in conserving energy. He levers his boots off the road, balances his pack on the rifle, leans backwards, and relies on the resulting triangle, like a photographer's tripod, to support him. The bush must have schooled him in acceptance, which prepares him for this involuntary journey; the look he gives the photographer is cheekily direct and resilient. It would be good to know that he was not killed further up the road. Whatever happened to him, he has a descendant in the tired soldier photographed by Dupain during the next war. His hat is off, and he slumps on a wooden bench, which probably felt comfortable to him in contrast with other recent billets. His eyes remain open, as if he were dazed or traumatized. Rather than sleeping, he might be re-running inside his head a film of what he has experienced somewhere in the Pacific. The view outside the window, blurred by the train's movement, hints at the contents of that private movie, not available for exhibition to non-combatants.

138
Unknown photographer
An Australian infantryman easing his load,
Henencourt, Feb. 1917

139
Max Dupain
Tired soldier in Queensland train 1943
© Max Dupain 1943. Licensed by VISCOPY, Sydney 2003

The foreign wars to which Australians so eagerly rallied during the twentieth century were the new nation's blooding. Australia itself had nothing to gain; the point of these exercises was to earn international respect by demonstrating a suicidal bravado. Shackleton, exchanging what he called 'the white warfare of the Antarctic' for 'the red warfare of Europe', made a speech in Sydney in 1917 calling for Australians to enlist, which he described as 'the supreme opportunity offered to every man of our race to justify himself before his own soul'. This sacrificial self-justification became part of the national cult. In Canberra, the axis of power extends along an avenue linking Parliament House and the War Memorial, which glower at each other from opposite hills. There were no victories to boast about, so instead Australia resolved, in the necrotic rites of Anzac Day, to celebrate defeat. It was a day that always depressed me during my childhood. The tramping hordes in a frosty dawn like battalions of ghosts, the flags limp at half mast, the disconsolate, wailing bugles at the cenotaph. Later, the rowdy swilling of the survivors: the gloomy commemoration was followed by a drunken wake.

140
Sam Hood
Anzac March
(*George Street, Sydney*)
1930s

Sam Hood photographed the parade in Sydney during the 1930s. He makes no judgment, but the stalled trams, the shut shops and the ranks of spectators obediently lined up on the kerb are enough to alarm me. George Street could be the valley of death. Even demilitarized, this was still a uniform society, where you joined the ranks and marched along unquestioningly. Axel Poignant, daring to be more sceptical about the morose ceremony, photographed the dawn service in Perth at the end of the 1930s from a chartered plane. The angle conveys his disenchantment, as Roslyn Poignant commented when she first published the photograph in 1992. A meagre crowd surrounds the obelisk; paths extend radially across a bushy park, but – as Poignant sees from high above – they do not succeed in organizing people and narrowing them into an orderly defile, as George Street does. Soon the marchers run out and, as always in Australia, the trees resume.

The dawn service at Torquay in Victoria, photographed by Laurie Wilson, is a frieze of shuffling shadows. The horizontality of the image, with ragged flags hanging from a leaden sky, makes it all the more oppressive: Cinemascope, as Fritz Lang grudgingly snarls in Godard's *Le Mépris*, is good for photographing funerals. Here the procession doubles back and continues in the opposite direction, with a pipe band distantly droning as it passes the gun emplacement. Local worthies stand to attention, as do the microphones into which they utter their platitudes. The centre of the procession, thanks to one of those accidents that grace good photographs, is occupied by a man blowing his nose. Fokkema's documentation of Anzac Day concludes his book on Wilcannia: rightly so, since this is the ritual by which society ensures its moral cohesion – though here that society looks so piteously sparse that children are conscripted to make up the numbers. Fokkema follows the parade down the main street, with some Aboriginal people looking on from the shaded verandah of the pub. At the wreath-laying ceremony,

141
Laurie Wilson
Dawn Service, Torquay 1976

the veterans spread themselves out, but still cannot cover the acreage of empty grass around the war memorial, where there is room for a frisking dog and someone's temporarily abandoned baby. Wilcannia does not run to podia or platforms; the speeches are made from the back of a pick-up truck, onto which a piano has been hoisted to accompany the hymns. A child plays on a swing just behind the parked truck. The secretary of the Returned Servicemen's League – with a moustache modelled on a recruitment poster, wearing a suit that emerges from the wardrobe only once a year – shows off his organization's marching band: a cassette player. Photography discloses what you cannot see, and also – more impolitely – what you should probably overlook. In this case it is impossible not to notice the state of Ted Davies's fingernails, and the blood blister probably left behind by a hammer blow. Like anyone who lives in the underpopulated hinterland, Ted is an expert at making do.

142
Gerrit Fokkema
RSL Secretary Ted Davies
holds the Wilcannia Anzac Day
Marching Band tape recorder
from the album
Wilcannia: Portrait of an
Australian Town 1982
© Gerrit Fokkema

Roger Scott, on Anzac Day in Sydney, has usually concentrated on the detritus that the parade leaves behind. Drums and trumpets lie discarded on a corner at Chifley Square as a band breaks ranks; the banner belonging to the Australian Intelligence Association, with a legend calling for rearmament, broadcasts its warning to a few indifferent girls in Elizabeth Street; and a stupefied loyalist, the cigarette between his fat fingers concealing his medals, manages to hold his divisional sign more or less erect, though the parking meter that takes his weight leans at a boozy angle. Photography, with its fickle eye, specializes in sideways glimpses that question the official solemnity. But Scott's peripheral view also suggests an affectionate understanding of the day's real significance: the march is a tiresome obligation; the true act of communion is the piss-up that follows. Anzac Day starts as Australia's Halloween, with the dead revisiting the darkened streets, and ends as its raucous Saturnalia.

143
Roger Scott
Anzac Day 1973

In Wilcannia, the afternoon's revelry includes a game of two-up behind the pub. The spinner stands on a square of bedraggled carpet laid down on the dirt, and tosses two coins into the air from a strip of wood. A man still in uniform has been entrusted with the winnings, and grips a few dollar bills in his fist. Boys in cardigans gaze up hopefully as the coins twirl; the Aboriginal observers know better than to get excited about the prospect of instant enrichment, and cling to their bottles of beer. Over the page, Fokkema's book ends with his photograph of a freshly-made grave. The juxtaposition is another example of Australia's morbid laughter. No wonder two-up was so popular with the diggers in the trenches, who were photographed playing it by Hurley. The game expresses the doomed nonchalance of the national mood (which may be why it was banned by successive Australian governments). Australians like anything aleatory, from betting on the Melbourne Cup to a tussle with a metallic, unforthcoming poker machine or a solitary session with a scratch card, but two-up is an especially revealing pastime. No element of skill influences the outcome of the spin; the players who bet on which way up the coins come down cannot read a form guide or compute averages, and must simply take their chances. Two-up also allows a whole crowd to gamble, grouped around a circle scrawled in the sand or, out of sight of the law, on concrete in a back alley. You cannot play unless you first convene what is called, with characteristic sarcasm, a 'school'.

Dymphna Cusack's novel *Come In Spinner* takes its title from a poem by Ian Mudie which sees two-up, like life itself, as a divine joke: '"Come In Spinner" laugh the gods'. Once more chartering a plane, Poignant spied on a two-up school, from what might have been the viewpoint of the gods, outside the mining town of Kalgoorlie in Western Australia. The angle was a sensible precaution: if he had approached the illegal arena more directly, the players would have beaten him up. But the gods, diving downwards for a closer look at mortal folly, do not seem to be laughing. The image is a panoramic

144
Axel Poignant
Two-up School
1936

145
David Moore
Two-up at Betoota,
South-western Queensland
1961
© Estate of David Moore

study of futility, as the anxious ring of men hoping for profit fades into the impermanent scrub. The sand here is a playing field, scraped at random by the tyres of cars; the
lines will soon be wiped out by the wind – leaving no trace, like the trajectory of the
tossed coins. The circular school inside its half-built shelter rhymes with the open,
unguarded mouth of a mine, which is a vertical shaft sending you straight to perdition.
It is sunset, and every car and bush casts a long, premonitory shadow.

At Betoota in Queensland, David Moore photographed a two-up game at the
racetrack. His lower angle enabled him to study the emotions of the players, sema-
phored by their body language. Again the shadows are ponderous: it is the end of the
day, after the races are over. Some of the men stare up into the sky, where the coins are
pirouetting. The rest are glumly stoical, looking down or to one side. One has his hands
behind his back, signalling helplessness. Another self-defensively grips his groin. The
men squatting on the ground with their beer cans look amused because they are not
involved. Further off, another clump of sitting figures pays no attention at all. At the
edge is a rare intruder, sliced off – except for an arm and a scrap of clothing – by the
frame: a woman, necessarily excluded from this male pastime, who drags a child home.
The expectancy of the players soon dissipates as the endlessness of Australia, sketched
by those lengthening shadows on the dirt, takes over. Whereas Poignant looks down
with bleak omniscience, Moore respects those who, braced for disappointment, insist
on holding out hope. In 1985 he came across twin two-up schools in the bush outside
Kalgoorlie, the descendants of the one Poignant photographed over forty years earlier.
He declared that these crude structures were among 'the best buildings in Australia',
though neither was 'really a building in municipal council terms'. They were starkly
minimal: a summer ring was partially enclosed beneath an iron roof, with a central
opening like the Globe Theatre, and the ring used in winter consisted of low benches
inside a circular fence of galvanized iron, 'as simple and precise as a Zen garden'.
Moore's allusion to Ryoanji is brilliantly apt. If the dusty earth of the winter ring corresponds to the gravel so assiduously raked by the monks at Kyoto, then these rough metal
shelters are temples after all, and two-up is the Australian version of Zen.

At a football match in *Kangaroo*, Lawrence describes people 'gazing spellbound on the evolutions of chance', which he calls 'this very Australian state'. I was often told as a boy about the importance of being a good sport, which meant that you must be willing to lose; on occasion my father even addressed me as 'sport', to ready me for the rough and tumble. It is all only a game, and therefore you can allow yourself to admire an enemy or opponent who outplays you. During the bushfires in early 2002, a reporter on Sky News marvelled at the velocity of a blaze that was incinerating the Blue Mountains: he compared the fire to a Raging Bull (meaning Martin Scorsese's prizefighter, not a steer) and then to a celebrated local footballer unstoppably making his way through the opposite team's pack. Hurley, I later discovered, had likened a bombardment in Flanders to the pace of 'a Gippsland bushfire'. Combustible nature and high explosives both remind us of our impotence, while the trajectory of a football and the spinning of two coins demonstrate the flippant, chancy injustice of our world. A cheerful fatalism is another of Australia's undervalued bequests to mankind.

In Australia, the Marlboro cowboy dismounts. The country rode to prosperity on the sheep's back, not the horse's, and its pastoral economy determined its early self-image.

When the Sydney Harbour Bridge opened in 1932, a historical pageant trundled across the span. An allegorical Australia had her golden chariot drawn by six merinos, with cows, milking cans and separators bringing up the rear. In 1934 in his *Melbourne Odes*, Frank Wilmot described a bank teller who travels by tram to the Agricultural Show at Flemington and thrills to the idea of the outback with its 'life of fevered effort, of wool and tortured love!' Only in Australia could wool-growing be associated with fever and a fraught eroticism. Politicians took advantage of the myth by snuggling up to merinos. In 1961 Jeff Carter photographed Prime Minister Menzies, with eyebrows that need shearing, standing beside a prize specimen at the Sydney show. Menzies's wife pats a ewe with her gloved hand. Peter Porter, browsing through a copy of Hesiod's *Works and Days* bought at an English rural fête, instinctively connected the husbandry of Boeotia with the hard lives of his compatriots, who inhabited the kind of rude, self-reliant pastoral society idealized by classical poets. Australians quietly tended their flocks, and – before the introduction of blade shears – scraped the wool off their sheep with kitchen knives. Artists still see these frugal smallholders as colleagues: Les Murray celebrates the solidarity of 'us primary producers, us farmers and authors'.

Marcus Clarke called the bush a 'wild dreamland'. Those who lived in it spent much of their time dreaming. In Cazneaux's *Billy Meditation*, a swaggie stares reflectively into the fire as his tea stews. The contemplativeness of these pastoral characters is vouched for by the amount of reading they do. Nicholas Caire's *Lone Bushman* pores over a newspaper outside his handmade shack. A naked Pitjantjatjara boy in a touching photograph by David Moore kneels in the hot dust with a book spread open in front of him, his finger tracing the abracadabra of the strange letters. Jeff Carter photographed a black jackaroo at Starvation Bore in South Australia, sitting on his disused saddle beside some tree stumps with metal rings – used for tethering refractory horses – driven into them. Carter's man is rapt, detached from his surroundings: he is reading a paperback entitled *Wyoming Jones For Hire* and imagining another, more violently extroverted frontier. But would the Marlboro Man use his saddle as an easy chair, and spend his time with his head in a book? In 1992 Anne Zahalka measured the difference between two national creeds in her photographic pastiche of Frederick McCubbin's *Down on his Luck*, painted in 1889. McCubbin's prospector, who has not found gold, hunches on a log and glumly pokes his campfire with a stick. Grey smoke drifts across a clearing in the chilly bush. It is here that Zahalka has placed her addition to the painting: a Marlboro billboard, which might have been dreamed up by the man staring into the fire. On the poster, a strapping American cowboy shoulders his saddle, admonishing the defeated Australian. 'Come to America with me,' says Joe Byrne to Ned Kelly near the end of Carey's novel. When they ford the flooded Murray River, crossing into New South Wales to escape the police, Joe looks to Ned as if he were 'swimming to America'. As Lindt's photograph testifies, he did not arrive.

Epic demands the heroic transcendence of natural limits. Americans braced their continent together with rails, and constructed towers that besiege the sky. Pastoralism is more sympathetic to those who lack the energy or the opportunity to perform such feats. It enjoins a settled, meek contentment; for this reason Christianity, annexing the classical myth, declared it to be a blessed condition. Christ the good shepherd forgivingly views mankind as a herd of sheep, which are liable – as the chorus bleats in Handel's *Messiah* – to go astray. Australia amended the literary fiction and the religious fable to fit the circumstances of its grazing stations. On one of these, Kerry's mob of twenty thousand sheep, with no shepherds to look after them, chews the land bare, leaving only a couple of unbowed, indigestible trees. The huts, grouped around the station woolshed, keep a cautious distance, like shacks on a beach looking out at a white, eddying ocean: how can men control this collective, brainless mass? Yet the title of the photograph does not condemn the sheep for their mobility; Australians, who fondly refer to themselves as a mob (and sometimes a weird one), are happy to

146
Charles Kerry
Mob of 20,000 Sheep c. 1890

recognize an affinity with the somnolently munching animals. The connotations of 'mob' are usually derisive. Shakespeare's Roman politicians despise the mob for its inconstancy, and take pride in their own principled fixity. Australian English ignores the word's snooty history. At the opening of the Sydney Olympics, the Aboriginal actor Ernie Dingo introduced himself to the television audience by saying 'G'day mob, how are you?', and then explained that a reconciliatory tribal dance signified the hope that 'we can all be one mob'. A mob is indiscriminate, a jostling, multifarious chaos, and that – just as much as the entranced study of the way balls or coins behave – is a state Australians regard as a happy one.

Literary pastoral, with its meditative calm, emphasizes the vigilance of the shepherd keeping watch in the fields. Australia concentrates on a figure situated later in the production line: the shearer, who converts wool into wealth. Between 1888 and 1894 Tom Roberts painted two tributes to what he called 'the great pastoral life', benign visions of a vernacular Arcadia. In *Shearing the Rams*, horned merinos gently submit to barbering; shearers bestride them, clipping away at their lucrative coats, while a squatting, white-bearded elder keeps watch and smiling barefoot boys gather armfuls of fleece or sweep the floor. Roberts's second painting, *The Golden Fleece*, admits the commercial uses of the myth. A girl at a sorting table, beaming at the painter, holds up a coat that the shearers have cleverly eased off a sheep.

The woolshed in the paintings is a recess of shade, with glimpses of baking paddocks through the narrow doors. Samuel Sweet, lining up the shearers outside, exposes the shaky fabrication of the shed: metal panels nailed together, making the interior a sweatbox, and a door of palings that hangs askew. Roberts's shearers are young and athletic, bending double as they work; formed into a team, they look alike, equalized by physique, facial hair and the costume of their trade. Sweet's men, less exemplary, are a matey rabble. Like Kerry's sheep, they constitute an unkempt mob, solidifying into a wall that is stronger than the creaky shed – shearers unionized themselves in 1886, when the bosses attempted to slash their wages – but not renouncing their grizzled individuality. What they have in common is their grubbiness. The sheep they grip all day under their left arms leave greasy stains on their shirts, though Roberts ignored this unpicturesque filth. Their posture, now they have stopped working, sends out mixed, complex signals. The men with crossed arms are truculent, like the 'shearing knights' (as a ballad called them) who organized the unions, but the way those in the front hold their tools hints at emasculation. Roberts made sure that the points of the implements disappear into the fleeces they are loosening; Sweet's men aim the scissors at the shorn sheep but also at themselves. Their job enriched the coastal cities, so it is hardly surprising that *Shearing the Rams* was bought by a Melbourne stock agent who hung in it a Collins Street boardroom. At the feet of Sweet's shearers slump the woolly exoskeletons of the sheep, outer casings that the shrivelled, ashamed animals have abandoned. Eventually the shearers too would be no more than husks. Like swagmen and bushrangers, stockmen and prospectors, they are still venerated in Australian folklore as symbols of doughty independence; the myth is kept alive to console urban and suburban men for the nomadic freedoms they have lost. Why else would Dr Kennedy in *Neighbours* have a sheep grazing beneath the rotary clothes line in his backyard?

147
Captain Samuel Sweet
Sheep Shearers, Canowie Station
c. 1880

148
David Moore
Sheep Crutching, South Australia
1963
© Estate of David Moore

According to the spirit of Christian pastoral, shepherds develop an affectionate affinity for their sheep. We are all silly creatures, easily frightened, needing supervision. Tom Roberts admired 'the patience of the animals whose year's growth is being stripped from them for man's use'; the shearers during the 1880s also felt they were being fleeced, though they reacted more impatiently. The photographs by David Moore and Jean-Marc Le Pechoux are not concerned with the social order and its economic justice. Their focus narrows from the industrial division of labour in the shed, painted by Roberts, and the consolidated show of strength in Sweet's photograph. Moore and Le Pechoux concentrate on isolated anecdotes, moments when individual shearers relax into a tender fellow feeling with the animals. In a nineteenth-century ballad about a dance at Eubalong in New South Wales, the cavorting shearers, awkwardly clasping their female partners, are described as stringy wethers. They are more at ease when getting to grips with their sheep. The man on the left in Moore's photograph is dealing with a delicate area of the animal's anatomy; it spreads its legs in a gesture of trust. The man on the right, manoeuvring his ungainly sheep into position, seems to be dancing with it, or at least teaching it the correct steps. Once again, the sheep consents, permitting itself to be eased off the ground by the shearer's embrace. Le Pechoux's shearer, also attending to the animal's crutch, has got to grips with it even more snugly. He leans over its groin, it nestles in his. Barbering is an intimate transaction. Hair-dressers are supposed to listen to the confidences of their female clients, and in more covert days they used to discreetly sell men contraceptives. Exercising the pathetic fallacy, we can imagine a smile on the ewe's face; the shearer's face is hidden, as are his clippers. In her 1991 series *Pet Thang*, Tracey Moffatt replaced these male shearers with a woman, whose cosy proximity to a sheep is openly and dangerously erotic. The woman sleeps, and dreams of a lamb floating above her. Her naked breast nudges the tangled woolly coat of an adult sheep. Roles are reversed: now she is trussed, prepared for a sacrifice that she seems to be relishing. The shearing shed, for Moore and Le Pechoux, becomes a secretive salon. For Moffatt, it is a drowsy boudoir or – when the setting changes to an abbatoir – a recess of delectable pain.

149
Jean-Marc Le Pechoux
Man Shearing a Sheep 1975

We are a long way from the American rodeo, with its disciplinary domination of insurgent nature. Although the frontier is supposed to be a school of toughness, in pastoral Australia it produced men who were humbled and seasoned by hardship. They protected themselves against the land by recoiling into a guarded introversion, or by relying on one another. Lindt's woolly-bearded sundowners make a characteristic couple. The tree against which they lean – with its second trunk sprouting to keep them at a distance, like a partition between rooms or an agreement about different sides of the bed – is their overnight house. The man sitting on the rolled-up swag is in charge of the evening meal, and pours tea from his billycan. His mate, lolling on the ground as he waits to be served, has a smile that could be philosophical, or perhaps faintly crazy. Lindt's inventory of national types also included a miner, posed in the studio with his kit. The miner is more downcast than the two swagmen, who at least have no mercenary hopes that can be dashed. His back is bent, his expression listless. His hand trails vacantly, with nothing to grasp. Australians from the first were inured to disappointment.

This lassitude has overtaken the chorus of Egyptian soldiers and priests that Jack Cato photographed during a performance of *Aida* in Melbourne in 1929. The priests in Verdi's opera are the rumbling voices of a belligerent theocracy. They rally the army for war against Assyria, march in triumph after the battle, and implacably condemn the traitorous commander Radamès to die. But these supposed Egyptians are actually Australians, and Cato catches them between scenes reverting to conduct that comes more naturally to them: taking it easy. Though the plaster deity rigidly maintains his pose, they slouch at the base of the monument in a cloud of stage dust that could be cigarette smoke. The same posture – not so much relaxed as depressed by a pensive calculation of the odds against success – appears in another confidential backstage photograph. In the dressing room at Wimbledon in 1957, Lew Hoad seems to be steadying himself against collapse by planting his hands on his knees. His neck and back carry an intolerable, invisible strain; he stares at the floor, closely guarding his distress, and refuses to show his face to Moore. Barefoot, wearing only shorts, he is uncomfortably stranded between the camouflage of the street – discarded on those hooks – and the costume required by the stage, the arena, the court. He has cast off his private self. A public role awaits him, announced by the glare of light that pushes its way through the open window, but he is unprepared to confront it.

Moore's subject is hardly the man commemorated by the International Tennis Hall of Fame, which enthuses over Hoad's epic attributes: his 'gorilla chest and iron wrists', his 'assault-minded' style, the way he 'blistered the ball'. According to this description, he was a cross between an ape and an armoured vehicle. What Moore saw, however, was a recruit before the battle, worrying – as Australians have always done – about his adequacy. Luckily Hoad recovered his fighting spirit. The light through the window already awards him an aureole, as it sets fire to his blonde hair; after this photograph was taken, he strode out to win the mens' singles trophy for the second successive year.

152
David Moore
Lew Hoad in dressing room
before winning at Wimbledon
for the second time 1957
© Estate of David Moore

Jack Cato consorted with gods, but, as a staunchly demotic Australian, could not convince himself to believe in them. Melba, who adopted him as her protégé, was pleased that he treated her as plain Nellie Mitchell from Melbourne. When she introduced him to Caruso, Cato noted that the squat, swarthy tenor was boosted to heroic stature by four-inch platform soles. Cato's memoirs contain a chapter called 'Debunking the Spirits', about his campaign to expose the fraudulence of photographers who claimed to have taken portraits of wraiths and revenants, shimmering in ether. These ghosts, he remarked, were 'extremely out of focus, and therefore spiritual'. No wonder his photograph of *Aida* brought the grandest of operas down to earth by showing the extras nursing their tired feet and dreaming, probably, of a cold beer.

153
Axel Poignant
*Swagman on the Road to
Wilcannia* 1954

Australian photographers even demythologize myths that they themselves have created. This is the case with two images that have come to be venerated as icons, almost literally consecrated: the *Swagman* photographed on the road to Wilcannia by Poignant, and Dupain's *Sunbaker*. Both are portraits of national characters. It is convenient that both lack faces, like Nolan's Ned Kelly inside the rectangular helmet he hammered together from ploughshares. Anyone looking at these photographs can graft features of his or her own choosing onto the archetype. On her husband's behalf, Roslyn Poignant challenged what she called the 'iconic status' of his photograph during the early 1990s by licensing its use on a change-of-address card. She disliked the way this image of intrepidity in the outback had been cosily adopted by an urban society; it irritated her that the figure of the solitary battler was being patronized as one of Crocodile Dundee's ancestors. Near the end of his life, Dupain protested against the political and commercial conscription of his photograph: 'It's looked on as a symbol of Australia, which of course it isn't'. How could it be, as the model — so the nationalists were dismayed to learn after Dupain's death — was a young Englishman? Endlessly reproduced and imitated, images like these can be symbols of whatever you choose. Variants of the sunbaker have been used to sell suntan lotion, a cream to retard hair loss, and a cure for obesity. During 2002 Poignant's swagman appeared in a newspaper supplement touting a 'cultural feast' to be held in Alice Springs, with seminars on 'sustainability' and 'desert knowledge'. Can he be passed off as a New Age seeker? His bike would hardly have taken him into the Northern Territory. As so often, the photograph appeared in the newspaper uncredited. It now belongs to all Australians, and the artist must surrender his proprietary rights.

The Poignants met the swagman near Wilcannia in 1954, talked to him for a while, and then, as he walked away, Axel photographed him from a platform on top of their van. The high angle allows the photographer to glimpse a destination that his subject could not see: a sunlit open plain, like a promised land. The road beyond Wilcannia leads to the mine at Broken Hill, and we are free to assume that the swagman has set his course towards wealth, or at least employment. Roslyn Poignant, discouraging such sentimental reveries, points out that the country had already been 'spiritually occupied' by the Aboriginal people, so it needs no mirage of enrichment on the horizon. In any case, a happy outcome looks unlikely. The dwarfish bow-legged figure might be Chaplin at the end of *Modern Times* — except that the tramp scampers along a road that is bouncy and resilient because it is American, and also he has Paulette Goddard for company, whereas the swagman pushes a bicycle that lacks pedals and a chain, and must make do with a solitary bedroll. Everything about him looks tenuous, pitiful. His braces hold up a pair of pants that are too big for him, strapped at the ankles to keep them out of the wheel spokes. The bicycle itself is a wistful, footsore admission of weakness. Perhaps, daunted by what lies ahead, the swagman might turn tail, or simply lie down beside the road. Roslyn Poignant remarked to her husband after the encounter that she could easily imagine the bush reclaiming his listless, mouldering body. A sundowner, like an elegiac veteran on Anzac Day, thinks about the going down of the sun even when it is confidently rising.

The kangaroos above a Balmain shop photographed by Missingham in 1956 do a better job of exemplifying the archetype. At least there are two of them, although they appear to be setting out in opposite directions. It's not so much that they are mates who have arrived at a parting of the ways; rather that they have both decided to turn their backs on the pile of architectural flummery — bays, niches, triangular peaks, all over-grown with curlicued foliage — that ennobles the grocer's establishment and vouches for the pompous solidity of the city he serves. These marsupial pioneers are strong

155
Hal Missingham
Balmain Pediment 1956

enough to sling their blueys over their shoulders, while Poignant's swagman relies on the bicycle to carry his load, and they jauntily swing their billycans from their other paws. They are wearing work boots, though locomotion will be no problem for them: they can vault across Australia, using their tails to propel them. Despite this admiration for the bounding energy of the animals, Missingham's image ironically teases the national myth. The two free spirits are immobilized in stone, and cemented to a balustrade on a rooftop, from which they survey the Sydney suburbs.

Poignant's photograph permits sedentary suburban Australians to imagine that they are trekkers in the outback. Dupain's photograph encourages the opposite delusion. If it symbolizes Australia, it imagines a lucky country of tanned bodies where, absolved from the need to work, you can doze in the sun. Coastal Australia needed a mythical hero to match the explorers who confronted the interior. Jeff Carter, introducing his book on *Surf Beaches of Australia's East Coast* in 1968, fantasized about a marine Genesis, competing with Aboriginal legends about the primal creators who wandered over the land and moulded its tumuli: 'In the beginning there were waves. Then land appeared and the waves beat upon the land. After some time man came on the scene and eventually he rode upon the waves.' Old and New Testaments are abruptly and scandalously conflated here. God is omitted, being irrelevant to Australia; Adam, in this pagan genealogy, is fused with Christ, who does not merely walk on water but dances on it, thanks to his surfboard. Was the surfie Australia's incarnation of the new man? A long-limbed boy in florid shorts, photographed by Ray Leighton for a book on *Sydney Beaches* published in 1950, is described by the caption as 'typical of the Australians' who 'own the future of this vigorous young nation'; his qualification for ownership is his skill at 'mastering the hazards of the sea'.

But Sydney is not Malibu or Santa Monica, just as Starvation Bore is not Wyoming. Attractive as the myth may seem, the language of ownership and mastery is misleadingly American in its emphasis. The sunbaker is prostrate. In 1936 Dupain photographed a female nude, and called the result *Impassioned Clay*. The title comes from Keats's sonnet about *King Lear*, with its 'fierce dispute' between 'damnation and impassioned clay'. Dupain, however, omits the dispute and the possibility of damnation; in Australia the human clay is cooked like terracotta by the sun, not agitated by destructive Shakespearean passions. The sunbaker's inertia makes him monumental. Unfocus your eyes and this could be the outline of Uluru on the molten horizon. Though Australia is a furnace in which the earth is charred, the drops of water on his arms and his wet, slick hair save him from desiccation or burning up. Dupain's angle is as low as Poignant's in the portrait of the swagman is high, but the looming bulk of the sunbaker is not ponderous or oppressive. He floats on the sand, as weightless as a cloud. The figure has grown back into the landscape; like those Aboriginal ancestors, he is looking through the surface into the subsoil, seeking to be embedded there. His head is almost buried, and his fingers are crusted with grains as if he were digging himself deeper. Was this how life began, fertilized by the sun rather than (as in Jeff Carter's account) irrigated by the sea? The paganism of the image recalls the Greek belief that heat guarantees vitality and determines gender: foetuses turned out to be male, according to Aristotle, if they cooked in the womb, whereas females were cooler, more emollient. D. H. Lawrence in his Sicilian story *Sun* refers to the erectile sun as 'he', and describes it inseminating a woman who enjoys a 'procreative sunbath'. According to this physiognomic theory,

Dupain's figure is an androgyne. The Greeks expected men to show off their vigour, while women were allowed to lapse into docile passivity. The sunbaker's body is masculine, but Aristotle would have thought his posture feminine; the opposites here reach a peaceful equilibrium.

When Australians undressed at the beach, Dupain saw the world's innocent beginnings restored. An attempt was made to dramatize this moment of creation during the opening ceremony of the Sydney Olympics, when young Nikki Webster knelt on a beach towel that was both a prayer mat and a magic carpet; she then levitated on the towel and looked down at the burnished continent, surrounded by oceans of rippling plastic. Before the pantheistic ballet began, she smeared on a coating of sunscreen. Dupain's elemental religion, we now know, is likely to prove carcinogenic.

Sandwiched between earth and sky, the sunbaker may be in a state of pantheistic grace. Or he may simply be asleep, glutted after lunch or exhausted after a swim. Poignant's photograph hesitates between seeing the swagman either as a quixotic adventurer or a sorry derelict, and Dupain registers a similar ambiguity about his national character. Does this body have a brain, let alone a soul? That is the question Lawrence asked about Australia in *Kangaroo*, which contains a scene that could have suggested both the *Sunbaker* and Dupain's later photograph of the baths at Newport Beach. Lawrence sends himself, in the guise of Somers, on an excursion to a beach north of Manly, which could easily be Newport: there is a 'salt pool where the sea had ebbed in' and 'a state reserve – a bit of aboriginal Australia' with a spit of sand between the lagoon and the surf. Here Somers notices a youth, who could be the one leaning against the pool at Dupain's Newport, with 'huge massive legs', and reflects that 'they seemed

157
Geoffrey Powell
Intellectual, Bondi Beach
c. 1946

to run to leg, these people'. He then sees another young man 'lying on the warm sand-hill in the sun', who is surely the sunbaker. This figure 'had rolled in the dry sand while he was still wet' and 'lay like an animal on his face in the sun'. Somers concludes that these Australians are 'like real young animals, mindless as opossums'. But what if the sunbaker were to roll over and show his face? The *Tribune* photographer Geoffrey Powell included a man on the beach among his portraits of young Communists, and character-ized him – perhaps sarcastically – as an intellectual. During the 1940s, the pipe was certainly a prop that betokened thoughtfulness, even if a beach was hardly the place to smoke it. The hair in the man's armpit is also a testimonial: an intellectual is just another kind of worker. Socialism has its own version of pastoral, populated by brawny doctri-naire proletarians rather than musing shepherds. As so often, the fence has a story of its own to tell. It is made of barbed wire, as if the beach were a prison camp. Powell's man is not communing with nature like Dupain's; inside the fanged perimeter of the pleasure zone, he dreams of freedom. The sun is the opium of the Australian masses.

At his Institute of Physical Education and Medical Gymnastics, Dupain's father enrolled Australians in a cult of masculine vigour that was also an ideological prop of the Nazi regime. When Hoppé in 1931 called Australians 'children of the sun', he was using a phrase that, in Germany, soon became a coded encomium of brutishness and brawn, exemplified by Arno Brecker's statues of square-jawed thugs with chests like armoured breastplates. There is an Ocker equivalent to this hormonal conformism. In Michael Powell's film of *They're a Weird Mob*, made in 1966, a chorus intones an anthem as the hero's migrant ship docks at Circular Quay. A thousand baritonal oafs bellow an introduction to Nino Culotta's new home, and warn him that

> There are many manly things that must be done.
> A man's gotta prove he's a man.
> Wear your shorts, bare your chest, build a barbecue.
> It's a man's country, sweetheart,
> From the chain marks on its ankles right up to its short back and sides.

Some of Dupain's images now seem to be colluding with this physiological fascism: a discus thrower he photographed in 1938 could come from the prelude to Leni Riefenstahl's film about the 1936 Berlin Olympics, in which frowning athletes limber up on a beach beneath a sombre, thundery sky. But he was aware of the need to relax his father's rigorous standards. In 1939 he photographed a couple from behind as they surveyed the surf. Dupain called the photograph *Form at Bondi*, but the figures are as informal as Cato's unhieratic Egyptians. The man, a wrestler from his father's gym, has a roll of fat around his midriff, and his hands rest on his hips with uncalculating casualness. The woman, meanwhile, tweaks her swimming costume, which has stuck to her leg. These are not quite the 'living statues', bronzed rather than marmoreal, that Hoppé described forming 'unconsciously geometrical patterns' on Australian beaches.

Dupain's photograph of Newport Beach goes further in amending this muscle-bound classicism. He called the leggy Lawrentian boy 'Adonis-like', though an Olympian god would have done without those patterned trunks. Dry marble changes to wet flesh, and the Greek agora – the public space where men demonstrated their commitment to the shared life of citizenship by freely exhibiting their nakedness – is replaced by a pool, a landed sample of the shark-infested sea. There is room here for a woman in a bathing cap, who in classical society would have been compelled to stay indoors. Jung believed in an 'oceanic feeling', which is our sense of immersion in a collective unconsciousness. Dupain's people are clambering out of or diving back into that buoyantly communal state. At Newport, on the populated coast, Dupain located his own smaller version of that safe, hospitable inland sea that explorers in the nineteenth century hoped to find.

He returned to Newport in 1978, taking with him a fragment of a Greek sculpture that he had inherited from his father. He placed the woman's head, with its implacable stone coiffure, at the water's edge, allowed it to be swirled and tossed by the bubbling surf, and fitted six photographs of its misadventures into a single panel. It was a complicated act of purgation, a cleansing that could only have been performed at the beach. The fixity of the Greek ideal, which his father had applied to actual Australian bodies, begins to dissolve and erode as the head rolls in the water. During the 1980s, toying with souvenirs towards the end of his life, Dupain forced the same Greek head

158
Edward Cranstone
'They Had Their Fun',
The Northern Camps
from the album
Design for War, vol. II
1942–44

159
Jon Lewis
Retired Beach Inspector, Bondi
1985

into a confrontation with the grizzled, frumpy faces of the women in a queue for rationed meat that he had photographed in 1946. Again he assembled a montage. The sculpture with the chiselled profile, untroubled by possession of a body, sits in a corner staring up at the harassed middle-aged shoppers. But it is the women from the meat queue Dupain chose to honour, separating them from the crowd and enclosing each face in a painted frame, like images of ancestors on a mantelpiece. They belong in the national family album. It is the classical matron who is a stranger in Australia.

At Cranstone's rude tropical resort, a sign lewdly ridicules the ethos of fitness extolled by Dupain's father. Nakedness is a leveller, and the Australian beach is a plenum of average flesh. A sunbather photographed by Jeff Carter is bald, with a hairy sagging chest; sitting down, he removes his flip-flops and picks gritty sand from the crevices between his toes. Jon Lewis's retired beach inspector is even further from the ideal. His belly has swollen like that of a pregnant woman, and his plump thighs leave little room for the pouch containing his genitals, which may have retracted into that marshmallowy mountain. His ovular tent, swelling around him and obliterating Bondi, could be a sac that contains his private ocean, a tank in which he floats. Two fat-dimpled legs gape open at the left, with a child – who might have clambered into the world from between them – standing in the cavity. Perhaps the beach is where these flabby monsters come to spawn and to hatch their eggs, after which they will roll back into the water.

The sunbaker has the sand to himself. Dupain, who spent his hours of leisure rowing alone in the harbour off Castlecrag, valued such solitude: Australia is an empty space, available for monopolistic possession by a romantic ego like that of Voss. The dreamer, asleep in the sand or trudging through the desert, owns the world he has imagined. What happens if the angle of vision is widened to include all those jostling other existences excluded by the frame? Rex Dupain, Max's son, has photographed a Bondi now populated, like Australia itself, by a variety of urban tribes, amiably and rowdily coexisting. His subjects include Japanese surfers, dark-

160
Roger Scott
Bronte Beach (No. 2)
1979

complexioned immigrants from the eastern Mediterranean, and a pair of men (defined as a couple by the title of his photograph) gossiping on towels that have been positioned suspiciously close together. In the tidal pool at Bronte beach, photographed by Roger Scott, the members of the tribes paddle in a companionable scrum, with newcomers pushing down the steps to join in. A fence, as usual, stands guard, but everyone has breached it: the welter of people is itself fluid, easily bypassing such obstructions. Dupain at Newport stands at a distance and watches the drying bodies compose themselves into a sculptural frieze. Scott, however, is in the water, only just managing to keep his camera above waves that churn and heave with the pressure of romping bodies. The disapproving woman in the foreground, protecting her back and insisting on a respectful perimeter, has misunderstood this promiscuous democracy. The scene is messily baptismal, as an entire society – lodged, in more solid form, in the houses piled up on a distant cliff at the right – liquefies.

Lawrence's image needs to be amended. You do not walk out of the world into Australia. Preferably you jump into it, and enjoy the splash as your body breaks the surface and then resiliently bobs up again. Perhaps your head remains immersed, while your legs, like those of the upside-down diver Scott photographed along the same coast at Queenscliff, communicate your frothy joy to the air. You can use the water as a trampoline, and the headless figure's toes signal delight as eloquently as fingers. Here too, as at Bronte, the headland is occupied by piles of brick boxes, with windows parcelling the view into horizontal slices like photographs. But the contours of these sandstone cliffs narrate their own erosion, and the blocks of flats will eventually be consumed by the ocean. Was it our primal mistake to clamber ashore and stand upright? The blue is not beyond, as Lawrence thought. It is beneath you as you look down, then above and all around you. Once you divest yourself of an old identity, cast off all landed, dressed differentiations and take the plunge, you are at home.

161
Roger Scott
Queenscliff Legs
1975

7: Artworks

The process of home-making involves making art. The image is a fusion of subject and object, of inner and outer; it marries the mind to nature. But according to the local slangwidge, an artist is a wastrel whose only talent is for self-indulgence or self-delusion. Hence those lovable Australian ogres, the booze artist and the bullshit artist. Australian nature itself qualified as art or architecture, and photographers were content to catalogue its wonders. The stereoscopic views of the Jenolan Caves by J. Rowe during the late 1890s have titles like *Alabaster Column* or *Crystal Cities* entered in ink on the cards, defining the rock formations as impromptu architecture. When Peter Dombrovskis photographed the rivers on the west coast of Tasmania, he felt he was discovering art, not inventing it. The recess of jewelled rock that he called *Masterpiece Alcove* demands to be admired as one of nature's artefacts; gems begin as stones, and here the cutting and polishing has been done, with the slow patience of the perfectionist, by water rather than a human craftsman.

The photographers of the Australian landscape studied nature in the hope of glimpsing what lay behind it. The shutter opens at the instant when the eye senses that the world is about to become transparent, allowing matter to be lit from within by spirit. Wordsworth saw 'splendour in the grass' and 'glory in the flower'; a clump of daffodils constituted a host, like an army of gold-bedecked angels. Henri Mallard's clouds at sunset testify to the same imminent divination. A photograph writes with light, which is why the earliest practitioners described it as nature's pencil. But the original calligrapher must be a deity, whose inscriptions perplex us. The Aboriginal people studied a scripture that lay underfoot, tracing tracks across the land; their white usurpers, abstracted as ever, preferred to scrutinize the sky. Mallard, using Wordsworth's word, considers the sunset to be splendid, though it could equally well be an augury of apocalypse. Behind the dense, thundery clouds, the rays form themselves into the shape of an upraised hand.

Photography lent itself to this earnest decipherment of nature. Alfred Stieglitz set out 'through clouds to put down my philosophy of life', and in March 1909, above the Megalong Valley at Katoomba, Harry Phillips photographed an allegorical combat of 'cloud figures', acting out the imperial frictions of the northern hemisphere. As Phillips read the scene, 'a cloud resembling the German eagle…with outstretched wings' blotted out the sun and clutched in its talons a fragile wisp representing Belgium. Another black cloud formed itself into the likeness of the British lion, while a certain indefinite blob was surely 'our late beloved Queen Victoria with a white cap on her head', revisiting her former colony as ectoplasm. The Russian bear hovered

menacingly nearby; if the picture was turned upside down, it became a leopard, symbolizing 'anti-Christian power'. All these geopolitical portents were inscribed on the evening sky in letters of drifting vapour.

Phillips was convinced that a seance had taken place inside his camera. Mallard's symbolism is vaguer, but the pattern of light he photographed still transmits a supernatural message. That radial flare from the sinking sun is mysteriously analogous to the array of girders on the Sydney Harbour Bridge, which Mallard photographed and filmed while it was under construction. In 1932, when the bridge was complete, he made the affinity explicit in a photograph taken at sunset. The sun drops behind a rampart of dark clouds, but sends out a last burst of radiance through a break just above the highest point of the span. It is, in the mystical sense, a sign: the bridge is a prophetic emblem of connection, like the Brooklyn Bridge of Walt Whitman and Hart Crane. The religious aspiration is deliberate. Art in Australia preached salvation, and set out to transfigure the hellish penal colony by pointing to the heavens that blazed or scintillated above it. The drover in 'Banjo' Paterson's ballad *Clancy of the Overflow* sleeps rough, but he witnesses 'the wondrous glory of the everlasting stars'.

In 1925 George J. Morris photographed the entrance to the Art Gallery of New South Wales. He called the image *The Spirit of the Ionic*: the columns with their florid, curling capitals are spirits, emissaries – like Phillips's clouds – from another, loftier world. Cazneaux's photograph of the same building takes a more sceptical, sideways look at the manifold mission it was meant to serve. At first the colony's few imported treasures were housed in a wooden shed with a sawtooth roof, nicknamed the 'Art Barn'. Early designs for a permanent gallery equipped it with domes, arches, turrets and pinnacles, making manifest its uplifting bequest to Sydney. In 1909 the architect Walter Liberty Vernon replaced the warehouse with this classical temple. Hal Missingham, director of the gallery from 1945 to 1971, enjoyed exposing the ornate front as a fraud. Behind it, he knew, crouched a utilitarian structure that resembled a workshop in the outer suburbs. He preferred the lowbrow factory to the ostentatious temple, because Australia itself had been cobbled together. Missingham laughed at architecture that organized society into 'a hoped-for permanence': so much for the art gallery's eternal pantheon.

163
Harold Cazneaux
*Exterior of Art Gallery
of New South Wales* c. 1930s

A grandiose roll-call of artists, mostly unrepresented inside the building, unfurls in bronze around the outside of the gallery. Morris's view singles out the name of Michelangelo. Cazneaux's vantage point unluckily accentuates the forgotten sculptor Jean Goujon, sandwiched between Canova and Pythagoras: a symptom of the perishability of this supposedly immutable classical canon. Sculptured panels on the façade show art in the service of empire: Assyrian and Egyptian monarchs inspect the palaces and triumphal avenues that will immortalize them, a Roman emperor visits a building site in Gaul. On either side of the Ionic portico stand equestrian statues, added in the 1920s, which display the Offerings of War and Peace. A slogan at the base of the figure who symbolizes war hopes for mercy and justice, but the winged emblem of victory on the rearing warrior's staff implies that civilization is a benefit of conquest. Peace, photographed by Cazneaux, flaunts an olive branch and claims the 'real and lasting victories'. A cornucopia of trophies spills from this figure's saddle: comic and tragic masks that announce the origins of drama, a painter's palette and a sculptor's mallet, as well as the lyre played by Orpheus (or by birds in the Australian bush, with their lyres of flaunting tail feathers). Peace also offers a harvest of fruit and fleece. Is culture then a by-product of agriculture, rather than the victor's armed imposition?

It's a pity that Gilbert Bayes, the sculptor, had to prop Peace on horseback. The figures needed to be symmetrically balanced, although they propose different ideas of art and its function in society. War is an epic swaggerer, gripping swords and broken spears. Peace yearns for a pastoral reconciliation with the earth, but the flowering ground is trampled by the horse. In the interconnecting parks outside the gallery, a debate about the meaning of Australia rages, with buildings and statues silently quarrelling. The Botanic Gardens – where the city's first, temporary art gallery stood, and where Roger Scott photographed the coy white nymph in the shrubbery – define the country as an exotic Arcadia. Across the Domain in Hyde Park, the War Memorial, the destination of Sam Hood's Anzac march, remembers Australia's obligations to an unhappier world elsewhere, and counts the mortal cost of its involvement in history. The Art Gallery, a sandstone Parthenon, stands a little way from St Mary's Cathedral, photographed during construction by Bayliss: the two institutions promulgate different faiths, with opposing ideas of salvation. Outside the gallery on the lawns of the Domain, the argument becomes audible at the weekend when speakers – lacking the stone pedestals of Bayes's horsemen – mount their soapboxes and denounce the government or promote the sect, cult or ideology of their choosing.

The angle of Cazneaux's photograph is duly deferential. The horse and its rider both look away from the photographer, whose art – which was not accepted as such at the time, because it did not derive from classical Greece – was excluded from the building. Should the Australian artist plead for admission to a gallery like this, or was a new country bound to arrive at its own vernacular definition of culture? Peace brandishes the kind of palette used by Victorian academicians, but the young Sidney Nolan, unable to afford the proper equipment, made art with the help of scavenged materials: slates from a leaky roof instead of canvas, the streaky blade of a windscreen wiper in place of a brush. As each art was reinvented in Australia, such self-reliant improvising became the rule. The reply to the letter sent to Clancy of the Overflow arrives in 'a writing unexpected', clumsily traced by 'a thumb-nail dipped in tar'. In *We of the Never-Never*, describing efforts to settle the outback, Mrs Aeneas Gunn vows to 'begin at the very beginning of things'. The native women on the station therefore cook up a supply of ink by burning water lily roots. But writing is a luxury, and has to wait; the ink is used 'to make guiding lines on the timber for [a] saw', which cuts up trees to build a house. That Northern Territory dwelling remains, as Mrs Gunn says, 'unpapered': it is not yet a house of fiction. Richard Flanagan's painter-convict in *Gould's Book of Fish* still trusts in art as a 'Divine Redemption of Nature', though he too must self-reliantly manufacture his own materials, and he writes one chapter of his memoir in ink confected from his own shit. Snugglepot and Cuddlepie enjoy a concert of music scraped and scratched on native instruments. The pianola is a hollow tree with pedals of bark, and the notes are supplied by a colony of resident frogs peeping through eye holes in the wood. Crickets and birds join in, forming an unsymphonic ragtime band that is resident in a boronia bush. In May Gibbs's White City, a photographer hollows out a gum nut to use as a camera, with a gum leaf stretched over it as a hood.

Despite this ingenious contrivance, photographers are not free to make their implements. There is no getting round your need for a camera, which someone must construct for you. But Australian photographers pay tribute to artists whose work is a handicraft, and whose hands dabble in the earthy substance of the country. The *Artist's Hand* photographed by Poignant belonged to Missingham. They were on a trip to the bush outside Perth with some naturalist friends when their vehicle broke down; Poignant, unable to help with the repairs because of an injured back, took photographs instead, including this study of Missingham's hand, filthy with axle grease. The title is subtly ironic. A first glance might take this to be a black hand, since the grease has inkily picked out the lines and creases in the skin. Placed on a slab of wood, the palm prints are aligned with the splintery grain of the timber, claiming a connection between man and nature; open, the hand displays a native map, on which the paths are genealogical trails. A second guess might be that it is an artisan's hand. Who, without Poignant's prompting, would imagine that its owner was an artist? But the artist in Australia must know how to mend a car in the outback; he should be professionally prepared to dirty his hands. The image also slyly glances at the psychology of the vocation. Though photography is a white-collar occupation, painters are licensed mess-makers, like unregenerate children. Artists belong in the bush, or on the frontier: they are, after all, wild men.

David Moore photographed the brush in John Olsen's hand stirring the lake of lush pigment that became his ceiling painting *Summer in the You Beaut Country*. The huge canvas could be the flat expanse of Australia itself, waiting for some instigating hand to stretch out – as God does on the ceiling of the Sistine chapel – and animate it with dabs of flushed colour: turbid snaking rivers, deserts of hot ochre, a frothy ocean, the throbbing sun. A few years later, Olsen completed *Sydney Sun*, now in the National Gallery of Australia. This too was a ceiling painting, with the molten sun exploding into life overhead like a squeezed, oozing orange; the three plywood panels were to be coextensive with the sky. Moore also photographed Fred Williams in his studio, spattering flecks of paint on canvases that sprawl on the floor or are propped against the wall. The portly god, clutching his brushes, stands back to survey his work and wonders if it is good. He operates on all fronts simultaneously, colouring in what remains of the world after Olsen has taken care of the sky.

In Moore's photograph, the stripes and squiggles of Olsen's brush cause life to pullulate. Roots burrow, insects scuttle, people play. Moore, looking horizontally across

164
Axel Poignant
Artist's Hand 1941

the canvas, cannot read this seething detail, and because his medium is black and white he is unable to convey Olsen's celebration of colour as energy. But these sacrifices are worthwhile, because Moore wants to show the artist in action, not the finished product. Olsen's gesture is casual, which suits a painting with such a colloquial title; the brush rests between his fingers rather than being gripped by them. If you look at outback Australia from the air, its topography consists of scrawls and striations, roughly daubed by a splapdash hand. A brush mediates between the invisible artist and the wet, unformed surface. But the distance is abridged by the puddle of paint on Olsen's palm and the splashes that extend down his arm. His is the dyer's hand, stained (to paraphrase Shakespeare) by what it works in. Aboriginal makers kneaded the land into shape, and Olsen is bringing it alive as if transfusing blood into it. Rather than reproducing a world that already exists, Australian artists make a new one with their bare hands.

Aesthetes, in the country's earlier days, had to be brave missionaries. Like Oscar Wilde lecturing the Colorado miners on dress reform, they made propaganda for style in a society that had no patience with ruffles, flounces or fanciness.

In 1928 L. Hey Sharp photographed a white egret with preening feathers, and called it *Mannequin*. Such flaunting narcissism issued an invitation to artists: Robert Helpmann choreographed a ballet, *The Display*, about the courting antics of the lyrebird. It took courage for a man to mimic its vainglorious strutting. Exhibitionism was better left to the forces of nature, or to statuesque foreign show-offs. In Mallard's photograph of the Archibald Fountain in Hyde Park, taken in 1938, the water exuberantly sprays the night sky, while Apollo, holding the lyre that he awarded to Orpheus, contorts his rippling body in order to admire the view; the title Mallard chose for the image was *Display*. Inanimate domestic objects could do their own cavorting, if they were artfully arranged. Olive Cotton's *Teacup Ballet* in 1935 positioned half a dozen cups and saucers on a table, backlit them, and allowed the shadows they cast to turn them into a corps de ballet, with their handles as arms daintily cocked on hips.

166
L. Hey Sharp
Mannequin c. 1928

During the 1920s Ruth Hollick took the first Australian fashion photographs, and introduced a new breed of superciliously refined creatures to the callow, ragged country: a Whistlerian lady wrapped in pelts, who poses next to a table with a vase of emblematic peacock feathers, or the line-up of Regency dandies and bonneted shepherdesses who advertise an emporium selling clothes for 'the man of taste' and 'artistic furnishings'. The captions attached to her photographs when they were published in The Home daringly emphasized the gratuitousness of fashion, its obsession with novelty and inutility. The decoration on one garment had a mind of its own: 'some frills are so perverse that they insist on running up and down instead of round about'. These clothes liberated the bodies that wore them, casting off Victorian strictures. 'There's sheer romance,' according to another caption, 'about a suit that permits itself to swing from the shoulders for all the world as if it were a cape'. This was an inflamed, seditous language, treating perversity and permissiveness as virtues. The spirits Caire photographed in his fern gullies had come to town, and now enticed the citizens to adorn themselves with butterfly wings or velvety fur. The editors of The Home claimed that 'Fairy Fingers worked upon these frills for fairy girls to wear'.

Hollick's four couples look shy. They cower against the wall, not quite able to live up to their top hats and hooped skirts, and the bare room hardly qualifies as a bower. Only the man in the middle, with his hand pugnaciously on his hip, seems ready to face down anyone who calls him effete. Their successors proved more intrepid, and set out on a series of colonizing expeditions that brought the gospel of art to the interior, or to Australia's outlying fringes: Le Guay's model even reached Ayers Rock, where she attempted to enfold the monolith with her gauzy arms, and Helmut Newton took Maggie Tabberer to Papua New Guinea and photographed her coolly scrutinizing the native produce, her hat nestling beneath the grass roof of a hut. The women, in both cases, were more outlandish than the settings in which they had been placed. Henry Talbot, in photographs taken for the Wool Board, despatched his models to pastoral Australia. Like all mannequins, they are futuristic beings, who show us what we will look like next season or next century, but Talbot photographed them revisiting the past, stranded in a run-down country town. The figure on the left rests on her rifle; all three women keep one hand on their belts, as if they might need to reach for their guns. Their stance is militant, aggressive, in contrast with the man in the doorway whose arms are folded, and thus useless. They are female equivalents to the Wild Colonial Boy in the ballad – violently modish, outlawed for being so haughtily perfect – who have come to beautify the backblocks by force. But they fail to impress the listless local, and the sheep turns away from them, not recognizing its fleece in the lurid colours that they wear. The backdrop undoes their endeavour: the sign on the wall fades, the curtain hangs in tatters, the corrugated iron of the verandah rusts and corrodes. The town decays, the sheep snoozes. Both are immune to the accelerated tempo of fashionable lives, which demand perpetual change. Luckily the women can propel themselves out of this dozy idyll: a reflection in the window shows the car in which they do their time-travelling. Talbot's image has the humorous despair of the best fashion photography. Beauty begins to perish as soon as the shutter clicks, innovation leads to obsolescence. The immemorial continent ignores those who think they can redesign it.

167
Ruth Hollick
Robertson and Moffat 1920s

168
Henry Talbot
Wild Colonial Colours Campaign for the
Wool Board 1970s

Olive Cotton photographed a pretended fashion assignment on Cronulla Beach
in 1937, with Max Dupain playing the role of the photographer crouched over his camera. The model extends her skirt to form a windbreak, and makes use of the setting sun
as her lighting designer, pointing with her other hand to the elongated, elegantly thin
shadow she casts. She seems not to have noticed that the would-be photographer is
behind her. In any case, the boggy trail of footprints demonstrates the absurdity of
photographing fashion in a location like this, where the weather cannot be controlled
and the model's heels will sink into the sand, dirtying her hem.

Other photographers sent their models on ambassadorial tours of the inner city.
A Le Guay mannequin, with her blouse falling off her shoulder and a floral hat drooping
from her hand, attitudinizes in the rubble of a Sydney slum. One of Athol Shmith's
subjects, in a 1958 photograph, kicks up her heels among the sacks of onions and
potatoes in a Melbourne market; a worker stands aside to admire her, though in contemporary terms he – with his leather apron and faded shirt – is just as fashionable as
she is, a prize specimen of rugged proletarian chic. In *Fashion Queue*, taken at a Sydney bus
stop, Le Guay arranged a frieze of figures to dramatize art's impatient ambitions for a
crassly materialistic society. Two men in suits, on their way to work in offices, slouch
against the poles of the bus shelter. Between them are two mannequins, tall and glacial,
dressed in white and poised on teetering heels. One stares ahead as if looking for the
bus, though public transport is hardly the place for her. Two more women complete the
queue. One is fashionable, dressed in the same compulsory white, the other –
baggily and casually dressed – is not, and a pile of books in her arms implies that she
considers an interest in clothes to be frivolous. A pair of schoolboys with satchels have
inserted themselves into the queue. One has a slingshot, which he is aiming at the
second, who wears a simian carnival mask. The third model play-acts alarm when she

sees the monster, and pretends to emit a squeak of distress; the bookish woman studies the antics of the boys through her glasses. Le Guay's four couples perform a stationary dance, acting out a debate between overlapping ideas. Beauty accompanies business, because fashion, like art, is a luxury, the product of economic surplus. Intellect stands back and casts a contemplative eye over the scene. The boys express creativity in their own way by playing games: art is an alternative to work, granting the fortunate few an indefinite prolongation of childhood. And the boy in the mask, who has retired behind an alternative identity, is an artist already, whether he knows it or not.

Fashion is not only about being fashionable. The word holds a memory of art's miraculous power to fashion or fabricate a world. The capacity to revamp the self by updating your wardrobe or redesigning your hair is a lesser manifestation of the impulse. The disorientated models stranded in slums, in markets or at bus stops are emissaries of art. But should reality be compelled to beautify itself? Art has learned to appreciate what once seemed ugly or merely utilitarian. The camera, with what Edward Weston in 1943 called its 'innate honesty', disdained artifice, which is why those fashion shots are apologetically staged as parodies. For Weston, 'photographic sight' involved the patient, affectionate scrutiny of the world in which we actually live. Paul Strand commanded his colleagues to forget about making pictures and 'look at the things around you'.

Look, for instance, at corrugated iron. Australia is inconceivable without it, since it adaptably replaces the stone and wood that are lacking. A world made this way, of course, could easily be unmade. Hoppé repeats a bush legend about an Aboriginal prisoner who escaped from a corrugated-iron gaol in Darwin by using a can opener. In 1976 Jeffrey Smart painted a *Corrugated Gioconda*, imprinting Leonardo's mysterious woman – along with a line-up of torn, tatty posters – on an undulating metal wall: the work of art, he seemed to conclude, cannot survive in an age of mechanical reproduction. But corrugated iron, seen photographically, can be beautiful. Mark Strizic, as if following Strand's orders, got as close to it as possible, resting his camera on the surface of the roof and allowing it to see something that the human eye probably could not.

170
Mark Strizic
Corrugated Roof from the
series *South Melbourne*
c. 1967–72

Which of us would be on the roof in any case, unless we were mending it? The silvery sheets have an almost organic rhythm, which cannot be restrained by the nails or nuts and bolts that clamp them down. They buckle and gather into frills, like those on Hollick's dresses. In contrast, the planks of weatherboard under the eaves look lifeless. The metal induces a physiological recognition: its texture is mottled, discoloured and veined like ageing skin. Is it, too, biodegradable? Jeff Carter reports that, because there were no trees on the Birdsville Track, the dead were buried between two sheets of corrugated iron, 'riveted together to form an envelope'.

The beauty salon in south Melbourne has been abandoned, and its window is papered with bad news – of dangerous weather, unemployment, sporting upsets, and continuing political problems in south-east Asia. The columns of small print at the bottom right probably record deaths. Nevertheless, Strizic honours the social and psychological need that kept the salon in business, and even recognizes the appropriateness of using newsprint – abstractly placed sideways, to signal that you are not supposed to read it – as a window covering. The hand-painted letters on the glass reproach the mechanized type on the paper. Whoever did the lettering tried hard to make the alphabet dance: the capitals R and B are twisted like wrought iron, the w allows for flicking lateral strokes of the brush, the ys drag tails along the floor behind them, and the l, stretching out its legs to sit down, splits the word containing it in half. A home-grown artist was at work here, and took pride in demonstrating his skill.

If you can read the date on that copy of *The Age*, the photograph, like the newspaper, becomes a chronicle of your time, your life, your fading hopes. Judgments about beauty and ugliness are irrelevant, as they are when we study the faces of our pets, our children, our partners or our parents. Whitman, imagining a culture for democratic America, thought it should consist of 'facts…showered with light', not expensive, abstruse and probably foreign artefacts. A photograph like Strizic's is a fact illuminated, and the light striking the glass in that Melbourne slum is so intense that it writes the capitalized, conceptual word Beauty all over again on the smudged, parched paper.

171
Mark Strizic
Ridgeway Beauty Salon
from the series *South Melbourne* c. 1967–72

★

In *The Tree of Man*, young, guileless Australia is at first suspicious of art. When the deranged Mr Gage hangs himself, he leaves behind 'a kind of oil paintings' that show dead trees and Jesus Christ, 'mad things'. Amy Parker is equally mistrustful of books, because they are 'different from what things are'. Towards the end of the novel, Australia grows up into an understanding of the need for art, which enables us to stand aside from our world and consider it anew while we re-enact the mystery of its making. Stan and Amy bemusedly attend a performance of *Hamlet*, and their daughter Thelma goes to a concert at which 'a grave Jew with a violin' plays 'a great concerto'. Back at the homestead, Amy takes her grandson, who will be a poet when he is older, for a tour of the pantry. As the boy marvels at jars of pickled meat and preserved fruit, Patrick White comments that 'There is a mysticism of objects, of which some people are initiates'. Those people are often photographers: a chunk of crimson glass that the boy looks through is a lens, tinting and refracting reality. He asks if he can keep the glass, which he will treasure as 'a secret thing'. The secret is the power of vision.

Photographs invest objects with that numinous glory, and make symbols of them. Sometimes a camera is not necessary, as long as you have an eye. I spent my childhood gazing at one particular object in my parents' house. After my mother's death, I carried it off, along with the box of photographs. I have found a place of honour for it in my house, though only I can see the glow it still emits, like a magic lamp with wish-fulfilling powers. It is a chipped china salt and pepper shaker, made to mark the opening of the Sydney Harbour Bridge in 1932. It more or less copies the pylons that anchor the bridge, though there are nozzles on either side for the salt and pepper (which, of course, it never dispensed). The white china has a gilded trim, like ribbons arranged for the opening ceremony; the side is decorated with a painting of the bridge itself, with two or three ferries beneath it in the blue harbour. Those castellated pylons with their granite facing were a decorative afterthought. Because they have no structural purpose, Robin Boyd excoriated them as as a lie 'of Goebbelsian proportions'. The lie would not have bothered me, even if I had known about it: I wanted fiction.

For me, the little ornament symbolized an alternative world which, as yet, I could only imagine. The bridge itself was also a symbol. As a work of engineering, it stretched across the water efficiently enough. But as a work of art – photographed and painted during its construction and ever since, described and inventively modified by writers – it had other functions to perform. For artists, the bridge was a launching pad, not an assemblage of roadways and rail lines. A 1932 linocut by Ailsa Lee Brown, *Moths around the Quay*, looked down on it futuristically from the viewpoint of a pilot high above: the quay is a vortex of agitated shipping, whipped up by the plane's propeller. The bridge's very existence transfigured Australia, and abridged the distance between reality and dreams. Was the historian Alan Moorehead joking when he declared in 1953, on behalf of other expatriates, that 'we liked Sydney Harbour much better before the famous bridge was built'? A man professing such an opinion deserved to live in exile.

The planning and building of the bridge, extended over nine years, was a protracted, anxious re-traversal of evolution, summing up and completing the travail of settlement, cultivation and acculturation in Australia. Cazneaux photographed it from the beginning. In one of his earliest images, the stone pillars are as stumpy as chopping blocks of wood, and grimy heaps of scaffolding litter the northern foreshore. But in *The Old and the New*, the bridge has begun its task of renovating or modernizing the city. The old is the colonial rookery of The Rocks, with washing strung out to dry on a fence, paths straggling down an overgrown hill, telegraph poles tilting at sick angles, and listless children – strays, like the dog – guarding their dusty turf. The new rears unexpectedly at the end of the street, as cranes tug the arch of steel into the air. Cazneaux punned on the same dichotomy in *The Bridge Book*, which he published in 1930: his photographs of the steel girders as they started to vault upwards from the anchorage were called 'old shots of new shoots'. Shoots are organic growths, groping their way wherever they please. The bridge, however, required a more precise calibration. Girders projected outwards from either side of the harbour, and the city waited to see whether or not they would meet in the middle at the exact point determined by the engineers.

172
Harold Cazneaux
'*The Old and the New*',
Harbour Bridge, Sydney c. 1929

The photograph Cazneaux called *Streamers of Steel* emphasized the implausibility of the equation, as if the connecting girders were loose, flapping, not braced to withstand pressure and support loads. Because the pedestrian track curved alongside the span, he likened it to a ribbon. How could such windblown things be stiffened and riveted into place? Could an idea be given physical form?

A bridge, like a metaphor, is a transporter. From the first, this one had more to do than carry traffic. Eleanor Dark's novel *Waterway*, published in 1938, regards the bridge with a 'wilful mysticism' like the boy in *The Tree of Man*. Her hero likens the span to a 'ghostly arc', or – when the sun rises, ridging the sky with flame – to a rainbow. Rather than grey steel, it displays the polychrome sign of a covenant, which might perhaps harmonize the conflict-ridden society of the novel. It is, in this view at least, a harbinger of 'ultimate good'. *The Bridge Book* includes an image of the span – near completion, though the deck has not yet been lowered into place – seen through a haze. The caption, sharing the word with Eleanor Dark and Patrick White, calls it 'Mystic, wonderful'. The phrase is quoted from Tennyson, who applies it to the arm of the Lady of the Lake when she reaches up from beneath the water to grasp Excalibur, discarded by the dying Arthur. The bridge, to those who watched it rise unsupported, seemed just as phantasmal.

In 1933 Robert Emerson Curtis published fourteen lithographs that treated the construction as a technological epic. The gods in machines who ruled the classical world have been usurped by god-like machines, which deify the men who operate them. Curtis's commentary strove to invent an appropriate Homeric diction, ennobling the workers with capital letters: 'From his lordly seat in the clouds, the Driver of the Creeper Crane is the High Master, the Weaver of Steel'. His metaphors hallowed the bridge – he called his image of the shadowy nave beneath the pylon 'Cathedral' – but they also hinted that such marvels may, like the skyscraping modern city, be a product of demonic magic. The twisted cables, not yet braided, reminded Curtis of 'Medusa's locks'. More startlingly, a *Sydney Morning Herald* reporter in 1928 watched the riveters lobbing incandescent lumps of steel from hand to hand and likened them to 'playful Satans'. Sin and Death build a causeway over Chaos in *Paradise Lost*, and Pandemonium, the parliament erected by the devils, effortlessly rises 'like an exhalation'.

The Reverend Frank Cash, who watched the construction from his rectory verandah in Lavender Bay, published his own interpretation of it in 1930. His qualifications for this photographic exegesis, entitled *Parables of the Sydney Harbour Bridge*, were technical as well as clerical: he had studied metallurgy and mining in Kalgoorlie before taking holy orders. His photographs of the pillars and cranes are sharp and stark, rigorously modern. But this mechanistic structure was for him, as he boomed in bold lettering, **'a visible sign/ of the invisible originative power'**, and his parables expound the stratagems of 'the Divine Mind', which has bestowed a 'spiritual Ark' on Sydney Harbour and helped the country to rise above its scurrilous penal beginnings. From his verandah, Cash saw the promise of redemption. In David Malouf's *An Imaginary Life*, Ovid is banished from Rome. Beside the Black Sea, he might be looking over the Nullarbor Plain: he reports with a shudder that he has seen 'the unmade earth'. The bridge belonged to what Cash called 'the created world', and it revealed the process whereby **'the Most High completely furnished His universe'**.

At the end of his book, Cash rhapsodizes about the bridge's patterning, which he reads allegorically as proof of God's intricate, benign superintendence. Once the bridge had opened, Cazneaux too enjoyed its artfulness, the way its mechanistic kit of parts plays visual games with steel and empty air, light and shade. His *Bridge Pattern*, photographed in 1934, sees the girders as a spider's web, transparent and diaphanous because of the sunny glow within them. Dupain's *Bridge Construction* takes a similar patterning of crosses and triangles beneath the roadway and uses it to ponder the baffling recessiveness of perspective. With no point of orientation to establish whether we are looking up, down or sideways, the mind loses its balance in an abyss of endless duplication and recession. This is not quite Cash's theodicy: the more closely you look at Dupain's bridge, the harder it is to believe in it. What Dupain photographed is a cat's cradle of deranged, ensnaring intricacy, or – as in his nocturnal view of the walkway – a sharply tapering tunnel in which the lights, hovering inside milky spheres of halation, disappear over the edge of space and go on shining, unseen, in some remote galaxy. An observatory stands on a bluff next to the bridge's southern anchorage; Australia is the best place for viewing the Magellanic Clouds, and if you look up on an average night you can supposedly see straight into the depths of the universe. The bridge, unrecognizable because Dupain compressed and foreshortened the arch, is here a telescope focused on that outer limit of speculation.

The Sydney Harbour Bridge jolted Australia into abstraction. Its structural puzzle abstracted people from a world with which they were familiar, and forced them to think about the contention of energies, the management of stress, and the precarious equilibrium of physical forces. It demanded diagrams, not pictures. Grace Cossington Smith painted the curvature of the span, still with a gap in the middle, as an essay in cubic and volumetric forms. A souvenir edition of *Art in Australia* rejoiced that the bridge's construction had stamped out the 'dissolute streets and crazy buildings' of The Rocks, seen in Cazneaux's *The Old and the New*. Those streets, according to this severely modernist reckoning, were dissolute because of their picturesque crookedness, not because of the brawling pubs situated in them. Dupain, in a photograph taken at night in 1938, showed the bridge as a laboratory in which the conundrums of physics were clarified. Glaring vectors represent cars that passed during the exposure; the bridge permits accelerated movement, which was the impetus of modernity, but in doing so it demonstrates how objects in motion disintegrate into streaks of travelling light.

In retrospect, Dupain was convinced that the bridge imposed a 'new vision', like the rectified optics promoted at the Bauhaus. Introducing a collection of Mallard's photographs, he argued in 1976 that the bridge forced his mentor Mal to renounce his

174
Max Dupain
*Sydney Harbour Bridge
Walkway* 1940s
© Max Dupain 1978.
Licensed by VISCOPY,
Sydney 2003

'arty' style and reconsider his fuzzy pictorialism. The bridge, in Dupain's estimation, had no ambition to be art; it was an heroic example of 'machine form and function', and thus 'blood brother to the camera'. (Somehow, in this description, the practicality of the Bauhaus has been fused with primitive sanguinary oaths like that sworn by Wagner's Siegfried in *Götterdämmerung*. As in Curtis's lithographs, the bridge can only be explained by coupling ancient epic with up-to-date technology.) Dupain declared that the bridge itself demanded that photographers should use 'no pretence' and rely instead on 'pure observation and the application of photographic technique'. He followed his own edict in a photograph taken from the southern pylon in 1938, which organizes Sydney into a geometrical theorem: seen from up here, Circular Quay is actually square, which – in its revision of natural contours – is even more remarkable than a circle. But Mallard's photographs deviate from this austere creed. For one of them he enticed a young woman in a cloche hat and fashionable shoes to clamber over the side and prettily pose on one of the four gigantic hinge-pins that carry the weight of the arch. The bolts and the tensioned cables were not allowed to speak their own 'graphic language'.

It is Moore, in a series of photographs entitled *Steel Construction* taken in 1981, who approaches the bridge in the way prescribed by Dupain, admiring the physique of a mechanomorph: its intersecting girders and riveted joints, studied in close-up, store the energy and fortitude it needs for its leap across space. Dupain wondered whether 'Mal loved the Harbour Bridge', but is it possible or even desirable to love a machine? Affection demands that you humanize the object, and Moore might be scrutinizing the lean limbs and bunched muscles of an athlete. In his aerial view, the bridge's physiological valour in crossing that gap turns into a daring metaphysical feat. The harbour, seething in reflected light, reveals a world still unfixed, malleable, as at the moment of creation. No division has yet been decreed between the waters and the dry land. Water overflows, eating into crevices, threatening a deluge. The land is as dark as the water is bright, so the sails of the Opera House, the high-rise buildings around Circular Quay and the cranes at the Wooloomoollo docks blur into bumps or peaks that are part of the terrain. The bridge, occupying the centre, is precious evidence of human habitation in and power over this inchoate, fluid world. Eventually you notice other, less assertive bridges further up the Parramatta River, as well as a ship (though it could be the snout of a submerged alligator) making its way in a straight line towards The Heads. But initially it is the bridge that makes the connective gesture, and braces together all that the water, relentlessly clawing at the shores, presses apart. And because the span photographically duplicates itself as a reflection, the arc turns into an oval and acquires new symbolic meanings. Is it an allusion to the sketch of a fish that was an emblem of the early Christian church, or perhaps a cosmic eye, signifying purpose – forethought and foresight – in this random welter? The roadway now consists of two exactly matched parallels. Since such straight lines do not occur in ragged, spilling nature, we have evidence of mental intervention. Hoppé liked the bridge because it improved 'nature's scheme' by blocking off the mazy meandering infinitude of water to the west. In Moore's photograph, it supersedes nature and – like the oblong monolith that startles the apes in Kubrick's 2001 – vouches for the possibility of evolution.

The bridge became a white Uluru: a hearth and an altar, a sacred place where rites could be performed. As at the rock, a climb has become obligatory, a way proving

that you are worthy to be at home in Australia. For her *Leisureland* series Anne Zahalka photographed a chained party of mountaineers trudging up the arch and down the other side. Depending on whether you are looking east or west, the sun rises or sets in alignment with the Harbour Bridge, as if the grid of steel were redefining the sky as a stained-glass window. There was a suggestion that, on the night it opened in 1932, the illuminations should form a rising sun and crown, the badge of the Australian Imperial Forces. In the suburb of Rozelle, a war memorial stands by the water in the grounds of a former mental hospital. It takes the form of a miniature harbour bridge, with a stagnant pool of sludge in a concrete tub beneath it. The pylons mark the beginning and end of both world wars; the arch of thin, twisted metal extends from life to death. More optimistically, the global television relay on New Year's Eve 1999 started with fireworks above the Harbour Bridge, so that the new millennium officially began here. On the same night two years later, the clump of Uluru suddenly ignited on the span, flowering in fire beneath a pyrotechnical Southern Cross.

To Dupain in the 1930s the bridge constituted 'a wonder'. It soon lost its other-wordly aura, and came to be treated more fondly and familiarly. Robert Emerson Curtis called the iron case of the cable anchorage 'one of four immense "warts" on [its] buttock'. It is hard to imagine Whitman or Hart Crane noticing such a defect, but Curtis saw the bridge warts and all. It is lovable because it shares human imperfections, and can be snugly reduced in size to fit, like my pylon, on a mantelpiece. Australian house-wives crocheted soft bridges during the 1930s, stitching its image onto doilies and tea cosies; it acquired the jocular nickname of the coat-hanger. In Sydney once I bought a plastic coat-hanger in the shape of the bridge. I hung it on the wall rather than hanging clothes on it, but its uselessness simply serves to underline the flexibility and symbolic utility of the structure: the bridge will support any meaning you suspend from it, and tolerates any act of appropriation. Hence Effy Alexakis's photograph of the Greek flag above it, with the pole stuck in the roof of the Sydney Opera House, or the versions of it sculpted in shells by Lola Ryan and Mavis Longbottom. Alexakis, born in Australia to a Greek family, is making a point about dual nationality and divided allegiances, but the photograph at the same time comments on symbols and their shorthand: parallel lines and a cross stand for a country, though the arch with its diagonals and the curving peak of the sail also laconically signify Australia. Peter McKenzie's photograph is another exercise in making and remaking symbols. Shell assemblages like these are a specialty of women of Aboriginal descent living in the suburb of La Perouse, near Botany Bay; Lola and Mavis have reclaimed one of the invading culture's totems and reconstructed it using indigenous materials collected along the coast, not steel and concrete. The dupli-cated icons belong in this homey setting, on a cluttered porch where you might expect these smiling, hospitable women to offer a batch of scones rather than bridges. Mavis told McKenzie that 'To match all your shells and get the colour into it you've got to be an artist'. His photograph shows the indiscriminate rubble they work with: a crate of small, nondescript shells, from which they have pieced together their jewelled icons.

In 1996 Rex Dupain photographed a crowd of tourists with cameras on the bridge: everyone who sees it wants to take it away with them, and photography, as in the family album, is a means of emotional annexation and conservation. Two photo-graphers make different choices. A lanky youth with his back turned concentrates on the arch, while an Asian tourist steadies his camera on the parapet and focuses on the skyscrapers behind Circular Quay. There is a third option: the bridge offers a platform for photographing the Opera House, and – if you point the camera through the lozenge-shaped girders, as Rex Dupain has done on other occasions – a means of framing it.

When the architect Harry Seidler first saw Jørn Utzon's design for the Opera House, he sent him a cable acclaiming it as 'pure poetry'. It was an apt tribute. What Mallarmé called 'la poésie pure', the earliest announcement of linguistic modernity, was dispensed from having to mean anything in particular: its words were signs, free to signify whatever they pleased. Robert Hughes described Utzon's earliest sketch as a

176
Effy Alexakis
Greek Flag, Sydney from the series
Greek Australians: In Their Own Image Project 1984

177
Peter McKenzie
Lola Ryan and Mavis Longbottom

'magnificent doodle'. Even more bracingly than the Harbour Bridge, the Opera House offered Australia a lesson in abstraction. Bridges are necessary, or at least useful. Opera houses, strictly speaking, are neither (and this one – after penny-pinching bureaucrats tampered with the plans, reducing the size of the stage and narrowing the orchestra pit to a trench – has trouble serving the purpose for which it was built). The Sydney Opera House exists to be ambiguous, to be looked at from very available angle, and to be quizzically represented or described by artists. It has the relativity of the true symbol, like porous, pliant Uluru. The metaphor-makers can reconstruct it, as Clive James surreally does by calling it a portable typewriter stuffed with oyster shells. Eric Thake domesticated the Opera House in 1973 on a linocut Christmas card which applied the profile of Utzon's sails to a tilting row of white cups, plates and saucers in the rack of a dishwasher. Thake's title was *An Opera House in Every Home*. That democratic promise extends to the wardrobe of every home as well as its kitchen: Dame Edna Everage sometimes wears the building on her head, or has its roof copied in rhinestones on her spectacles. Though Frank Cash and Eleanor Dark described the Harbour Bridge sacramentally, we are now too ironic to see the Opera House that way. It is an icon of popular culture, and happily blushes pink on posters for the Gay and Lesbian Mardi Gras. These humorous desecrations do not make it any less mythic: we have come to understand that myths are consciously contrived to serve a social need.

Robert Emerson Curtis sketched at the site for nine years, and called the album he published *A Vision Takes Form*. In his commentary he likened the Opera House to a prehistoric monster, an octopus, a butterfly and an Arab stallion; he drew the sails sublimating, rising in an imaginary gale to spread their gleaming wings over the city. Max Dupain also chronicled the building works, and in his essay on Mallard said he had tried to 'encompass the whole gigantic movement in cryptic pictures'. The building was already cryptic, since its form belies its function; Dupain set himself to encrypt it all over again. Rather than imagining it to be organic, like Curtis, he concentrated on details which, disjoined from the whole, are dazingly unfamiliar, almost extra-terrestrial. A close-up of the roof tiles makes them look like feathers. On another vault, he shows what lies beneath this white cladding: a machine-made infrastructure of concrete. Standing further back, one of the arched shells, with a ladder for the workers still clamped to it, could be a radio telescope scrutinizing the sky. Like the Harbour Bridge before it, the Opera House forcibly renovated artistic vision.

Moore took intrepid advantage of the same opportunity, hovering above the sails in a helicopter or exploring the cellarage. His Opera House looks most alluring when still unbuilt in 1962: he found a bare concrete amphitheatre under the podium, and in the cavity beneath the staircase photographed the patterns made by the sun as it pierced slats that had not yet been filled in. The play of light resembles musical notation, or the indentations on a piano roll; these are the abstract formulae that can be translated into sounds. Such photographs literally show the building's crypt, a hidden depth that disappeared as construction continued. A telephoto view taken from the Botanic Gardens in 1966 presses the Opera House up against the Harbour Bridge and makes the two merge, so that the three red cranes used for assembling the roof also seem to be working on the span of the bridge. The sails are ruled into squares by a grid of scaffolding. Is the bridge also simply a skeleton that will later grow flesh? As the photograph was taken, a train began to cross the bridge from Circular Quay; it looks as if it is about to speed through a tunnel inside one of Utzon's acoustic shells. The jumbled apparatus, like the city itself, is the Meccano set every boy, in the pre-electronic era, used to dream of owning. Moore's aerial view, also dating from 1966, allows us to take the Opera House to pieces and then put it back together again, which is how modern art has always dealt with the obtuse physical reality of our world. The sails are unclad, and expose a chequerboard later covered by the tiles: the peaks have to be read as structure, not ornament. The site looks like a constructivist toy. Here, laid out in order, are all the spare parts you need to make your own opera house, or to conduct what the physicist Eddington, explicating Einstein, called an exercise in 'world-building'. Before you can begin, some decrypting is necessary. The angle equalizes parked cars and crates of tiles; bafflingly, there is no evidence of human initiative, because at this height men disappear. But the temptation to metaphor is irresistible, and in looking at the image we make bridges between this unintelligible technical diagram and a nature it seems to deny: the clustered red cranes are praying mantises around a honeycomb. Even when the Opera House was complete, Moore enjoyed making it evanesce, blurring it into a soft white fog during the winter of 1973.

Throughout the process, Moore marvelled at the way the Opera House unfolded from a shaky scale model, which the engineers dared to make solid and workable. He used the incomplete building, its roof flayed and with cranes rearing above it, as a backdrop for the miniature model, admired by crowds of stick figures. But the Opera House

178
David Moore
*Opera House Under
Construction, Sydney* 1966
© Estate of David Moore

had been visited on a society not yet reconciled to the superb folly of art, and Moore, with his journalistic eye, also documented the political tribulations of the scheme. In 1962 he photographed a group of architects touring the site; they frown behind a fence of spiky rods that are meant to reinforce concrete. In 1966, after Utzon's departure, he photographed a board at the gate with a list of contractors' names. The panel crediting the architect had been removed, and the top honour went to the Ministry of Public Works. Moore seized the opportunity to photograph the minister whose interference forced Utzon to resign: grizzled, beefy, with his thick hands spread proprietorially on a plank as he stands with his back to the building, he is the very antithesis of an aesthete.

Hoppé thought that the bridge completed the view, and so it seemed until the Opera House arose on Bennelong Point in the early 1960s. Then the view had to be recomposed: the city and even the harbour are unfinished artworks. The revision continues, for good or ill: an apartment block locally likened to a toaster now looms on Circular Quay across from the coat-hanger. Meanwhile photographers struggle to enclose these disparate icons inside a single frame, or break the frame in order to release them into the open, airy space outside.

Inside Seidler's office on the north shore, Dupain found a way of encapsulating them. The harbour and its velvety night sky are an extension of the architect's transparent room, which is itself a display case for modernist virtues: taut, resilient Bauhaus

chairs, designed for modern bodies that spurn inertia, and a table-top ornament that denies its own solidity and seeks to take wing. Nature has come indoors, and thrives in controlled conditions rather than being left to its own unkempt devices. Hence the plant on one glass table and the bowl of yellow daisies on the other. Life inside a work of art requires rigorous discipline, which is why it is perhaps convenient that the human users of this room have gone home for the night. Dupain may have been able to move the furniture around, but he could not alter the disposition of the objects on the other side of the glass: the Harbour Bridge, the Opera House peeping out from behind a pylon on the far side of it, and the lighted towers of the Luna Park funfair at Milsons Point on the near side. Still it looks as if he had painted it all, like the artists in Russell Roberts's office touching up their photo-mural. The lines of perspective breach the glass barrier and meet at the exact centre of the bridge's span; because the glass wall serves as a mirror, the bridge with its radial sunrise of girders sends out another lunar flare, like a searchlight raking the sky. The line of lamps on the walkway of the bridge looked sullen and bleary when Dupain photographed them in the 1940s, like the backdrop for a crime scene in a film noir. Now, extending across the middle of the view, they constitute a galactic horizon, standing in for the rim of the world that you seem to see when you stand on the cliffs a few miles east and look at the ocean – which like the nocturnal sky is sapphire flecked with white foam. The incandescent turrets of Luna Park, cheekily poking through the floor and rhyming with the penile propeller of the glass ornament on the table, subliminally explain the meaning of the panorama. By day, you work. When night comes, electricity supplies a thousand alternatives to sleep. This is, to rewrite 'Banjo' Paterson, the vision splendid of the neon-lit city extended: Sydney's joyous answer to the bush.

Yet it is artificially lit and enclosed within glass, like a framed, glazed photograph hung on the wall. How likely is it that Seidler, who admired Utzon's architectural poem, would have paid a similar compliment to Luna Park? Between those towers is the face of a leering woman. You enter the amusement park through her crimson mouth with its portcullis of teeth. For all Dupain's efforts, there is an imbalance between the hushed purism of the room and the raucous excitements of the city outside.

John Gollings has attempted another rearrangement of the scene, a juggling act that looks at it by day from the other end of Dupain's axis: beneath the span of the bridge you can see the building that houses Seidler's office. The view, which Dupain controls and orders, here bursts free, in a jittery, ricocheting explosion that tries to catch the flickery, distracted motions of the eye and also the competitive, unsynchronized activities of the city. Everything is kinetic, despite photography's necessary stilling of life. Ferries plough the water, jumping to and fro because of the gaps in time and space between the separate images Gollings has glued together. Even the Opera House gets up from its pedestal and vaults through the air as if on a pogo stick. Those triple shells were designed to be dynamic, as they overlap and redirect themselves so that they can encompass the sights and sounds of the harbour; now the building triplicates itself, in a bounding arc that upstages the gentler and more continuous curve of the bridge. Sea and sky are happily confounded in a hurly-burly of elements. A man is fishing, but his catch could be floating in the air above him: a single dirigible, reproduced and redistributed by Gollings, becomes a school of tadpoles. Like the thrust of the roof beams in Seidler's office, a central trajectory impels us into the scene. But in Dupain's photo-

graph, that barrier of glass restricts us; the tapering rail that Gollings places in the centre offers no obstruction. It invites us to go for a promenade, and even provides seats on which we can sit to look at the harbour or to study Gollings's assemblage. David Hockney, explaining his own photocollages, said in 1987 that 'Modernist art hasn't triumphed yet', because 'we're still stuck with the Renaissance picture – which is the photograph'. Chinese scrolls liberated Hockney from the regimentation of Western space, and permitted him to construct composite images that conveyed what it feels like to walk across the Brooklyn Bridge or around the Grand Canyon or to drive along Mulholland Drive. Gollings's photograph laughs at the amateur artist kneeling to touch up his canvas: why should any rectangle presume to make sense of the exhilarating anarchy of the scene? Sydney, after all, is a city of licence, a playground for the eye and for all the other organs.

As *The Tree of Man* concludes, Amy's grandson prepares to write 'a poem of life, of all life', an epic that will find room for trains and false teeth and scraps of torn letters as well as apples, trees and the smell of bread. The first task of art was to aestheticize Australia – to make it look beautiful, even if that meant photographing it through a lens smeared with vaseline or covered by muslin. But art, growing less defensive, comes to question the snobbish strictures of beauty, and eventually is able to comprehend everything that the country contains: not only lyres and peacock feathers but advertising blimps, toasters, coat-hangers, roofs of corrugated iron and men with dirty hands.

8: Remaking the Map

In my youth, the great Australian rite of passage was a passage out of Australia. Cazneaux photographed the jubilant rupture in 1928, as another boatload of passionate pilgrims set off from Circular Quay to visit a foreign land they still self-deceivingly called 'home'. Passengers on overseas liners used to throw streamers down to the friends who gathered on the dock to wish them farewell. The paper tightened as the boat backed out, and tore to signal the instant when physical contact with the country and the people in it ended. The moment mimed a death, but these occasions were happy wakes. Weren't the dear departed going to a better place?

Like all the best photographs, this one seizes on a spontaneous configuration of lights and lines that somehow compress an emotion. All is whirling confusion, and thanks to the pall of black smoke above the white blizzard of paper you can almost hear the dolorous foggy sound ejected from the funnel as the ship edges out. Two years later,

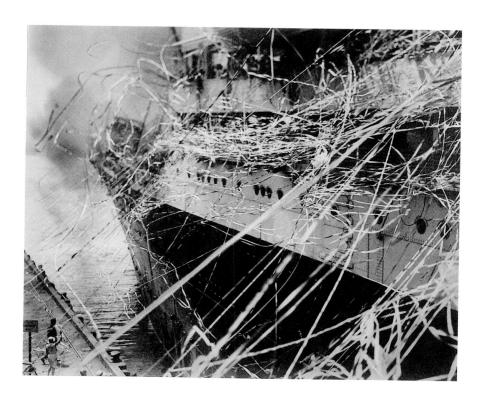

181
Harold Cazneaux
Departure 1928

Cazneaux described the motorized rhythms of the modern city as 'all messed up and doing jazz'. The same syncopated 'jazz of moving shapes' is visible here, despite the slow, stately departure. But from the randomness Cazneaux has salvaged formal control. A diagonal line slants across the image. It is the streamer that will break next; most of the others have already snapped, and are snarled in the giddy air. It leads from an upper deck to that corner of the pier where two figures left behind – the only people who can be identified in the blurred, hectic scene – stand staring at a future they will not experience. One of them, bravely making the best of it, manages to wave. I remember my mother crying as she said goodbye to me at the airport in Hobart, when I flew off to catch my own ship from Melbourne forty years after Cazneaux's photograph was taken. She knew it was a kind of burial ceremony, the interring of the child she once possessed. I did not feel ashamed at not sharing her emotion (or rather at feeling its exact opposite, as I waited for the engines to rev up and the propellers to whirr). When I returned a decade later and saw her at the same airport, she blinked before she recognized me. 'I wouldn't of known you,' she said as my father drove us back to what they insisted on calling my home. I was a revenant, an intruder from another world.

The tangle of paper in Cazneaux's image, if you sort it out, could be stretched out to map the shipping routes across the oceans. These were the lines I always followed when, as a boy, I opened the atlas to measure what seemed to be our geographical disconnection, our castaway status. The map showed Australia as a centrifuge. From its ports those dotted tracks set off to traverse endless blue expanses; you had to follow them over the page, or around the edge of the world, before you arrived at the destination you dreamed about. Nowadays, at long last, the country is centripetal: we seek the centre, rather than fleeing from it. The ritual trip, for young Australians, is to the interior, not overseas.

To depart, as I remember, was to rejoice. Homecoming, or your first arrival if you were what we used to call a 'new Australian', involved more dubious emotions. The widow David Moore photographed as she arrived in Sydney in 1966 mutely says it all. She is stranded between cultures. Her headscarf is left over from the Mediterranean village she has quit, but her handbag announces her preparedness for a new life in the suburbs. Still, she seems unable or unwilling to imagine her own reincarnation. Her face is weathered, incised with ancestral miseries. Her costume is funereal, as is her mood. With one gnarled hand she steadies herself on the railing; the other is planted more confrontationally on her hip as she squares up to the bright, brash city. She is too old to be assimilated, which is what Australia expected of newcomers in those days. Presumably her relatives sat her in a corner, let her lose herself in reverie, and waited for her to die.

At least Bill Florence, who could have been her contemporary even though he arrived in Australia so much earlier, was young enough to undergo this enforced adjustment. His assimilation is commemorated when Alexakis rephotographs an image made in 1922. Bill used to be called Vasilis Florias, when he lived in the depopulated village of Platrithia in a house eventually occupied by stray goats; Australia has approximately translated his name, offering him an Anglo-Saxon identity. Aged fourteen, he has got himself dressed up for entry into a new life, which officially began in the Melbourne studio of the original photographer, S. Raftopoulos. Cranstone's *Design for War* includes an image marked with the hand-lettered legend 'ALIENS'. It shows a group of

182
David Moore
Southern European Migrant
Arriving in Sydney 1966
© Estate of David Moore

183
Effy Alexakis
Bill Florence (Vasilis Florias)
Being Welcomed to Australia
(Melbourne 1922)
from the series *Mavri Xenitia*
[*Black Foreign Land*] 1991
part of *Greek-Australians: In Their*
Own Image Project 1982–
[copy of a 1922 studio portrait
by S. Raftopoulos, Melbourne]

184
John Williams
Greek Wedding Reception,
Newtown 1971

185
Narelle Perroux
Australian Rules Football at
the Sports Weekend 1989

southern European migrants at meal time at a workers' camp in the outback. The grins on their faces announce that they have successfully learned how to be Australian by drinking milky tea and eating buttered bread. Bill's initiation requires him to step into a cut-out map of the continent. The Australia that welcomes him is an empty space, its arid centre occupied – in a spot of creative map-making – by a chimerical painted ocean; the welcoming committee consists of a kangaroo and a kookaburra, and although the steamer at the bottom aims its prow directly up Bourke Street towards the pompous headquarters of state power, Bill's new home could just as well be that bush hut erected somewhere off the coast of Queensland. The country's name is not written on the photograph's placard, which means that Bill is welcomed by a blank. He grips the Great Australian Bight at either end, to fix and fasten this vacancy that he, in his small way, has come to people.

As so often, photography conducts people through the stages of life, and here it marks a second baptism. Bill is framed by his adopted country, and the image entitles him to citizenship. But photographs are as mortal as their subjects, and in the seventy years that intervened before Alexakis assembled her series of *Greek-Australians: In Their Own Image*, the original had been blotched and scarred. A fissure travels like lightning from Cape York across the Northern Territory, slices Bill's ear and continues on to his chest. It is a sad epilogue to this new beginning. Could it have been made by an angry, ungrateful heir, or by a stranger indifferently disposing of Raftopoulos's archive? Families, like all communities, are held together by acts of affection, which include the circulation of photographs. In retrospect we are reminded how difficult it was, and still is, to fill the hungry outline of Australia with love. Easier, perhaps, to imagine the space occupied by an inland sea.

John Williams caught up with an assimilated clan at a Greek wedding reception in the Sydney suburb of Newtown. The guests wilt with tedium on their uncomfortable chairs, while litter accumulates on the bare floorboards. This banquet predates multiculturalism: the tables are laden with Australian beer, American soft drinks and sausage rolls, without a culinary trace of Greece. Williams, disgusted by scenes like this, unassimilated himself and became 'a man without a country – an anti-nationalist'. This is a convenient identity for a photographer, perpetually ready to jump on or off a plane, professionally detached because he sees himself as a camera, cold-eyed and neutral. But your native character clings, and even when explaining his rootlessness and his sense of being an internal exile, Williams relies on an aboriginal image. He says he is 'a neurotic unreconstructed hunter-gatherer' whose quest is for images, not food.

Williams first fled overseas with his camera in 1965, three years before me. Now, looking around a country that no one could possibly want to leave, I wonder what we were running away from. There are photographs to remind me. I can sympathize with Narelle Perroux's bored Aboriginal spectators at the football match. That is how I remember the Australia of my restive childhood and adolescence: an empty space that we encircled. Sometimes deputations were sent out to occupy the void, to inscribe ideograms on it. On St Patrick's Day 1937, Sam Hood photographed thousands of pious children arrayed on the Sydney Showground, where they form themselves into a rosary, a crucifix, a shamrock, and spell out 'WE CHERISH THE ROSARY' with their aligned bodies. That is one way of colonizing a continent. More often, as I remember, the thousands stayed in the grandstand and watched as the distant figures in shorts merged in a flailing-limbed composite known as a pack, fighting for possession of a ball. In the

absence of other values or allegiances, the side for which you cheered defined you. 'What team do you barrack for?' I used to be asked by my uncles, who met on Sunday mornings to drink their way through a replay of Saturday afternoon's football game. When I shrugged, they looked shocked. 'A bloke's got to have a team,' they said. I soon learned to pretend that I belonged to one.

Attendance at the sports weekend is an indoctrination for Perroux's subjects, who must learn what it means to play by Australian rules. An oval is scratched in the dirt. The lucky few are inside it; everyone else clusters admiringly around the rim. A kind of community is being convened here, as it was at the gymkhanas and cricket or football matches to which I was dragged, though all I can see is the arbitrary placement of the goal-posts, set down illogically in that level waste, and their needless height, a reminder of the trees they once were. The players, so far away, seem likely to disappear into the scrub on the horizon. Nearer to the camera, the ground clots into stony rubble. All concerned are imagining a green field, but their combined wishing does not quite manage to transform the desert.

Though the Sydney Cricket Ground provides a pampered lawn for its teams, David Moore's photograph is essentially the same as that taken by Perroux: here is another distended vacant space, with a crowd gathered expectantly around it. The scene could be taking place on the beach in the poem by T. S. Eliot, where the last men stand together and avoid speech. An artificial hill has been added to the landscape for the benefit of the spectators, who – unlike Perroux's Aboriginal crowd – bring their sub-urban comforts with them, lying on rugs beside their supplies of drink. The horizon, too, is less dismal than in the outback, where it surely discloses, if you ever reach it, another instalment of weary infinitude. The pavilions erect a skyline of minarets, and every pinnacle flies a flag: the sky, vaguely prodded by Perroux's goalposts, has to be annexed. But the game itself is, once more, a flea circus. The men in white dwindle to insects in that yawning emptiness.

Philip Quirk's image of the headmistress, with her pompous rump and her buttressed chest, brings other miseries back to me, and the white knee-socks of her colleague with the loudhailer still induce a chill of alarm. At school, I remember classes being assembled in straight lines in the playground, and barked orders telling us to stand to attention. On Wednesday afternoons we had sports, which consisted of running around in circles. The chairs in Quirk's photograph, stacked on a scruffy athletic field, sum up the inequity of it. The troops who are being harangued through the megaphone are expected to hurl themselves into motion. Their overseers, meanwhile, will make themselves comfortable and smile as their underlings roll in the dirt. I find myself irrationally enraged by the headmistress's sunglasses: a privilege that goes with her position, hinting at lofty inscrutability. The pair of displaced balls behind these bossy female warders, not yet kicked into the fray, explain my alarm. Here are the emasculators, megaphonically telling you how inadequate you are.

187
Philip Quirk
Headmistress, Sports Day
1975

At least David Moore's traffic cop is merely depressing, and does not incite the same terror and anger as Quirk's figures. Positioned on a rise where six streets converge, he guards the gateway to Kings Cross, which Christopher Koch – recalling his days there as a refugee from Tasmania – describes in his novel *The Doubleman* as 'a southern hemisphere Montmartre'. I remember hopefully climbing that hill on early visits to Sydney, wondering whether any of the women walking in the street might be streetwalkers. On the summit, I knew, were all the vices not available in Hobart. I managed to overlook the fact that William Street itself was a dreary succession of car showrooms, and once I had reached the Cross I thrilled to the jangling music, the eye-popping lights, the smell of rancid frying oil, and the importuning of the sallow-faced youths, not much older than I was, who tried to lure customers downstairs into their girlie shows. A city, for me, had to be an erotic lair, a place of dreadful, delectable night. All this the policeman denies by raising his hand. His silhouette has been sharpened and darkened by Moore, which makes him look like a superimposition; indeed he is exactly that, inkily imprinted on the city. He prohibits motion, and once the urban jostling and fretting and itching – the city's jazz, as Cazneaux called it – has been stalled by the photograph, you suddenly notice how charmless the scene is, without the blowsy mystery of darkness and glowing neon. The view looks towards the west, but there is no shining horizon, only a lowbrow sky blurred by smog, webbed by tramlines, annexed by corporate logos, and further flattened by the terraced verandahs of shops. I define a city as a place where everything is possible. Moore's policeman has narrower notions about what is permitted.

Authority is impersonal, so – like the long-suffering group at the sports weekend and the slumped, broiling spectators at the Sydney Cricket Ground – he is seen from behind. Bodies without faces form a phalanx, flabby but impregnable. Perhaps we should be grateful that all these figures are looking in the opposite direction. What if they turned round, saw you spying on them, and denounced you? This happens in the photograph taken by Roger Scott at an election rally in 1975. Malcolm Fraser was addressing a meeting at the Randwick race course in Sydney – or rather he was being

188
David Moore
William Street Looking West,
Sydney 1961
© Estate of David Moore

189
Roger Scott
*Prime Minister Malcolm
Fraser, Randwick Race Course*
1975

addressed by his baying supporters, who waved placards that alliteratively ordered 'guilty' Gough Whitlam to go and warned Australia to secure itself against communist subversion. With no horses in evidence, Randwick is the forum for a rampant mass society that will trample opposition. Les Murray has described the roar of the crowd at a Melbourne football final, heard from a park a mile away; he happily surrendered to the tidal emotion, as Australia itself yelled and bellowed. To me, a noise like that sounds feral, ferocious. It announces that they have formed a hallooing posse, and are coming to get you. Scott, radicalized by the protest movement against the Vietnam war, has sneaked onto the podium behind Fraser. The crowd agitates its placards and chants its slogans, not knowing who he is. Even the civic worthies on the podium go on inanely applauding, unaware of the invasion. But Fraser, with the politician's inborn paranoia, has eyes in the back of his head. He wheels round and extends an accusing finger, like Lord Kitchener on the recruiting poster. Your country needs you, and if you decline to answer its call or presume to question its reasons, you declare yourself unfit to live in it. The inequality is terrifying: one man stands up to several thousand others who disagree with him. At such moments photographers derive courage from their cameras, which are buffers and also retaliatory weapons. Scott pressed the shutter before he was ejected. Power, in Fraser's petulant outrage, exposes its impotence, and the dissenter wins his argument with the like-minded majority.

The individual took a long while to emerge in Australia. Solidarity, as in Sweet's line-up of unionized shearers, overruled the loneliness of a singular existence. In my box of photographs, along with the expected weddings and christenings, there are recurrent scenes at football matches and in saloon bars. The pack and the five-o'clock swill were both initiations into the communal life of Australia: immersions in mud or in booze.

The first photographers treated individuals as items in a set, a series. The society distributed across the continent was small enough for them to conceive of photographing all its members, one by one if not all at once. A photograph is a likeness, but not one of us thinks that we look like our portraits. Photography is better at showing how we resemble one another: a family album is a genetic map. George Baron Goodman, licensed to take daguerreotypes, moved to Hobart from Sydney in 1843. A newspaper in Launceston hoped that 'when he has taken all the people of Hobart Town', he would come north to complete the census. During the 1860s William Davies assembled several thousand people on a five-tiered grandstand at a racetrack, with a supernumerary crowd – better behaved than Scott's obstreperous mob at Randwick – filling the paddock. His carte-de-visite strains to find room for everyone in Melbourne, or at least everyone who could afford to attend the races. The ambition persists in Murray Bail's *Contemporary Portraits*, in which a fictitious photographer called Douglas Huebler sets out to document the existence of everyone in the world. Bail wishes him luck, though his story jokes about the superficiality of the medium. Huebler wants to start by photographing a person incapable of sin, a person who may outlive art, a person whose existence is normally uneventful, and so on until his survey is complete. Such internal histories can only be narrated, not photographed. The analysis of character, Bail implies, is best left to novelists.

Yet Australian novelists were at first reluctant to deal with differentiation and idiosyncracy. Introducing the bush-folk in *We of the Never-Never*, Jeannie Gunn makes an effort to separate them from the landscape, placing them 'distinct in the foreground'. But how distinct are they, since they are given composite, complementary identities? Mrs Gunn lists them as The Boss and The Little Missus, The Head Stockman and The Quiet Stockman, with a few black 'boys' and 'lubras' and a dog or two. Only the Chinese cook is allowed to be unique, for racial reasons: 'Cheon was Cheon, and only Cheon; and there is no word in the English language to define Cheon…simply because there was never another Cheon'. In fact there were many millions, who would all – if Mrs Gunn had seen them – have looked the same to her. Lindt arranged his photographs of bush workers into a taxonomy of *Australian Types*, and Cranstone's albums include a photograph of two workers on a building site in the Torres Strait, which he labelled *Northern Types*. The types are bluff, grinning and grimy. One of them wears his shorts gaping open at the waist, the other has a swelling belly. A photograph Cranstone entitled *Making of an Anzac* displays a more idealized type. A man in a greasy bush hat outside a hut with a corrugated-iron roof pours himself a glass of milk. Anzacs can be manufactured, apparently, with extra doses of calcium.

Even in cities, unrepentant individualists were once so rare that they acquired a mythical aura. Sydney had Arthur Stace, a born-again alcoholic who chalked the word Eternity on its streets and walls fifty times a day for thirty years, and a vociferous, versifying bag lady called Bea Miles, who used to declaim Shakespeare on the steps of the Mitchell Library and commandeered taxis for expeditions to gather wild flowers.

The cleaners and the cabbies indulged them, recognizing – perhaps with a holy dread – their privileged status. The authorities treated W. J. Chidley, a harmless follower of Havelock Ellis, less kindly. Mallard photographed him in 1911, campaigning for sexual hygiene and a simpler life. He sports his usual filmy Grecian frock of tussore silk and carries a bag emblazoned with his usual motto, 'THE ANSWER'. He is not wearing a hat, which in the Australia of those days marked a man as a social outcast. But the Gladstone bag makes a compensating allusion to Victorian values: my father carried his lunch to work in one of these, and prepared me for adulthood by giving one to me when I went to high school. The clerks on George Street, slouching against lamp posts or shop windows in their drab, stuffy three-piece suits, would have been more comfortable if they had followed Chidley's suggestions for dress reform. Australians dream, as Les Murray says, 'of wearing shorts forever', and a less filmy version of Chidley's tunic is now – coloured khaki and trademarked Yakka or King Gee – the national costume. Even cashiers in banks wear shorts to work in the summer. Doing housework in a swimsuit or wearing pyjamas all day is, as Murray says, 'real negligée', a blissful reprieve from ambition and its pressures. It recognizes that happiness cannot be pursued; you just loosen your clothes and relax into it. But Chidley was arrested and charged with offensive behaviour for buttonholing passers-by. In despair, he poured kerosene over himself and ignited it; he died in an asylum in 1916.

Jack Cato, having returned to Hobart and opened a portrait studio, remained uncertain about the propriety of photographing individuals unless their social status or occupation made them notable. Lindt's bushmen could be presented as representative types, but Cato worried about the crankily or crazily self-sufficient characters who loitered on Hobart's streets or did odd jobs on its waterfront: Bill the bent man, Cackles the dwarf, Loony Fred, or Silly Snorky. In 1924 he exhibited a round-up of 'all the old

newsboys, billposters, pedlars, old fishermen, cranks, morons and identities that everyone knew'. Since his previous show had been home portraits of society women, he
worried about the acceptability of these indigents, and did his best to soften the affront:
the shadow of Snorky's sou'wester obscures his silly face. To Cato's relief, his bourgeois
customers found the eccentrics 'picturesque', because they were 'capable of being made
into salon pictures'. When illustrating his autobiography, Cato placed Snorky immediately after a group of scenes from ballet and opera, which include the baritone John
Brownlee as the captive Ethiopian king in *Aida*, dressed in pelts, with a necklace of teeth.
Snorky, a professional character, keeps company with the fancier performers, especially
the one who impersonates a savage.

   Traditional typecasting produced restrictive definitions of the sexes, each in its allot-
ted sphere. With the cruel, disengaged eye of the expatriate, the novelist Colin MacInnes in
1965 assigned Australian women to 'two types – either a rather stringy, small-breasted, leggy
girl with a sun-baked complexion, or else one with a large-hipped figure and an easy grace
of posture'. It is a summary judgment, an execution. Still there are no faces, only breasts, legs
and fructifying hips. The other sex, represented by lifeguards, swaggered along the beach in
what Dupain called a 'parade of masculinity'. He photographed the hormonal drills of the
lifesavers at Manly, awarded its name because an early colonist admired the manliness of the
Aboriginal people who lived there. Masculinity also makes its headquarters in the corrugated bog photographed by Ricky Maynard for his essay on *The Moonbird People*, the Tasmanian
Aboriginal people who catch, clean, salt and pack muttonbirds on the wind-lashed, depopulated islands in Bass Strait. Here maleness has its secure, minimal, windowless enclosure.
Positioned at the edge of the land, it marks a border: immediately behind it, wildness – in
the form of the agitated water – resumes. Yet for all its starkness, it has a certain delicacy.
The privy, which seats just one person, at least recognizes the need for privacy.

On the frontier and in the suburbs, Australia disposed of individuals by relegating them to clans. When Stan meets Amy in *The Tree of Man*, he asks 'You one of those Fibbens from Kelly's Corner?' Eager to fit in, she says she is, even though she is not. A touching, homely poem by Les Murray describes two taciturn men erecting telegraph poles. The first man introduces himself by saying 'I'm one of the Mitchells', while the other says exactly the same. My own relatives customarily referred to themselves as one of the Conrads or (on my mother's side) the Smiths, while inconclusively wondering who on earth I 'took after'. Over their sandwiches, Murray's men enjoy an Australian epiphany. He admiringly comments that 'Nearly everything/ they say is ritual'. Like communicants in church, they mutter formulaic responses. All very well, but what if you want to say something that no one has said before? In my extended family, anything described as 'different' – a new kind of food, or a new Australian – was suspect. Himmelfarb in Patrick White's *Riders in the Chariot* invites martyrdom by proudly declaring that 'In the factory where I work I am considered the most different of all human beings'. Such resistance is punishable by death, since 'normality alone was recognized in Paradise East'. Blue, the thug who leads the lynch mob that hunts down Himmelfarb, could be any of the faceless bodies photographed by Moore at the Sydney Cricket Ground or Dupain at Bondi: he is 'primarily a torso'.

From *Voss* to *The Vivisector*, Patrick White's recurring subject is the torso's acquisition of a querulous mind and a freakish imagination, which together disrupt the social norm. Not long before his death, he persuaded William Yang to collaborate in a photographic imposture that acted out the final stage in the evolution of Australian individuality. For the frontispiece of White's last novel, Yang made a flamboyantly rouged and powdered tranvestite portrait of him. The book, *Memoirs of Many in One*, was supposedly

192
Ricky Maynard
Men's Toilet from the series
The Moonbird People 1985

193
David Moore
Lifesavers at Manly
1959
© Estate of David Moore

written by the polymorphous Alex Xenophon Demirjian Gray, a courtesan and erst-while nun whose serial incarnations extend from Smyrna to the Australian outback, where – like the drag queens in *Priscilla, Queen of the Desert* – she leads a theatrical tour through Philistia, performing *Antony and Cleopatra* in towns such as Lone Coolabah, Peewee Plains, Kanga Kanga and Aberpissup. The doomed sortie of Voss is replaced by Alex's assault on the 'mediocrity of the Australian bush' with its 'dust and trees, trees and dust, or simply dust'. White pretended merely to have edited his friend Alex's memoirs; to Yang he admitted 'She is me'. At least she was one of his many selves. Having arrived at the idea of individuality, we need to progress beyond it, as White did in creating his androgynous sibyl.

Photographs like Yang's had begun to explore what David Moore calls 'the theatre of the self'. The phrase marks an exhilarating liberation: men are permitted to play, not just to work or to fight, and the playing need not be confined to the sports field. Women too now delight in flouting the approved types and demonstrating their multiplicity. Hence Sue Ford's periodic self-portraits, which show how all of us metamorphose as we advance through time, or Tracey Moffatt's repertory of roles (including a photographer with half a dozen cameras slung round her neck, apparently stalking big game in the bush), or Polexini Papapetrou's studies of her daughter Olympia, dressed up as a Chinese princess or Supergirl or any other optional, variable fantasy. God is not one, despite the admonition of Eric Thake's guru, and no human being is merely singular.

At the same time, making images of a new Australia, photographers looked again at our archetypal pin-ups. Surfers in the age of Aquarius scoffed at the goose-stepping antics of those who professed to guard them. In 1968 Jeff Carter, in his book about the beaches of the east coast, ridiculed the formulae of the belt-and-reel method of rescue, with its 'marching and military-style drilling' and 'standing rigidly in line from the largest to the smallest'. His attack on 'strict formation' could be applied to Quirk's headmistress and Moore's traffic cop. For Carter, the surf, like the outback, is a paradise for loners. 'For everyone,' he comments in the text that accompanies his photo-graphs, 'surfing is a gateway to his own little promised land'. The surfies Carter quotes speak of 'going to church among the waves', and also of 'a new art form'. Their artistry, sculpting the water, licenses both their individualism and their exhibitionistic virtuosity. Already in 1959, Moore had studied the lifesavers at Manly with probing irony. In their chaste costumes, they are giving a balletic performance, but do they dare to admit it? The man on the left grimaces as he grips the leg of his shamming mate, conscientiously pretending that this is a genuine rescue. His colleagues seem less convinced: the next in line is frankly puzzled, and the man on the right does not bother to act, letting the rope droop in his hand while he glances down at the earnest, elaborate posture of the supposed victim. Masculinity is itself a charade, and cannot help betraying its own anxious theatricality. The slumped man the others are carrying has been choreographically trained to impersonate a dying swan (a female role).

Moore caught the covert sexual display and shamed self-disbelief in the scene; Martyn Jolly flexes and twists the image of such occasions by rephotographing the work of his predecessors. For his 1993 series *Wonderful Pictures in Colour*, he laid their books 'open on a table, allowing the pages to curve upwards (very erotic)', then photographed obliquely across the pages and manipulated his view camera to achieve what he calls an 'anamorphic, fishtailed spatiality'. Can lifesavers, who pride themselves on being amphibious, object to being given fishtails as if they were mermaids? Jolly's blurred, grainy, elongated teams form a colonnade, but the twin columns are purely decorative, and the diagonal stripes on their costumes turn their bodies into specimens of Op Art. Telescoped by the lens, the water piles up behind them into a solid wall; a surfer hovers halfway up it, not needing their ministrations.

194
Martyn Jolly
Lifesavers from the series
Wonderful Pictures in Colour
1993

To tamper with icons as Jolly does is to question the values they uphold. He has played the same distorting tricks on the frieze of wounded soldiers around the Anzac memorial in Canberra, and on the predatory aluminium eagle – a bizarre acknowledgment of American support in the war against Japan – that glares down from its perch on a column outside the Defence Department. Craig Holmes's subaqueous volleyball player, from an advertising campaign for Speedo entitled *Underwater Achievers*, goes even further in disarming the official image. The strong rule the beach and may possibly inherit the earth, but their effectiveness is lamed and hampered once they are immersed in water. The player strains to lob the ball over a drowned net, and in doing so releases an octopus of desperate bubbles from his mouth. All the same, projectiles – and this rule applies alike to torpedoes and to Ian Thorpe – travel more slowly through water than they do through air. The Speedo logo is an arrow, yet that volatile point is blunted once it gets wet. Advertising sells products by manufacturing myths about them. The devious technique can be put to work on anything that is saleable: a brand of sportswear, or a country that wants to present itself as a tourist destination. The cleverest advertising photographers find ways to subvert the commercial pretext, like Holmes disempowering his athlete or Gollings sending the Marlboro Man to traipse through an unaccustomed wasteland of ice.

Such iconographic games testify to the way Australian life has changed – psychologically, morally and even spiritually – during recent decades. Malouf described the process in 1978, while purporting to write Ovid's *Imaginary Life*. Ovid, the poet of

195
Craig Holmes
Volleyball from the Speedo
Underwater Achievers
Campaign 1993

metamorphosis, understood the pain of the transformation that changes creatures from beast to man or from man to god. As he civilizes the wild child he adopts on the frontier, he too practises that art of metamorphosis, and in doing so he begins to transform nature into culture. Here by the Black Sea, everything is utilitarian, like Australia before Le Guay, Talbot and Shmith despatched mannequins to preen in the desert or the drab, gravelly city. 'The women wear no ornaments,' Ovid notes. In a subsistence economy, only the flowers he cultivates in pots are pointless and frivolous, like Olive Cotton's corps de ballet of teacups. Under his tutelage, the boy learns to pile up blocks. This summarizes the building of cities, and advances through the earliest and tardiest stages of evolution.

Remembering Rome, Ovid boasts that he personally 'created an age': the sybaritic time of Augustus. Yang simultaneously documented the creation of an age in his *Sydney Diary*, photographed between 1974 and 1984. A double page devoted to 'The Triumph of the Flesh' includes Stelarc's suspension from a tree outside Canberra, though priority goes to an Oxford Street leatherman, an urban Aboriginal whose chest is a jungle of green and red tattoos, with his nipples as the protruding pistils of flowers. Yang's Sydneysiders slither between cultures and genders like Ovid's experimental beings. David Gulpilil is here, grinning ferociously, and so is Joan Sutherland, resembling an over-bedizened female impersonator in a winged gown as she sings *La Traviata* outdoors in Hyde Park. For Malouf's Scythians, 'it is a new concept, play....Free is not a word that exists, I think, in their language'. Ovid shows them that 'we are free to transcend ourselves. If we have the imagination for it'. Twenty years after publishing *An Imaginary Life*, Malouf delivered the Boyer lectures, in which he discussed 'the making of Australian consciousness'. He called his series *A Spirit of Play*: that spirit – once as alien in Australia as in Ovid's Scythia, unless it could be organized into team games or drinking bouts – now pervaded society, gurgling through the open mouth of the hostess at the entrance to Luna Park along with gales of canned laughter, or erupting onto carnivalesque Oxford Street during the Mardi Gras parade.

The spirit of play impels Roger Scott's women at Luna Park, who happily poke their heads through holes and agree to wear whatever body has been scribbled onto the wall. One of them turns out to be a buxom nude, while her friend is cross-dressed in a gaudy tuxedo. The design crudely rearranges Circular Quay, placing the span of the Harbour Bridge on top of the Cahill Expressway. The topographical liberty discloses a new use for the versatile bridge. Here it is a route to the third dimension, and its stiff girders make way for these clowning faces which thrust through all obstructions. In his *Sydney Diary*, Yang confides that Luna Park was an 'obsession' he shared with the artist Martin Sharp, who salvaged some tacky artefacts when the park was closed down in 1979. The memorabilia he hauled home included the panel beside the one punctured by the grinning women. Its edge is visible in Scott's photograph; it shows Batman and Robin doing some caped crusading on the choppy harbour, in a shark-finned boat with 'LUNA PARK' on its prow. In Yang's photograph, Sharp and another enthusiast donate their heads to the figures. What Sharp called his Dreamuseum is a camp reliquary, but Scott's disillusioned angle shows up the tawdriness of the setting – the gap behind the painted boards or under the counter, and that forgotten, useless curtain rod – and attributes the high spirits of the women to the line-up of bottles that their painted hands are grabbing. Alcohol is still the most reliable means of self-transcendence.

196
Roger Scott
Luna Park, Sydney
1972

Ian Lever's men, warming up for Mardi Gras, transcend themselves by dancing, which releases the limbs from control by the head and allows them to behave ecstatically. A happy photographic accident has grafted an excited penis onto the tallest figure, who uses the lower leg of a female passer-by as a prosthesis. This organ graft bridges a gap between two different worlds. In the background, the people in clothes go about their business, bound in one disciplined direction. In front, the revellers, who have seceded from society for at least one night, wheel in giddy circles. They belong to a metropolitan tribe, whose identity is cemented by masks, make-up and play-acting. Is the world maintained by work, or does it need to be kept in motion by ritual and even riot, which – like the sacrifices of the Aztecs – ensure that the sun goes on shining? Dance is a profane pleasure but also a sacred compulsion. The tribesmen are braver than Scott's women. Rather than attaching their heads to pre-painted bodies, they prepare for the ceremony by stripping off and daubing themselves with unbelligerent warpaint. Although one of them is Asian, their skeletal markings evoke the alarm caused by the appearance of the sailors on the First Fleet: the Aboriginal people thought these white men must be ghosts. Here the ghouls or disco dervishes are resolutely earthy, and their cavorting is desire's protest against the killjoy idea of death. But the tall man prevaricates between the two worlds. From the waist down, he is a satyr. From the neck up, he looks more like an intellectual: the paint stops where his collar ought to be, and – since he has no pockets – he has kept his glasses on. A keen, amused mind supervises the torso's enjoyments. It is like making love while watching yourself do so in a mirror.

Such revelry leaves a mess behind it. John Williams photographed the aftermath of the Rocks Festival in 1972, with drunkards staggering through a dry surf of litter, and Yang's *Sydney Diary* includes glimpses of bedraggled Sunday mornings in grungy flats, with empty bottles and boxes of dildoes strewn on the floor. In 1978, while working as a labourer at Luna Park, where he helped to refurbish the wooden carousel, Max Pam registered his own verdict on Australia's unbridled hedonism. During his lunch break, he looked up as a cold front swept in, and was reminded of 'the sky over Ginza the last time Godzilla ravaged Tokyo'. The clouds were curdled, and the towers above the gate poked them like hypodermic syringes. With her electrified hair, the welcoming woman whose face is just outside the frame might have been screaming. With a certain apocalyptic glee, Pam added an epilogue to his photograph. Later that year 'there was a fire in the tunnel of love, and ten children perished in the blaze'. Luna Park closed down, which is how Sharp managed to get hold of those curios. Actually it was the ghost train not the tunnel of love that caught fire, and there were seven deaths not ten. 'The towers,' according to Pam's footnote, 'no longer exist.' Since then, they have been restored; defying retributive portents, the party continues. Carnival is supposedly a farewell to flesh. In the religious calendar, Mardi Gras is a last chance to gormandize before the abstinent regime of Lent begins. If we are now all pagans, can the indulgence be extended indefinitely?

The Mardi Gras Parade in 2002 was a march-past of icons, scurrilously and hilariously reinterpreted. The cathedral photographed by Bayliss during construction, now rechristened St Muscle Mary's, trundled up Oxford Street on the back of a truck. Female cardinals fished in their handbags and lavished condoms on the crowd, and male Spice Girls officiated at the altar as priestesses. The jiving shrine was followed by a sequinned Harbour Bridge, held aloft by some gentle ruffians in leather. Its girders were coloured streamers, and a flotilla of balloons bobbed above the span: the bearers had adopted it as the symbol of their charity, which looks after people who suffer from dementia caused by HIV. The Opera House, incarnated by three drag queens with billowing tulle skirts and golden satin sails, brought up the rear. A group of lesbian mothers took their theme from The Wizard of Oz, and brandished a placard announcing 'There's No Place Like Home'. Though this is the title Paula Dawson used for her holo-gram, the Sydney women had something less suburban in mind. Home is no longer the place I remember, a weatherboard box containing a conventional and supposedly happy family. The country has experienced a rebirth or perhaps – if we risk using the capital letter – a Renaissance, and we are all new Australians now.

At the end of my excursion, I find myself staring at some images that signal Australia: the flag, the name, the map. They are what the linguists call floating signifiers, buoyant and breezy, amiably content to mean whatever you please. The young Bruce Chatwin 'never heard the word "Australia" without calling to mind the fumes of the eucalyptus inhaler and an incessant red country'. Neither notion has much to do with Australia. The inhaler announces that pinched English ailment, sinusitis; sheep, a plague introduced by the Eng-lish, need to graze, so the land where they congregate is green, not red. Such reveries are easy enough. Instead I want to anchor the signifier, and coax it to reveal something about the place it refers to. The debate goes on about what kind of country its citizens want it to be. How does the visual evidence help to understand the country now, or to guess at its future?

My gaze is directed, to begin with, in two directions at once: up into the night sky, down into the nether region between a woman's legs. On Australia Day 1983 David Cronin photographed a contestant in a beauty contest, swaying on high heels at Rymill Park in Adelaide. At least, he photographed some of her: here is another cropped, trun-cated Australian, a counterpart to Dupain's faceless sunbaker. She is patriotically attired, with the national flag and the Southern Cross emblazoned across the bottom half of her bikini. Yang photographed a warehouse party in 1981 at which one of the sweaty male dancers, seen of course from behind, wears nothing but a pair of boxer shorts with an outline map of Australia on them. Either he has the shorts on inside out, or the map has been printed back to front – arsy-versy, you might say. Is Australia, which began as Britain's cloaca, now the pudenda of the envious earth? I remember my chauvinistic delight when I heard one of the scrawny Manchester lads in the television series *Queer as Folk* wonder why a recent handsome pick-up had bothered to spend the night with him. 'I can't be the best shag he's ever had,' mused Vince. 'After all, he's Australian!' A friend in the bar flapped an appreciate wrist: 'Ooh, Australia, nice.... Down under, didgeridoos – all sorts of possibilities.' The country gave birth to us, so it is both pleasant and apt

199
David Cronin
Australia Day,
Rymill Park, Adelaide
1983

to think of Australia as an erogenous zone. All the same, the beauty contest in the park raises the question of what Australia Day actually commemorates. There must be more to the country than beach barbecues and nubile flesh. Cronin notices the makeshift instability of the scene and its discomforts: the shaky platform on its spindly metal legs, the ragged tent that serves as a changing room, the cluster of spectators squinting into the glare of an overexposed sky, the amplifiers dispensing a battery of upbeat noise, and the knees of the woman that bulge under the strain of her upper body. The stars that make up the Southern Cross hang in a void. Beneath the tight triangle of fabric on the woman's groin there is also emptiness.

Later the same year, David Broker photographed another festivity in Adelaide: a parade of monsters, rather than the exemplary male or female types who swagger or wiggle through Dupain's beach carnivals or Cronin's pageant. The image is enigmatic in a way that only photographs can be, because it selects a specimen of reality and shows it to be surreal. It is possible to demystify the scene. The occasion was a children's party, which took its theme from the nursery rhyme 'Come out, come out, wherever you are'. The cuddly mutants who accepted the invitation wore floral masks or costumes made from garbage bags, cardboard boxes and ice-cream cartons; one of them borrowed the face of a koala. Framed in the curtained windows of the bus as if on a stage or a screen, they might be Priscilla's passengers or Alex Gray's thespian troupe. Childhood is the time of uninhibited imaginative play. Twenty years later, the children in the photograph have probably turned into bureaucrats and home-makers, husbands and wives. What especially intrigues me is the sign on the side of the bus, which acts as a teasing footnote

to the faces at the windows. The image and the word are forced into an equation: this is Australia, or at least (as the rest of the sign has been left out, and the connective preposition is snapped in half by the frame) one particular, peculiar aspect of it. In the 1950s we were often lectured about activities that were 'unAustralian'. The country had a rigid notion of itself, and you counted as a renegade if you queried its dogmas and were miserable when made to attend wood-chopping contests. But these monsters also belong in Australia; a monster, after all, is merely a creature difficult to categorize, a self-generated being or possibly a genius, not something for a grown-up to be frightened of.

Beneath the proud word naming the country, the rim of the tyre doubles as a glimpse of the globe seen from far above. Australia is one extremity on a planet that revolves through space, like the wheel of the bus. A searing sun flashes from the window and simmers on the metal, which is held together by the rivets. You can even pick out the bolts that fasten the metal plates in the middle of the word Australia. Is this the country: a precarious construction of sheeted tin that carries a precious human cargo? The sun pummels its sides, but the people on board this small ark have learned how to survive. They go native, camouflaging themselves as local fauna.

To paint a sign in Australia, whether it says Australia or not, is a challenge to nature. The sun will soon cause the paint to peel, which has blotchily happened in Stephen Roach's photograph. But even in decaying, the word unravels extra meanings. There are layered signs here, one on top of the other, like the strata of Australia's buried history. The subject is a mailbox at Taylor Square in Sydney, with a schedule of clearance times advertised by Australia Post: evidence of a society governed by bureaucratic schedules. But as the white paint flakes, it discloses another idea that has become synonymous with Australia. When the rest of the capitalized word is uncovered, will it read 'HOLIDAY'? Some of the letters posted here presumably went overseas, as Roach himself did soon after taking the photograph. He now lives in Italy, and thinks of this peeling Australia as a comment on his own disconnection from the country. The longer I look at the image, the more irresistibly the sign changes into a map. The white area is an ocean, the black specks and blobs and ragged fringes are peninsulas and scattered islands, like the archipelagos you fly over between Singapore and Darwin. Or else the ocean is black, the land white: it all depends on your decision about positive and negative spaces, and it makes no difference in the end. The impression is of an existential geography, a fractured, drifting mass of land on which we can alight, in which we can perhaps plant roots. As so often in photography, black and white engage in a battle which will never end, because neither extreme makes sense without the other.

Australia is named after the airy, premature supposition of its existence. For centuries before any navigator reached the edge of it, cartographers fantasised about a Terra Australis Incognita, an unknown southland. The laws of physics required that there should be such a place, a ballast for the northern continents, although no one could anticipate what it might contain. Getting there and then exploring the interior involved a confrontation with the unknowable. Before Voss sets out on his journey, his patron asks whether he has studied the map. 'The map?' he replies with supreme arrogance. 'I will first make it'. Artists are explorers too, making maps of worlds that need not actually exist. They can also obliterate what we take to be reality, and return to the epistemological vacuum that preceded Cook's voyages. In 1985 Max Pam took a photograph that he calls *No Australia*. The camera looks over the shoulder of a man reading a newspaper. A line of print at the top of the page says 'place in the world'. Beneath is a map of Asia, with nothing but water between Indonesia and Antarctica, where Australia should be. The paper was chiding Australians to recognize their region, rather than mourning a frayed bondage to Britain. Would they prefer to be outside the world, like castaways on a coral island? But the image is more than a geopolitical admonition. Though a continent does extend between the Indian and Pacific Oceans, Australia will not truly exist until we have filled in its alienated distances, attached ourselves to it by telling stories about it and making images of it. We do not expect Voss to leave an accurate record of the terrain he crosses. His task is to make a map of the spirit.

Jean-Marc Le Pechoux, recently arrived from Paris, noticed a map above a petrol station in Queensland in 1975, and blinked at its oddity. British Petroleum had hoisted a metal globe into the air to advertise a brand of petrol it called Super. The slogan Superlife, wafting above the map like a formation of puffy clouds, beams down on Australia and touts its virtues. The spiel looks antiquated: the frothy curvaceous lettering belongs to the 1960s, so this dream is already out of date. And though the globe might pretend to be lighter than air, rising like a helium balloon, it cannot escape into a sky that is closed off by telephone wires. Australia in this case does not peel like sunburned skin. Instead it rusts, bleeding in streaks as if from open wounds. Le Pechoux now refers to the image as his 'weeping Australia': could this be some sort of Antipodean miracle, like the statuette in the Neapolitan church on which painted blood liquefies once a year? My own reading of it adds an extra proviso. Whenever I see a map of the continent, I check the where-abouts of Tasmania, as you do when patting your pockets to make sure that you have not lost your keys, your wallet, your passport. Here, painted on a separate square of metal that has later been beaten into shape and fastened to the others, it clings to the slippery base of the globe. A tectonic fissure opens around it at right angles. Perhaps, in these incognito latitudes, there is a trapdoor through which my little island will be swallowed. The world-view on this map would be tragic if it were not so saltily funny.

The superlative or superior life, marketed by a British firm, belongs exclusively to Australia. Other countries have therefore been obliterated: India and China are squeezed into the far north, merging Asia with the Arctic Circle and allowing Australia, once again, to ignore the region to which it belongs. At least Les Walkling, flattening the globe into a map, makes an effort to situate Australia in relation to that daunting capital-ized concept 'THE WORLD'. But is this really the world that we inhabit? The curved bands of longitude can only be seen by a geometrizing god. We experience the earth differently, feeling stone or clods of dirt or drifting sand underfoot, never entirely sure where we are. Straight lines arbitrarily separate the Australian and American states. These applications of the ruler are mocked by the crumbling, eroded contours of the continents themselves, which owe their outline (which is only temporary) to the destructive and creative upsets of nature. At least the creased, wrinkled paper, tattered along its folds, sardonically tells the truth. The map seems almost as ancient as the earth, and equally subject – as those rips and tears imply – to its ailments. Australia may be a new country, but it occupies a hardbitten corner of a geologically old world. Looking at the space occupied by the Pacific, it is easy to imagine the submergence of our portion of the world; we live on a few tilted peaks, waiting for the water to rise towards us. The strip of flypaper pasted just off Australia's east coast is in a way a consolation. Though it marginalizes the country, it also serves as a mental dyke (and helpfully resists the influx of New Zealanders).

The adhesive strip, on which so many glued insects have already died, makes its own devious, shyly patriotic comment on the national predicament and our way of dealing with it. It sometimes seems as if the flies own Australia. I remember my mother's desperation to keep them out of the house, which had mesh screens over its doors. For a while, strips like this one, gaily coloured, dangled from our ceilings. If a blowie sneaked in, there was a battery of implements with which to swat it; it could also be stalked with a flapping tea towel. That insidious buzzing jeered at our desire to be sheltered, protected. In Canberra, on my morning walks along the lake to the National Gallery, that futile battle came back to me when, on a stretch of path unprotected by trees, the flies bombarded me, settling on my eyelids and in my ears, forcing me to put

203
Les Walkling
Flypaper 1980

down my briefcase and use both hands to fend them off. After a few days, I calmed myself down by remembering the Aboriginal guide who once took me to see the rock galleries at Kakadu in the Northern Territory. As he led the way through the bush, I stared at the back of his white shirt, blackened by the flies that had alighted on him. No doubt there were just as many hitching a ride on my back; I shook myself to dislodge an imagined swarm. But the guide never brushed them away. When he turned to explain a cliff painting, I watched one crawl at leisure across his cheek, closing in on his mouth. He was the proverbial image of grace, composure and goodness: here was a man who would not hurt a fly. He reckoned, surely, that because there was no way of defeating them – even if you pumped poison from a squirting can, as my mother used to do before aerosols were invented – it was best to let them live and to coexist with them. Didn't they have an equal right to be here? Walkling's pinioned flies are no more or less parasitical than the specks and spots of land stuck on that overwhelming expanse of water.

Remaking the map means revisiting and reinterpreting the past, which Australia has accepted as a national responsibility. Photographs, whose mood is inevitably retrospective, help us to arrive at this reckoning. But a map of the world, as Oscar Wilde insisted, must also make room for Utopia, which is our imagined version of the future. Maps are projections, and they should be able to see through time as well as organizing space. I end, accordingly, with two photographs that do more than record reality, even though they touch base near to each other in an actual Australia. They are glimpses of Australia's unconsciousness, and possibly previews of the society that it is in the process of becoming.

In *Sleep 2*, the snuggled geishas – copied from a hand-coloured photograph by Felice Beato, who photographed Japan in the late nineteenth century – are dozing at Darling Point on Sydney Harbour, with the bridge and the jutting pincushion of North Sydney in the distance. The faces that peep out of their bed are identical and unreadable, but the book that Lyndell Brown and Charles Green have suspended in the night sky suggests, like a thought bubble in a cartoon, what might be on their twinned minds. Its two pages document performances staged by Jacques Tingueley and Yves Klein: on the left, the aromatic exhaust from a 'meta-matic' engine inflates a balloon, and on the right a woman coats her naked body in blue paint. The puffery of Tingueley's balloon exhorted those who watched it to 'be free, live. Stop painting time....Live in the present', and Klein's model offered herself to him as an anthropomorphic brush. Why bother to make art, if a machine or a submissive female accomplice or someone else's book can do it for you? The geishas have been transplanted from feudal Japan, and the avant-garde performances come from contemporary Paris. Aesthetically, Brown and Green are citizens of the world (or of the library). Yet the world to which they belong consists of quotations, allusions and simulations. Printed onto plastic film and displayed hanging in the air not fastened to a wall, the painted and rephotographed photograph is an apparition.

Australia, rebranded for marketing overseas, has become just such a beguiling, illusory image. A small fable, very similar in structure and content to *Sleep 2*, appeared on British television during the winter of 1999. It began with a low, skimming flight along the Queensland coast – fuzzy mangrove swamps, glaringly white beaches – accompanied by the lulling drone of a didgeridoo. A somnolent, smiling face then swam into view. After that, words slid across the screen, announcing that 'The average person dreams only two hours per night', with a qualification tacked on after a pause – 'except in Qantas Business Class'. Finally the product responsible for the beatific smile was identified: 'The Qantas Dreamtime Seat', a recliner that lowers you into that sub-liminal stratum when you press a lever. A well-fed snooze while cruising between inter-national engagements is not quite what the Aboriginal people mean by Dreamtime, and you see very few of them in Business Class on Qantas. Photographs no longer vouch for a tough, undeniable reality, as they do in those early scenes of Australians struggling to construct an existence in bush huts or half-built cities. Images now possess value as a commercial opiate, and any fantasy can be realized if you have the money. You can see Japanese women like those in *Sleep 2* all over Sydney, though they tend not to spend their nights on the beach. They are more likely to be buying fluffy marsupials in duty-free shops, or photographing each other outside the Opera House.

A lantern in a paper shade glows beside the Beato geishas. This is their night light; it might also be a boxy camera, the chamber in which revelations occur. Shining more brightly, stretching sideways to encompass a land that is endlessly horizontal, it appears again in Anne Zahalka's *Open-Air Cinema*. The white rectangle is here a screen, set up in Farm Cove on the edge of the Botanic Gardens during the Sydney Festival. The screen lazes flat on its back beneath the waterline during the day, then in the evening rouses itself and stands upright. Fixed in place, it catches images beamed onto it from a Panavision projector. Behind it is the same shimmering array of icons seen from further across the harbour in *Sleep 2*: my pylon (here tinted a fiendish green), the girders of the bridge sketching their covenant, that sculptural cluster of polished shells, the

204
Lyndell Brown and
Charles Green
Sleep 2
2000–2001

mercantile towers staining the air and water with their own excited spectrum. The Japanese women, dreamily turning the pages of their memory book, are unaware of all this. They may not even know that a navigable futon has deposited them in Australia. But Zahalka's home-grown audience admires the view while waiting for the show to start, for the future to arrive.

Zahalka's screen, emerging from the water, is like a sheet of photographic paper removed from its chemical bath and hung up to dry. But by this stage, an image should have materialized on the coated page. The screen, so exactly positioned inside the frame, is like an inset photograph surrounded by a coloured mount – though the photograph is of nothing at all. Could this represent Australia? The oblong recalls a description of the country by Wim Wenders, who crossed from Indonesia to Darwin during the 1980s and set out from there to wander through the outback. He arrived without preconceptions. Australia was for him, he has said, 'ein weisses Stück Papier'. The metaphor is inappropriate, as Wenders soon realized. America may aspire to be a tabula rasa, a white expanse on which you can scribble your personal fantasy, but the Australian conscience forbids erasure: the country's troubling past haunts the present like a double exposure.

We have no idea what film the audience is due to see. Imagining myself in the grandstand, I remember my excitement on early trips to what we called 'the pitchers'. The images on view entranced me because they contradicted the stark daylight outside. This was my first experience of art, which can tell the truth but is also liable to entrance you with fiction and falsity; the lifelong sickness began here, encouraging my discontent and ensuring that I never felt at home – in Australia, or even in reality. Nowadays the film these people have gathered to see would not necessarily be set in one of the inaccessibly distant worlds that beckoned me during my childhood. It might even have

205
Anne Zahalka
Open Air Cinema from the
series *Leisureland* 1999

been made in a camouflaged Australia. In *The Thin Red Line* northern Queensland plays Vietnam, and in *The Matrix* Sydney is cast as any city in a globalized world where space has been electronically eliminated. On an average summer evening, the film shown here might feature Russell Crowe as a Los Angeles cop, a Princeton scientist or a Roman gladiator, or Nicole Kidman as a Russian mail-order bride, a French courtesan, a New England heiress or a Bloomsbury novelist. The country and its actors are expert at pretending to be anywhere and anyone else.

The people on the grass look up, hoping to see their own faces in a magic mirror. But what is Australia when it is at home, and allowed to be itself? No longer a remote tropical imitation of Britain, surely not a facsimile of America either. Perhaps the screen is blank because it depicts a society that does not yet exist – reconciled to its incongruous geographical position, uniquely able to connect and combine north and south; determined to understand and care for its arduous, beautiful land; adhering thanks to a matey, voluntary sense of community, rather than being unified by a creed or a birthright; more interested in play than in power. I could hazard some guesses about what this ideal state will look like by taking over the screen and warming up the audience with a slide show. It would include Cazneaux's stoical gum and Le Pechoux's shearer cradling a sheep, Caire's walker embraced by the tickling fronds of ferns and Stacey's legs skidding down Uluru, the blackened hand of Missingham photographed by Poignant and the hand of Whitlam photographed by Bishop as it trickles soil into Lingiari's palm. Lindt's weary swagmen could be followed by some of Cranstone's cheerful artisans, Fokkema's Anzac loyalists at Wilcannia by Lever's Mardi Gras dancers. I might slip in some images not reproduced in this book: a Jeff Carter photograph of arrivals at Sydney airport – Australians returning home, but also Indian women in saris and European migrants, all spilling down a rickety stepladder from the back of a plane and gratefully feeling the ground beneath their feet – along with Rex Dupain's multi-coloured tribes discarding differences as they shed their clothes at egalitarian Bondi. The episodic trailer could conclude with the uplifted arms of Charity Mango, photographed by Maureen MacKenzie as she throws out her fishing line. In spite of myself, have I compiled an anthology of happy moments?

In the epigraph to *Riders in the Chariot*, Patrick White quotes William Blake's mystical conversation with two of the biblical prophets who visited him. Isaiah – like Thake repudiating the phoney swami – denies that God can be simply and singly perceived, and says that the senses should seek out 'the infinite in everything'. Ezekiel insists that he too wants to raise men 'into a perception of the infinite', which is why, like 'the North American tribes', he eats dung. Without prescribing an excremental diet, photography does what the prophets recommend. It transforms sight into vision; it finds a glimmering of the infinite in an axe stuck in a tree stump, a lost sandal on a beach, a barbed-wire fence, or the span of a bridge. We are not looking at a blank when we ponder *Open-Air Cinema*. How different that white rectangle is from Tingueley's balloon, which dangles like a chilly moon above the harbour in *Sleep 2*. The screen is solar not lunar, white-hot not pallid. After dark, its incandescence is a reminder that the sun invented photography. Sun slices Mallard's clouds, lacily patterns Cotton's road, and tans the body of Dupain's bather; it also sparks the fire that destroyed Mrs Quigley's house. Through the burning glass of a lens, Australia is irradiated by the eyes of its artists.

List of Illustrations

53 Jon Rhodes (b. 1947), *YalaYala Gibbs Tjakamarrayi, Gibson Desert, NorthernTerritory* from an untitled bound album, 1974. Gelatin silver photograph. National Gallery of Australia (79.1954.19A). 76

54 Destiny Deacon (b. 1957), *Tax-free Kangaroos*, 1993. Gelatin silver photographs. National Gallery of Australia. Kodak (Australasia) Pty Ltd Fund 1997 (97.1764.A–D). © Destiny Deacon, 1993. Licensed by VISCOPY, Sydney 2003. 77

55 Eric Thake (1904–82), *Rathdowne Street Kangaroo*, 1967. Gelatin silver photograph. National Gallery of Australia (73.69). 78

56 Eric Thake (1904–82), *Bunyip at Mystic Park*, 1957. Gelatin silver photograph. National Gallery of Australia (73.55). 79

57 Grant Mudford (b. 1944), *Ayers Rock [Uluru]*, 1973. Gelatin silver photograph. National Gallery of Australia. Gift of the artist 1985 (85.1937). 81

58 Laurence Le Guay (1917–90), *Fashion illustration for Courtauld's Fabrics, Ayers Rock [Uluru], Northern Territory*, 1959. Type C colour photograph. National Gallery of Australia (88.1915). 83

59 Wesley Stacey (b. 1941), *Uluru in Morning Mists*, 1972. Gelatin silver photograph. National Gallery of Australia (89.882). 83

60 Wesley Stacey (b. 1941), *'The Digging Stick' on Uluru*, 1972. Gelatin silver photograph. National Gallery of Australia (89.895). 84

61 Wesley Stacey (b. 1941), *Looking Down the Climb*, 1972. Gelatin silver photograph printed 1989. National Gallery of Australia (89.885). 85

62 Wesley Stacey (b. 1941), *Hand Stencils, Mootwingee*, 1971. Gelatin silver photograph printed 1989. National Gallery of Australia. Gift of the artist 1990 (90.157). 86

63 Peter Elliston (b. 1940), *Couple on Platform at Giles Baths, Coogee, NSW*, 1992. Gelatin silver photograph printed 1995. National Gallery of Australia. Kodak (Australasia) Pty Ltd Fund 1996 (96.1007). 87

64 Tracey Moffatt (b. 1960), *The Movie Star: David Gulpilil on Bondi Beach*, 1985. Direct positive colour photograph. National Gallery of Australia. Kodak (Australasia) Pty Ltd Fund 1993 (93.677). Courtesy of Roslyn Oxley9 Gallery. 88

65 Mervyn Bishop (b. 1945), *Prime Minister Gough Whitlam pours soil into hand of traditional landowner Vincent Lingiari, Northern Territory*, 1975. Direct positive colour photograph printed 1994. National Gallery of Australia (94.1403). © Mervyn Bishop, 1975. Licensed by VISCOPY, Sydney 2003. 90

66 Francis Nixon (1803–79), *Aboriginals at Oyster Cove, Hobart*, 1858. Albumen silver photograph. National Gallery of Australia (93.56). 92

67 attributed to Daniel Marquis (active 1866-80), *Mummified Remains of an Aborigine* from an untitled bound album, c. 1866–80. Albumen silver photograph. National Gallery of Australia (85.1543.35:3). 93

68 Fred Kruger (1831–88), *Family of Civilized Natives* from the album *Souvenir Album of Victorian Aboriginals, Kings, Queens, & etc.*, c. 1866–87. Albumen silver photograph. National Gallery of Australia (81.2444.9). 93

69 Patrick Dawson (active 1860s), *Aboriginal Cricketers, First Australian Touring Team*, 1867. Albumen silver photographs. National Gallery of Australia (89.1607). 94

70 Captain Samuel Sweet (1825–86), *Mrs Philipson Bellamy*, c. 1886. Albumen silver photograph. National Gallery of Australia (86.1852). 95

71 Charles Kerry (1858–1928), *Meeting of the Waters, Katoomba* from an untitled bound album, c. 1890. Albumen silver photograph. National Gallery of Australia (85.189.21). 96

72 J.W. Beattie (1859–1930), *Where Twines the Path – to Pinnacle, Mount Wellington* from an untitled bound album assembled by W.A. Gosse, c. 1902. Albumen silver photograph. National Gallery of Australia (80.2252.36). 97

73 Nicholas Caire (1837–1918), *Giant Tree at Neerim, Forty Feet Girth*, c. 1889. Gelatin silver photograph printed c. 1900. National Gallery of Australia (83.3083). 98

74 Unknown photographer, *Stump at Botany*, 1870s. Albumen silver photograph. National Gallery of Australia (86.1860). 98

75 Gerrit Fokkema (b. 1954), *Alan Carrol, Owen Wyman and Robert Hunter*, from the album *Wilcannia: Portrait of an Australian Town*, 1982. Gelatin silver photograph. National Gallery of Australia (86.1254.39). © Gerrit Fokkema. 100

76 Nicholas Caire (1837–1918), *Selector's Hut, Gippsland*, c. 1886. Albumen silver photograph printed c. 1900. National Gallery of Australia (83.3079). 101

77 Nicholas Caire (1837–1918), *Fairy Scene at the Landslip, Blacks' Spur, Victoria* from the album *Colonies*, 1878. Albumen silver photograph. National Gallery of Australia. Joseph Brown Fund 1981 (81.2866.38). 103

78 Rose Simmonds (1877–1960), *Tall and Stately*, 1930s. Bromoil photograph. National Gallery of Australia. Gift of Dr J. H. Simmonds 1984 (84.1876). 105

79 John Kauffmann (1864–1942), *Victory*, c. 1918. Gelatin silver photograph printed later. National Gallery of Australia (80.3851). 106

80 Harold Cazneaux (1878–1953), *The Spirit of Endurance*, 1937. Gelatin silver photograph. National Gallery of Australia (82.1215). 107

81 Henri Mallard (1884–1967), *The Witches' Wood*, 1957. Gelatin silver photograph. National Gallery of Australia. Gift of Paul Mallard 1976 (76.1281.22). 109

82 Olive Cotton (b. 1911), *The Patterned Road*, 1938. Gelatin silver photograph. National Gallery of Australia (83.2894). © Olive Cotton, courtesy of Josef Lebovic Gallery. 110

83 Stelarc (b. 1946), performance artist, and Norman Ainsworth (b. 1942), photographer: image from the performance *Prepared Tree Suspension Event for Obsolete Body, No. 6, Canberra*, 1982. Gelatin silver photograph. National Gallery of Australia (84.443.4). 113

84 Jill Orr (b. 1952), performance artist, and Elizabeth Campbell (b. 1959), photographer: image from the performance *Bleeding Trees*, 1979. Direct positive colour photograph printed 1990. National Gallery of Australia. Kodak (Australasia) Pty Ltd Fund 1996 (96.904). 114

85 Wesley Stacey (b. 1941), *Woodchip Logging Aftermath (near Myrtle Mountain)*, 1980. Type C colour photograph. National Gallery of Australia. Gift of the Philip Morris Arts Grant 1982 (83.2730). 115

86 Kerry and Co. (1884–1917), *Native Climbing with Vine*, c. 1895. Albumen silver photograph printed c. 1900. National Gallery of Australia (85.1531). 116

87 Edward Cranstone (1903–89), *Men at Work* from the album *Design for War*, vol. I, 1942–44. Gelatin silver photograph. National Gallery of Australia. Gift of Edward Cranstone 1983 (83.2901.1.15). 117

88 Laurie Wilson (1920–80), *Derelict House with Axe*, 1970s. Gelatin silver photograph. National Gallery of Australia. Gift of the National Gallery of Victoria, from the Laurie Wilson Bequest 1981 (81.2316). 118

89 Gerrit Fokkema (b. 1954), *Tony Dell, Butcher* from the album *Wilcannia: Portrait of an Australian Town*, 1982. Gelatin silver photograph. National Gallery of Australia (86.1254.55). © Gerrit Fokkema. 119

90 Margaret Michaelis-Sachs (1902–85), *Wood-chopping Carnival*, c. 1945. Gelatin silver photograph. Gift of the estate of Margaret Michaelis-Sachs 1986. National Gallery of Australia (86.1384.275). Reproduced with permission of the Estate and executor, Serge Saubern. 120

91 Geoff Parr (b. 1933), *Fireplace Landscape*, 1976. Gelatin silver photograph. National Gallery of Australia (78.139). 121

92 Hal Missingham (1906–94), *Stayed Tree, Bouddi Park, NSW*, 1967. Gelatin silver photograph. National Gallery of Australia (74.83). 122

93 Optronics Kinetics Collective, *Cubed Tree April 1971*. Gelatin silver photograph. National Gallery of Australia. Gift of Daniel Thomas 1980 (80.1520). 122

94 David Moore (1927–2003), *The Impossible Tree 1*, 1975. Gelatin silver photograph printed 1976. National Gallery of Australia (76.1289.9). © Estate of David Moore. 123

95 Maureen Mackenzie (b. 1952), *Charity Mango Line-fishing in the Mowbray River Estuary*, 1986. Gelatin silver photographs printed 1990. National Gallery of Australia (90.1150.A–C). 124

96 Wesley Stacey (b. 1941), *Black Garden Ornament*, 1970. Gelatin silver photograph printed 1989. National Gallery of Australia (89.873). 125

97 J.W. Lindt (1845–1926), *Adelaide, Botanic Gardens, Temple* from an untitled bound album, c. 1887. Albumen silver photograph. National Gallery of Australia (85.192.5). 127

98 Wesley Stacey (b. 1941), *Canberra from the West*, 1980. Type C colour photograph printed 1981. National Gallery of Australia. Gift of the Philip Morris Arts Grant 1982 (83.2734). 128

99 Alfred Winter (c. 1837–1911), *Sandy Bay from St George's Hill, Tasmania*, c. 1870. Albumen silver photograph. National Gallery of Australia (86.1858). 130

100 B.O. Holtermann (1838–85) and Charles Bayliss (1859–97), *Panorama of Sydney Harbour and Suburbs from the North Shore* [detail: 2 of 23 panels], 1875 from the series *Holtermann's Exposition, NSW Scenery*. Albumen silver photograph. National Gallery of Australia (82.1159). 131

101 Unknown photographer, *Panoramic View of Adelaide, South Australia* from an untitled bound album, 1860s. Albumen silver photograph. National Gallery of Australia (84.2908.3). 132

102 J.W. Lindt (1845–1926), *Solferino NSW, Mining Town* from the series *Characteristic Australian Scenery*, c. 1872. Albumen silver photograph. National Gallery of Australia (91.722). 133

103 P.C. Poulsen (1857–1900), *Brisbane in Flood*, 1893. Albumen silver photograph. National Gallery of Australia (92.975). 134

104 attributed to Daniel Marquis (active 1866-80), *Graveyard* from an untitled bound album, c. 1866–80. Albumen silver photograph. National Gallery of Australia (85.1543.30:1). 134

105 Charles Kerry (1858–1928), *Esplanade, Manly*, c. 1890. Albumen silver photograph. National Gallery of Australia (85.189.3). 136

106 Unknown photographer, *'Enmore' Near Sydney – NSW* from an untitled bound album compiled by Robert Monckton, 1860s. Albumen silver photograph. National Gallery of Australia (84.2907.117). 137

107 Charles Nettleton (1826–1902), *General Post Office, Melbourne* from an untitled bound album compiled by Robert Monckton, c. 1867. Albumen silver photograph. National Gallery of Australia (84.2907.11). 138

108 Charles Nettleton (1826–1902), *Volunteer Fire Brigade, Ballarat* from an untitled bound album compiled by Robert Monckton, 1860s. Albumen silver photograph. National Gallery of Australia (84.2907.72). 139

109 Charles Nettleton (1826–1902), *Volunteer Fire Brigade, Ballarat East* from an untitled bound album compiled by Robert Monckton, 1860s. Albumen silver photograph. National Gallery of Australia (84.2907.73). 139

110 attributed to Charles Nettleton (1826–1902), *Congregational Church and Burke and Wills Monument, Collins Street, Melbourne* from an untitled bound album compiled by Robert Monckton, c. 1867. Albumen silver photograph. National Gallery of Australia (84.2907.25). 140

111 Stanley Eutrope (1891–1983), *Collins Street, Melbourne*, 1917. Bromoil photograph. National Gallery of Australia. Gift of Shirley Eutrope 1989 (89.298). 141

112 Edward Cranstone (1903–89), *Collins Street, Melbourne* from the album *Photography Lefevre Cranstone*, 1937. Gelatin silver photograph. National Gallery of Australia. Gift of Edward Cranstone 1983 (83.2902.1.7). 142

113 Edward Cranstone (1903–89), *Albany Coffee Lounge, Melbourne* from the album *Photography Lefevre Cranstone*, 1937. Gelatin silver photograph. National Gallery of Australia. Gift of Edward Cranstone 1983 (83.2902.1.20). 143

114 Wolfgang Sievers (b. 1913), *Escalator Site at Parliament Station, Melbourne*, 1977. Type C colour photograph printed 1988. National Gallery of Australia (89.1422). © Wolfgang Sievers, 1977. Licensed by VISCOPY, Sydney 2003. 144

115 Gerrit Fokkema (b. 1954), *The Post Office* from the album *Wilcannia: Portrait of an Australian Town*, 1982. Gelatin silver photograph. National Gallery of Australia (86.1254.15). © Gerrit Fokkema. 145

116 attributed to A.V. Smith (active 1854–74), *Lake Learmouth, near Ballarat, Victoria* from an untitled bound album, 1860s. Albumen silver photograph. National Gallery of Australia (84.2907.98). 146

117 attributed to Daniel Marquis (active 1866–80), *Driveway to Government House, Brisbane* from an untitled bound album, c. 1866–78. Albumen silver photograph. National Gallery of Australia (85.1543.25.4). 147

118 Wesley Stacey (b. 1941), *Fence Posts and Wire*, 1961. Gelatin silver photograph. National Gallery of Australia (89.857). 148

119 Eric Thake (1904–82), *Roadside Crucifix, Dumosa*, 1957. Gelatin silver photograph. National Gallery of Australia (78.1150). 149

120 John Kauffmann (1864–1942), *Street, Telegraph Poles and Church*, c. 1920. Carbon photograph. National Gallery of Australia (80.3887). 150

121 Mark Strizic (b. 1929), *Tree and Telegraph Pole* from the series *South Melbourne 1967–1972*, c. 1970. Gelatin silver photograph. National Gallery of Australia (74.459). 151

122 Max Dupain (1911–92), *Industrial Landscape*, 1935. Gelatin silver photograph. National Gallery of Australia (79.47). © Max Dupain, 1935. Licensed by VISCOPY, Sydney 2003. 153

123 Edward Cranstone (1903–89), *Prefabrication* from the album *Design for War*, vol. III, 1942–44. Gelatin silver photograph. National Gallery of Australia. Gift of Edward Cranstone 1983 (83.2901.3.14). 154

124 Gerrit Fokkema (b. 1954), *Somedaze No. 5*, 1977. Gelatin silver photograph. National Gallery of Australia. Gift of the Philip Morris Arts Grant 1982 (83.2248). © Gerrit Fokkema. 155

125 Tim Handfield (b. 1952), *Cairns*, 1978. Type C colour photograph. National Gallery of Australia. Gift of the Philip Morris Arts Grant 1982 (83.2334). 156

126 Tim Handfield (b. 1952), *Doncaster*, 1979. Type C colour photograph. National Gallery of Australia. Gift of the Philip Morris Arts Grant 1982 (83.2338). 157

127 Fiona Hall (b. 1953), *Adelaide, South Australia*, 1984. Gelatin silver photograph. National Gallery of Australia (92.990). Courtesy of Roslyn Oxley9 Gallery. 158

128 Fiona Hall (b. 1953), *Wantirna South, Victoria*, 1986. Gelatin silver photograph. National Gallery of Australia (92.991). Courtesy of Roslyn Oxley9 Gallery. 159

129 Jon Rhodes (b. 1947), *Hobart, Tasmania 1974* from an untitled bound album, 1974. Gelatin silver photograph. National Gallery of Australia (79.1954.17B). 160

130 Wesley Stacey (b. 1941), *Suburbia Forever*, 1970. Gelatin silver photograph printed 1989. National Gallery of Australia (89.876). 161

131 Lorrie Graham (b. 1954), *Bob Hawke, Labor Party Campaign Launch* 1982. Gelatin silver photograph printed 1992. National Gallery of Australia. Kodak (Australasia) Pty Ltd Fund 1993 (93.341). 162

132 Max Dupain (1911–92), *Short Dame at Jubilee Procession*, 1951. Gelatin silver photograph. National Gallery of Australia (82.1142). © Max Dupain, 1951. Licensed by VISCOPY, Sydney 2003. 162

133 Wesley Stacey (b. 1941), *Mythical Sight, Glenrowan*, 1988. Gelatin silver photograph courtesy of the artist. 164

134 Eric Thake (1904–82), *The Bushranger*, 1957. Gelatin silver photograph. National Gallery of Australia (73.54). 165

135 Frank Hurley (1885–1962), *Out in the blizzard at Cape Denison, adjacent to winter quarters*, 1912. Carbon photograph. National Gallery of Australia. Kodak (Australasia) Pty Ltd fund (92.1385). 166

136 John Gollings (b. 1944), *Lost in Snow* from the *Marlboro Series*, 1973. Type C colour photograph. National Gallery of Australia. Gift of Kate Gollings 1993 (93.841.55). 167

137 Unknown photographer (active 1914–18), *Gassed Australian soldiers at Villers Bretonneux 27.5.18* from the series *72 Miniatures from the War*, 1918. Gelatin silver photograph printed 1923. National Gallery of Australia (93.664.59). 168

138 Unknown photographer (active 1914–18), *An Australian infantryman easing his load, Henencourt, Feb. 1917* from the series *72 Miniatures from the War*, 1918. Gelatin silver photograph printed 1923. National Gallery of Australia (93.664.21). 169

139 Max Dupain (1911–92), *Tired soldier in Queensland train*, 1943. Gelatin silver photograph printed c. 1982. National Gallery of Australia (83.1354). © Max Dupain, 1943. Licensed by VISCOPY, Sydney 2003. 169

140 Sam Hood (1870–1953), *Anzac March (George Street, Sydney)*, 1930s. Gelatin silver photograph. National Gallery of Australia (92.968). 170

141 Laurie Wilson (1920–80), *Dawn Service, Torquay*, 1976. Gelatin silver photograph. National Gallery of Australia. Gift of the National Gallery of Victoria, from the Laurie Wilson Bequest 1981 (81.2353). 171

142 Gerrit Fokkema (b. 1954), *RSL Secretary Ted Davies holds the Wilcannia Anzac Day Marching Band tape recorder* from the album *Wilcannia: Portrait of an Australian Town*, 1982. Gelatin silver photograph. National Gallery of Australia (86.1254.68). © Gerrit Fokkema. 172

143 Roger Scott (b. 1944), *Anzac Day*, 1973. Gelatin silver photograph. National Gallery of Australia. Gift of the Philip Morris Arts Grant 1982 (83.2678). 173

144 Axel Poignant (1906–86), *Two-up School*, 1936. Gelatin silver photograph. National Gallery of Australia (84.142). © Axel Poignant Archive (Roslyn Poignant). 174

145 David Moore (1927–2003), *Two-up at Betoota, South-western Queensland*, c. 1961. Gelatin silver photograph. National Gallery of Australia. Gift of David Moore 1983 (83.3559). © Estate of David Moore. 175

146 Charles Kerry (1858–1928), *Mob of 20,000 Sheep* from an untitled bound album, c. 1890. Albumen silver photograph. National Gallery of Australia (85.189.33). 177

147 Captain Samuel Sweet (1826–86), *Sheep Shearers, Canowie Station*, c. 1880. Albumen silver photograph. National Gallery of Australia (89.1593). 179

148 David Moore (1927–2003), *Sheep Crutching, South Australia* [Photographed for Life Books], 1963. Gelatin silver photograph. National Gallery of Australia. Gift of David Moore 1983 (83.3535). © Estate of David Moore. 180

149 Jean-Marc Le Pechoux (b. 1953), *Man Shearing a Sheep*, 1975. Gelatin silver photograph. National Gallery of Australia. Gift of the Philip Morris Arts Grant 1982 (83.2459). 181

150 J.W. Lindt (1845–1926), *Sundowners* from an untitled bound album, c. 1890. Albumen silver photograph. National Gallery of Australia (85.191.19). 182

151 Jack Cato (1889–1971), *Aida*, 1929. Carbon photograph. National Gallery of Australia (91.93). 182

152 David Moore (1927–2003), *Lew Hoad in dressing room before winning at Wimbledon for the second time*, 1957. Gelatin silver photograph. National Gallery of Australia. Gift of David Moore 1983 (83.3413). © Estate of David Moore. 183

153 Axel Poignant (1906–86), *Swagman on the Road to Wilcannia*, 1954. Gelatin silver photograph. National Gallery of Australia (84.149). © Axel Poignant Archive (Roslyn Poignant). 184

154 Max Dupain (1911–92), *Sunbaker*, 1937. Gelatin silver photograph printed 1975. National Gallery of Australia (76.54). © Max Dupain, 1937. Licensed by VISCOPY, Sydney 2003. 185

155 Hal Missingham (1906–94), *Balmain Pediment*, 1956. Gelatin silver photograph. National Gallery of Australia (74.57). 186

156 Max Dupain (1911–92), *At Newport Baths, Sydney*, 1952. Gelatin silver photograph. National Gallery of Australia (79.61). © Max Dupain, 1952. Licensed by VISCOPY, Sydney 2003. 188

157 Geoffrey Powell (1918–89), *Intellectual, Bondi Beach*, c. 1946. Gelatin silver photograph. National Gallery of Australia. Gift of Geoffrey Powell 1984 (84.1864). 189

158 Edward Cranstone (1903–89), '*They Had Their Fun*', *The Northern Camps* from the album *Design for War*, vol. II, 1942–44. Gelatin silver photograph. National Gallery of Australia. Gift of Edward Cranstone 1983 (83.2901.2.13). 191

159 Jon Lewis (b. 1950), *Retired Beach Inspector, Bondi*, 1985. Gelatin silver photograph. National Gallery of Australia (89.258). 191

160 Roger Scott (b. 1944), *Bronte Beach (No. 2)*, 1979. Gelatin silver photograph. National Gallery of Australia. Gift of the Philip Morris Arts Grant 1982 (83.2695). 192

161 Roger Scott (b. 1944), *Queenscliff Legs*, 1975. Gelatin silver photograph. National Gallery of Australia (78.1143). 193

162 Henri Mallard (1884–1967), *Sunset Splendour*, 1959. Gelatin silver photograph. National Gallery of Australia. Gift of Paul Mallard 1976 (76.1281.37). 195

163 Harold Cazneaux (1878–1953), *Exterior of Art Gallery of New South Wales*, c. 1930s. Gelatin silver photograph. National Gallery of Australia. Gift of the Cazneaux family 1981 (82.1235). 196

164 Axel Poignant (1906–86), *Artist's Hand*, 1941. Gelatin silver photograph. National Gallery of Australia (84.143). © Axel Poignant Archive (Roslyn Poignant). 199

165 David Moore (1927–2003), *John Olsen Painting 'Summer in the You Beaut Country'*, 1962. Gelatin silver photograph. National Gallery of Australia. Gift of David Moore 1983 (83.3486). © Estate of David Moore. 200

166 L. Hey Sharp (1885–1965), *Mannequin*, c. 1928. Bromoil transfer photograph. National Gallery of Australia (78.859). 201

167 Ruth Hollick (1882–1977), *Robertson and Moffat*, 1920s. Gelatin silver photograph. National Gallery of Australia (7144). 203

168 Henry Talbot (1920–99), *Wild Colonial Colours Campaign for the Wool Board*, 1970s. Direct positive colour photograph. National Gallery of Australia (93.463). 203

169 Olive Cotton (b. 1911), *Fashion Shoot, Cronulla Sandhills*, 1937. Gelatin silver photograph printed 1988. National Gallery of Australia (88.2296). © Olive Cotton, courtesy of Josef Lebovic Gallery. 204

170 Mark Strizic (b. 1928), *Corrugated Roof* from the series *South Melbourne 1967–1972*. Gelatin silver photograph. National Gallery of Australia (74.498). 205

171 Mark Strizic (b. 1928), *Ridgeway Beauty Salon* from the series *South Melbourne 1967–1972*. Gelatin silver photograph. National Gallery of Australia (74.501). 206

172 Harold Cazneaux (1878–1953), '*The Old and the New*', *Harbour Bridge, Sydney*, c. 1929. Gelatin silver photograph. National Gallery of Australia (81.268). 208

173 Max Dupain (1911–92), *Bridge Construction, Sydney*, 1978. Gelatin silver photograph. National Gallery of Australia (79.11). © Max Dupain, 1978. Licensed by VISCOPY, Sydney 2003. 210

174 Max Dupain (1911–92), *Sydney Harbour Bridge Walkway*, 1940s. Gelatin silver photograph printed 1950s. National Gallery of Australia (99.60). © Max Dupain, 1978. Licensed by VISCOPY, Sydney 2003. 211

175 David Moore (1927–2003), *Sydney Harbour from 16,000 feet*, 1966. Gelatin silver photograph. National Gallery of Australia (76.1289.73). © Estate of David Moore. 213

176 Effy Alexakis (b. 1957), photographer, and Leonard Janiszewski (b. 1958), collaborating researcher, *Greek Flag, Sydney*, 1984 from the series *Greek-Australians: In Their Own Image Project 1982–*. Gelatin silver photograph. National Gallery of Australia. Kodak (Australasia) Pty Ltd Fund 1988 (88.2055). 215

177 Peter McKenzie (b. 1944), *Lola Ryan and Mavis Longbottom Demonstrating the Art of Shell Work*, 1987. Gelatin silver photograph printed 1990. National Gallery of Australia (90.1169). 215

178 David Moore (1927–2003), *Opera House Under Construction, Sydney*, 1966. Direct positive colour photograph. National Gallery of Australia (IRN 120352). © Estate of David Moore. 217

179 Max Dupain (1911–92), *Office of the Architect Harry Seidler, Milson's Point, Sydney*, c. 1971. Type C colour photograph. National Gallery of Australia. Gift of Harry Seidler 2001 (2001.247). © Max Dupain, 1978. Licensed by VISCOPY, Sydney 2003. 218

180 John Gollings (b. 1944), *Great Architectural Spaces: Sydney Opera House*, 1987. Type C colour photograph. National Gallery of Australia. Gift of Kate Gollings 1993 (93.870). 220

181 Harold Cazneaux (1878–1953), *Departure*, 1928. Gelatin silver photograph. National Gallery of Australia (76.1298). 221

182 David Moore (1927–2003), *Southern European Migrant Arriving in Sydney*, 1966. Gelatin silver photograph printed 1976. National Gallery of Australia (76.1289.70). © Estate of David Moore. 223

183 Effy Alexakis (b. 1957), photographer, and Leonard Janiszewski (b. 1958), collaborating researcher, *Bill Florence (Vasilis Florias) Being Welcomed to Australia (Melbourne 1922)* from the series *Mavri Xenitia [Black Foreign Land]*, 1991 part of *Greek-Australians: In Their Own Image Project*, 1982–. Gelatin silver photograph printed 1992 after a 1922 original print by S. Raftopoulos, Melbourne studio photographer. National Gallery of Australia. Kodak (Australasia) Pty Ltd Fund (93.1462). 223

184 John Williams (b. 1933), *Greek Wedding Reception, Newtown*, 1971. Gelatin silver photograph printed 1988. National Gallery of Australia (89.238). 224

185 Narelle Perroux (b. 1958), *Australian Rules Football at the Sports Weekend*, 1989. Gelatin silver photograph. National Gallery of Australia (93.661). 224

186 David Moore (1927–2003), *Sydney Cricket Ground from 'The Hill'*, 1963. Gelatin silver photograph printed 1976. National Gallery of Australia (76.1289.63). © Estate of David Moore. 226

187 Philip Quirk (b. 1948), *Headmistress, Sports Day*, 1975. Gelatin silver photograph. National Gallery of Australia (83.1421). 227

188 David Moore (1927–2003), *William Street Looking West, Sydney*, 1961. Gelatin silver photograph. National Gallery of Australia. Gift of David Moore 1983 (83.3539). © Estate of David Moore. 228

189 Roger Scott (b. 1944), *Prime Minister Malcolm Fraser, Randwick Race Course*, 1975. Gelatin silver photograph. National Gallery of Australia (77.761). 229

190 Henri Mallard (1884–1967), *The Answer*, 1911. Gelatin silver photograph. National Gallery of Australia. Gift of Paul Mallard 1976 (76.1281.64). 231

191 Jack Cato (1889–1971), *Snorky*, 1924. Gelatin silver photograph. National Gallery of Australia (91.90). 232

192 Ricky Maynard (b. 1953), *Men's Toilet* from the series *The Moonbird People*, 1985. Gelatin silver photograph printed 1990. National Gallery of Australia. Kodak (Australasia) Pty Ltd Fund 1990 (90.1508). 233

193 David Moore (1927–2003), *Lifesavers at Manly*, 1959. Gelatin silver photograph. National Gallery of Australia. Gift of David Moore 1983 (83.3498). © Estate of David Moore. 234

194 Martyn Jolly (b. 1959), *Lifesavers* from the series *Wonderful Pictures in Colour*, 1993. Type C colour photograph. National Gallery of Australia. Kodak (Australasia) Pty Ltd Fund 1996 (96.161). 235

195 Craig Holmes (b. 1956), *Volleyball* from the Speedo *Underwater Achievers* Campaign, 1993. Direct positive transfer digital print on polytech plastic laminate UV cured inks. National Gallery of Australia. Gift of the artist 1994 (94.260). 236

196 Roger Scott (b. 1944), *Luna Park, Sydney*, 1972. Gelatin silver photograph. National Gallery of Australia. Gift of the Philip Morris Arts Grant 1982 (83.2671). 236

197 Ian Lever (b. 1946), *Before the Parade*, 1993. Gelatin silver photograph printed 2002. Courtesy of Stills Gallery (NGA 120354). 238

198 Max Pam (b. 1949), *Luna Park, Sydney*, 1978. Gelatin silver photograph. National Gallery of Australia (79.2634). 239

199 David Cronin (b. 1957), *Australia Day, Rymill Park, Adelaide*, 1983 from the portfolio *Eucalypt*, 1983. Gelatin silver photograph. National Gallery of Australia. Kodak (Australasia) Pty Ltd Fund 1986 (86.2162.3). 241

200 David Broker (b. 1952), *Monster Parade, Adelaide*, 1983 from the portfolio *Eucalypt*, 1983. Gelatin silver photograph. National Gallery of Australia. Kodak (Australasia) Pty Ltd Fund 1986 (86.2162.1). 242

201 Stephen Roach (b. 1951), *Peeling Paint and Poster*, 1978. Gelatin silver photograph. National Gallery of Australia. Gift of the Philip Morris Arts Grant 1982 (83.2657). 243

202 Jean-Marc Le Pechoux (b. 1953), *Superlife*, 1975. Gelatin silver photograph. National Gallery of Australia. Gift of the Philip Morris Arts Grant 1982 (83.2461). 244

203 Les Walkling (b. 1953), *Flypaper*, 1980. Gelatin silver photograph. National Gallery of Australia. Gift of the Philip Morris Arts Grant 1982 (83.2778). 245

204 Lyndell Brown (b. 1961) and Charles Green (b. 1953), *Sleep 2*, 2000–2001. Digitally printed photograph on Duraclear film. Courtesy of Grantpirrie Gallery, Sydney (NGA 120423). 246

205 Anne Zahalka (b. 1957), *Open Air Cinema* from the series *Leisureland*, 1999. Type C colour photograph. Courtesy Roslyn Oxley9 Gallery, Sydney. 248

Index

Page numbers in **bold**
refer to illustrations